THE MAOISTS

Praise for the book

Nirmalangshu is smart and he cares. The best outcome would be if his book could contribute to a strategic debate for how to resist the land-grabs, expand India's fragile democracy, and most urgently, break the noose that the state is tightening around the *adivasis* and their lands.

—Justin Podur, in *ZNet*

Mukherji persuasively argues that the Maoists are at a brutal dead end. His solution is a desperate hope that reforms can be granted through an extension of democracy. He does dramatically demonstrate the consequences of revolutionaries setting themselves over and outside the class they purport to lead.

—Barry Pavier, in *Socialist Review*

Nirmalangshu Mukherji is a well-known scholar in philosophy and cognitive science. We can see the power of his analytical mind in this non-academic work as well.

—Probal Dasgupta, in *Anandabazar Patrika*

THE MAOISTS IN INDIA

Tribals Under Siege

NIRMALANGSHU MUKHERJI

AMARYLLIS

Copyright © Nirmalangshu Mukherji 2013

All rights reserved. No part of this book may be used or reproduced, stored in or introduced into a retrieval system, or transmitted, in any form, or by any means, (electronic, mechanical, photocopying, recording or otherwise) without the prior written permission of the Publisher. Any person who does any unauthorised act in relation to this publication may be liable to criminal prosecution and civil claims for damages.

Nirmalangshu Mukherji
asserts the moral right to be identified
as the author of this work

First published in London by Pluto Press, in 2012

This edition first published 2013

AMARYLLIS

An imprint of Manjul Publishing House Pvt. Ltd.
7/32, Ansari Road, Daryaganj,
New Delhi 110 002
Email: amaryllis@amaryllis.co.in
Website: amaryllis.co.in

Registered Office:
10, Nishat Colony, Bhopal 462 003

ISBN: 978-93-81506-26-4

Printed and Bound in India by
Thomson Press (India) Limited

CONTENTS

Introduction	1
1 Dark Clouds over Dandakaranya	13
2 Fragile Democracy	39
3 Role of Intellectuals	74
4 Arms over People	113
5 Forms of Resistance	142
6 Quest for Peace	183
Appendix I: Interview with Ganapathy, General Secretary of CPI (Maoist), 2009	215
Appendix II: Sanhati Statement against the Government of India's Planned Military Offensive in Adivasi-populated Regions	229
Notes	232
Abbreviations	252
References	255
Glossary	264
Acknowledgements	267
Index	269

INTRODUCTION

The word *tribal* is used in the subtitle of this book for familiarity. The indigenous people of India are commonly called *adivasis*, 'ancient inhabitants', in many Indian languages; it does not have the covert racist tone that the English word *tribal* has come to acquire. Gandhi called them *girijans*, 'hill people', which is inaccurate. From now onwards, I will use the word *adivasi* to denote my topic.

In this work, *adivasi*s are viewed as (Indian) citizens, period. They are not discussed in terms of their ancient culture, what they worship, and other forms of 'ethnic' distinction. There is no separate call to 'protect' their unique identity or to 'preserve' their special habitat. The 'sociology' and 'anthropology' of *adivasi*s are not my topics. *Adivasi*s are discussed because they are under attack by the Indian state and an insurgent group. Their democratic rights including right to livelihood – which they share with all people independently of ethnic categories – are seriously threatened in the context of an unfolding insurgency launched by the Communist Party of India (Maoist) or CPI(Maoist).

A Maoist party may be formally viewed as a communist organisation that subscribes to the doctrines of Marx, Lenin, and Mao Zedong (MLM). Given their loyalty to these classical doctrines, Maoist parties typically reject both (post-Stalin) Russian and (post-Mao) Chinese forms of communism.[1] Broadly speaking, these are widely viewed as egalitarian doctrines based on the enlightened principles of justice, equality, and freedom. Even if many commentators on the Left, especially in the West, view Leninism and Maoism as regressive doctrines by now, they continue to inspire a range of struggles for a just society across the world. For example, Maoists in India seek to create a paradise on earth … where no person shall go hungry; where no one shall oppress another, where there shall be no discrimination based on caste, religion or sex; where a new socialist human being will be born in whom greed, selfishness, ego, competitiveness will be replaced by selflessness, modesty and cooperation and where a concern for others will take precedence over concern for oneself.[2]

In any case, the salience of MLM is not under discussion here for it is a different matter how organisations which call themselves 'Marxist' or 'Maoist' behave on the ground, and what their presence means to the impoverished people they profess to liberate. History is replete with instances in which demonic, fundamentalist, reactionary, fascist, as well as progressive forces begin their career with elaborate promises for the poor and the attendant visions of a just society. The Nazi movement called itself 'National Socialist' and it emerged from ghettos of the poor, not from corporate headquarters. For this reason I will seldom engage theoretically with the classical doctrines themselves in this work; I will also largely ignore the intricate polemical debates around these classical doctrines that occur relentlessly in MLM party documents and journals.

Most Maoist organisations believe in an armed protracted war to seize state power to establish what Mao called a 'new democratic' order. In most developing countries with a large peasant population, the protracted war is supposed to be in the form of an agrarian revolution. Since the aim is to seize state power by force, most Maoist groups shun any form of electoral politics to access existing state power, although some also advocate participation in elections as a temporary tactic to reach the people. It is not surprising that when something as momentous as emergence of communist China happens in history — followed by heroic resistance put up by people of Vietnam, Cambodia and Laos with direct assistance from Chinese communists — it will inspire a variety of radical minds in the world.

There are literally hundreds of Maoist organisations operating across the world.[3] In Europe, there are Maoist forums in the Netherlands, Germany, France, Norway, Denmark, Sweden, Spain, Belgium, Britain, Portugal, Serbia, Austria, Poland, Slovenia, Greece and Finland, among others. In fact, there are several Maoist groups in most of these countries. In Latin America, Maoist groups are present in Colombia, Brazil, Argentina, Chile, Uruguay, Venezuela, Equador, Dominican Republic, Peru and others, with several groups in most countries. There are Maoist groups in US, Russia, Canada, New Zealand and Japan. Many countries in Africa and West Asia, including Morocco, Turkey, Iraq and Iran have Maoist groups. Maoist groups are present in other parts of Asia as well including India, Pakistan, Afghanistan, Nepal, the Philippines and Bangladesh.

The organisational strength and reach of these groups vary considerably. However, with the exception of Maoist organisations in India, Nepal, Peru, the Philippines and a few others, most of these groups appear to be small intellectual forums with insignificant penetration among people. There is little reason to believe that Maoist groups have played any noteworthy role in some of the recent and spectacular mass resistance movements in West Asia, Europe, Latin America and Africa. Even with respect to older resistance movements such as the fierce and controversial Revolutionary Armed Forces of Colombia – Fuerzas Armadas Revolucionarias de Colombia in Spanish, FARC for short – it is questionable if it belongs to the Maoist fraternity. FARC also started out decades ago as a guerrilla movement under the banner of the Communist Party of Colombia (Marxist-Leninist), but it is unclear if it ever adopted the Maoist doctrine. In fact, after nearly fifty years of operations, its adherence even to the classical Marxist doctrine has become questionable. Similar remarks apply to many armed insurgencies elsewhere.

Nonetheless, especially after the emergence of the neo-liberal era, the post-war 'Bretton Woods' world order is beginning to show signs of deep crisis, forcing vast sections of populations across the world into an increasingly desperate state even in erstwhile affluent zones. In the absence of avenues for peaceful and sustained resistance movements, Maoist and other militant forces can begin to play a more prominent role in these circumstances. Perhaps this explains the impressive, though largely dormant, proliferation of Maoist groups across the world in the last two decades.

On paper, most Maoist groups advocate very similar ideology and programme of action; only a detailed examination of their practice can reveal their specific political character. Labels such as 'Leninist' and 'Maoist' ultimately get their meaning, if any, only in the concrete context of people's lives. No doubt, in some cases, as in contemporary Nepal and the Philippines, Maoist organisations were able to organise genuine people's movements when they learned to adjust to the vastly changed world scenario after the Chinese revolution.

For example, the Communist Party of Nepal (Maoist) launched a peasant-based civil war more or less on classical Chinese lines against a ruthless monarchy and its royal army. However, as soon as the monarchy was defeated, the Maoist party there halted their armed insurgency and cooperated with the rest of the political organisations, including some right-wing ones, to establish genuine republicanism based on universal franchise. In the Philippines, a Maoist movement has continued for many years with widespread support and involvement of people against a token republic that subscribes to what Noam Chomsky (2011) has characterised as 'the Philippine model' favoured by the US for developing countries.[4]

Chomsky points out that the model is 'in place in the Philippines' which is 'the one US neo-colony that is still run virtually the same way it was run one hundred years ago – same elite elements, same brutal constabulary, different names – with the US in the background, but not very far.' Since these contexts leave little room for peaceful mass resistance, an armed struggle to enforce a drastic change in governance appears to be justified to that extent.

An armed struggle is no picnic for the masses. In every armed struggle mindless violence and atrocities are committed on unarmed people. This applies also to armed struggles in Nepal, the Philippines, Peru and Colombia which seem to have some salient features (Prashad, 2010). Also, armed struggles that appear to be uplifting from a distance, such as the ones led by the legendary Che Guevara in Bolivia and Ho Chi Minh in Vietnam might actually contain brutal elements that go against the very principles of resistance. Within this sombre perspective, however, it seems that, in some cases, an armed struggle might actually signal a historical step forward for the concerned people.

In contrast, in other cases, the growth of Maoist and other forms of (armed) insurgency may in reality impede available forms of democratic resistance such that, at least indirectly, they enable an otherwise beleaguered state to regain its illegitimate authority. In imitating the repressive forms of the ruling system, an ill-motivated armed struggle in such cases turns into another force of oppression for the impoverished masses. One could cite some cases of arguably 'predatory insurgencies' in Africa: Sierra Leone's Revolutionary United Front, National Patriotic Front and Movement for Democracy in Liberia, the Lord's Resistance Army in Uganda and so on. Questions have been raised also about FARC in Colombia and *Sendero Luminoso* in Peru.[5] Only a detailed examination of each case can tell whether a particular insurgency has advanced the cause of the people.

For reasons of familiarity and proximity, I will focus mainly on my own backyard to understand the rising wave of insurgencies in this unhappy world. I will discuss some cases in the South-Asian context itself such as Liberation Tigers of Tamil Eelam (LTTE) in Sri Lanka and Tehrik-e-Taliban in Pakistan to evaluate the political character of CPI(Maoist). To anticipate this, I will compare the Nepalese case with Indian Maoists and Sri Lankan militants repeatedly to bring out the crucial distinction between legitimate and illegitimate forms of armed struggles.

In India, with its rich tradition of communist movements, several dozen Maoist groups have emerged in the last few decades.[6]

Typically, most of the Maoist groups have very little presence in terms of people's participation. Among the more significant MLM organisations, CPI(Maoist) stands out as a formidable force with thousands of armed guerrillas and many thousands of square kilometres of *adivasi* habitats under its (military) command. To emphasise, I will not be concerned with the issue of whether these Maoist groups are 'genuine' MLM organisations. That is for the ideologues of these groups to squabble over. I will be solely concerned with their practices and their effect on the lives of the people.

As we will soon see, the life and livelihood of several million *adivasi*s, the poorest of the poor in India, are at stake. In terms of number of armed guerrillas and militias, range of area under control, and the ability to engage with the armed forces of the state, Indian Maoists are very much comparable to FARC in Colombia. Yet, in contrast to the huge international attention on FARC and its effects in the region, the Maoist phenomenon in India – especially the massive humanitarian disaster faced by millions of *adivasi*s – remains largely unknown to the international audience. Following his recent coverage of Maoist insurgency in India, Imran Garda of *Al Jazeera* television reports that a '40-year long civil war has been raging in the jungles of central and eastern India. It is one of the world's largest armed conflicts but it remains largely ignored outside of India.'

It is interesting that claims about the strength of the Maoists, made both by the Indian state and the Maoist party itself, are vastly exaggerated. These claims have found their way into some international quarters as well. A 'student paper' prepared and circulated by the US Army War College suggests that Maoists are now significantly present in 16 of India's 24 states; or, in 192 of about 600 districts.[7] The report claims that the Maoist party holds sway over a quarter of India's land-mass. These figures are frequently mentioned in corporate media and in 'expert' studies on insurgencies in India. The Indian prime minister has stated that Maoists are India's gravest internal security threat.[8] In what follows, we will try to understand the politics underlying these convergences on falsity (Nigam, 2010a).

In reality, the Maoists' strength is a fraction of what they claim it to be. For example, as a percentage of population and coverage of area, they are yet to reach the commanding heights attained by Maoists in Nepal at the peak of their power in the Nepalese countryside. In any case, India's 'gravest internal security threat' continues to be the abysmal poverty of vast sections of its people and the indignity meted out to women, minorities,

Dalits, backward castes and *adivasi*s which together constitute an overwhelming majority.

Still, it is undeniable that Maoists have emerged as a major force of insurgency. If we set aside the Maoists in Nepal – who have now joined the parliamentary system – Maoists in India could well be the largest MLM organisation in the world. The US Army paper thus may be right in suggesting that the impressive organisational strength of Indian Maoists might have led to a 'spill over effect' that has 'emboldened Maoist parties in Bangladesh, Bhutan, Sri Lanka and may reach Myanmar and into Southeast Asia'. Maoist upheavals in Nepal and India have led to the formation of a Coordination Committee of Maoist Parties and Organisations in South Asia (CCOMPOSA). The coalition consists of People's War Group (PWG), Maoists Communist Centre of India (MCC), Revolutionary Communist Centre of India, Revolutionary Communist Centre of India (MLM), all from India as well as *Purba Bangla Sarbahara Party* and *Bangladesh Samajwadi Party (ML)* from Bangladesh, Communist Party of Nepal (Maoist) and Communist Party of Ceylon (Maoist).[9] Thus, the Maoist issue has become even larger than its demonstrably disastrous effect on a section of the Indian population.

As we will see, a variety of increasingly assertive but peaceful resistance to the neo-liberal order is fanning out in India. Also, unlike monarchial Nepal and US-propped 'republics' of Colombia and the Philippines (the sites of FARC and the Philippine Maoists respectively), India continues to be a vibrant and stable parliamentary democracy whose electoral system is something of a model for the rest of the world. Specifically, it is reasonable to infer that the sustained presence and growth of parliamentary democracy in India has often acted as a trigger for movements for democracy elsewhere in South-Asia with uneven success. This applies to Bangladesh, Nepal, Sri Lanka, Pakistan even Myanmar

(Burma). Among the myriad political parties that participate in Indian elections, there is also a significant participation from the Left, including some Maoist groups. Sometimes this has led to significant action on national policy such as implementation of National Rural Employment Guarantee Act (NREGA), Forest Rights Act (FRA), Right to Information Act (RTI), Right to Education Act (RTE), and other progressive legislations.

In this fluid and otherwise promising context of resistance, the armed insurgency of Maoists provides the increasingly authoritarian Indian state with the golden opportunity to attack the entire spectrum of resistance under the pretext of the 'gravest internal security threat'. No wonder the ruling dispensation is inclined to exaggerate the strength of Maoists so that the Indian state can mount a 'suitable' response. In turn, the propaganda interests of the Indian state comes as a blessing in disguise for the secret Maoist party to claim that it has emerged as the 'only genuine alternative' for the struggling people of India.

What is the political meaning of these developments from the perspective of the Left? How do we understand the massive growth of Maoist insurgency in India in the rapidly shifting political order of the world? How do we appraise a formidable armed conflict in the context of neo-liberal attacks on the very foundations of democracy? How credible is a proclaimed resistance which places large numbers of impoverished people in the crossfire? More importantly and urgently, what options, if any, are now available to save *adivasi*s from mounting catastrophe?

In a recent searing piece on the situation in the war zone, Shoma Chaudhury (2011) observed: 'Life is only one of the sad casualties of the low-intensity war raging through India's heartland. The idea of justice, faith, freedom, free will, moral compasses, evidence, a simple sense of right and wrong – every human certitude that could give mental refuge even to the poorest of men – has fallen casualty here'. This book attempts to understand this 'casualty' of 'human certitude' in 'India's heartland'. Since the basic thrust of the book is to articulate the urgent humanitarian cause of saving *adivasi* lives, it should be viewed primarily as a political work. The facts discussed in this book are updated to the end of December 2011. I hope the perspective so reached will be sustained when the book is ultimately published in this fast-changing scenario.

To develop the humanitarian case, I will present a detailed criticism of the current operations of the Maoist party to bring out the serious flaws in their programme and in the ill-concealed Maoist propaganda voiced by some intellectual supporters of the Maoist movement. As noted, in criticising Maoists in India, I have refrained from evaluating the Maoist political doctrine itself, not to mention the broader Marxist perspective under which Maoism falls (D'Mello, 2009). This is because a range of naxalites are also severely critical of the Maoist party. Thus, even if I have protested the specific form of violence unleashed by the Maoist party in India, I have not adopted any Gandhian-pacifist outlook on the question of violence. In fact, I repeatedly applaud the armed resistance organised by the Maoist party in Nepal to overthrow a brutal monarchy.

Further, for roughly the same reason, I have not attempted a detailed evaluation of the history of Maoist-influenced naxalite movement in India, except for brief historical sketches to situate the discussion. There are a number of well documented studies on this topic.[10] The original naxalite movement of the late 1960s has branched into many strands most of which reject the politics of CPI (Maoist) party. So a specific critique of the Maoist party need not be linked to a general critique of the naxalite movement itself. This perspective on the Maoist issue is generally unknown – or, deliberately obfuscated – in the mainstream.[11]

The chapters that follow examine different dimensions of the Maoist issue to lead up to what, in my view, is the only rational and civilised option currently available to save *adivasi*s from further attacks by the state and Maoists. The proposal is based on the fundamental democratic principle that the safety of *adivasi* citizens is entirely the responsibility of the government and the rest of the civil society. It is a matter of sinister irony that Maoist guns were needed for the government to wake up to formidable 'developmental challenges' in *adivasi* areas. But no proposal for development carries any meaning when *adivasi*s are caught in a vicious war.

In writing a book like this in the prevalent ideological climate that borders on hysteria, I am reminded of some solemn words written in a different context: 'the correctness of the (not particularly profound) thesis it attempts to verify and establish virtually guarantees the pointlessness of the effort' (Noam Chomsky, 1986, xxviii).

1

DARK CLOUDS OVER DANDAKARANYA

As noted in the Introduction, this book is about the plight of *adivasi*s in the context of an unfolding insurgency launched by the Communist Party of India (Maoist) in some parts of East-Central India. The insurgency is mostly concentrated in some regions of the vast forests, locally called *Dandakaranya*, that span across the states of Chhattisgarh, Maharashtra, Orissa (now Odisha) and Andhra Pradesh. Maoists are also present in the forest areas of the states of Bihar and Jharkhand. To a lesser extent, they have some penetration in the forest areas in Karnataka and West Bengal as well. (See map of India).

Reportedly, there are thousands of Maoist guerrillas armed with sophisticated weapons confronting a vast array of paramilitary forces assembled by the Indian state especially in the state of Chhattisgarh, while the existing operations in the states of Bihar, Jharkhand, Odisha, Andhra Pradesh, West Bengal and Maharashtra have been enhanced. The offensive action of the state is (unofficially) code-named 'Operation Green Hunt' (OGH). As the forces raise their guns at each other, massive and protracted violence is breaking out in these hills and jungles affecting the lives of several million *adivasi*s inhabiting the war zone. As the catastrophe unfolds, it is important to understand its origins.

The communist movement in India with an explicit Maoist content found a new expression in 1967 with a peasant uprising in Naxalbari village and adjacent areas in the northern part of the state of West Bengal. In memory of that historic event, this phase of the communist movement is also called the *Naxalite* movement, as noted. One of the leaders of the movement, Kanu Sanyal, reported:

> Between the end of March and April 1967 almost all the villages in [the area] were organised. Where the membership of the *Krishak Sabha* [Peasant Association] never was more than 5,000, even there membership figures shot up to nearly 40,000. From 15 to 24 thousand peasants became full time activists. *Krishak Samiti*s [Peasant Unions] were formed in every village. At incredible speed revolutionary peasants set up *Krishak Samiti*s through hundreds of meetings and made them into armed bands of village volunteers.

'That the scope of such revolutionary activities,' Sanyal continued, 'could become so far-flung and extensive was due to the fact that among the peasantry 70 percent of the landless peasants led this struggle.'[1]

As we will see, however, it would be a mistake to identify the broad naxalite movement of the late-1960s with the current Maoist movement. When the uprising took place, the state of West Bengal was governed by a coalition of Left and centrist parties with the Communist Party of India (Marxist), CPM, as the dominant partner. In fact, the leader of the CPM, Jyoti Basu,

Map 1: *India with States and Union Territories*

held the police portfolio. The peasant uprising was essentially led by some local – including peasant – leaders of the CPM. As the uprising gained in momentum, the government, instead of entering into a dialogue for the peaceful resolution of the issue with their own comrades, chose to attack the uprising. To emphasise, the first attack on the naxalite movement was launched by the parliamentary Left itself. Thus, insofar as the naxalites are concerned, the parliamentary Left, especially the CPM, despite its Leftist labels, is indistinguishable from the Indian state.

Although the uprising was crushed by force, the movement soon led to a split in the CPM and a new organisation called the Communist Party of India (Marxist-Leninist), CPI(ML), emerged under the leadership of Charu Mazumdar. The split was already simmering due to a divide in the international communist movement between post-Stalin Communist Party of Soviet Union (CPSU) and Communist Party of China (CPC) led by Mao Zedong. The peasant uprising in Naxalbari led to the official split. While CPM continued its allegiance to Soviet Union, CPI(ML) shifted to the Chinese path. When the naxalbari uprising arose, the Chinese leadership announced to the world that a 'spring thunder' had broken out in India. After its initial promise, the naxalite movement also fragmented into a variety of factions under ideological division and severe repression by the state.

To appreciate the perspective of this book, it is important to note that factionalism was part of the naxalite movement from the very beginning. While the peasant uprising in Naxalbari was widely hailed by a range of non-CPM Left as a revolutionary development, many distinguished voices were ignored or silenced conspiratorially when the All India Coordination Committee of Communist Revolutionaries (AICCCR) was secretly formed in 1968. As a result, several groups and individuals started functioning independently of the AICCCR. Eventually, some founding members of the AICCCR also moved away when the party CPI(ML) was formally announced in 1969 (see Chapter Three). To emphasise, the original CPI(ML) did not represent the full spectrum of the naxalite wave. The party itself underwent several splits by 1972 as the programme of the party unfolded under the leadership of Charu Mazumdar. In this historical context, the politics of CPI(Maoist) is best viewed as a continuance of the remnants of that faction of the original naxalite movement which remained loyal to the politics of Charu Mazumdar. On the ground, therefore, there is a significant naxalite voice that rejects the politics and practice of CPI(Maoist).

Brief Chronology of Maoist Upheaval in India

Bold items denote existing communist groups

- **1964** Indian Communist movement splits into two parties, **CPI** and **CPM**
- **1967** Naxalbari Uprising (March)
  Broad meeting of communist revolutionaries mostly from CPM (November). *Dakshin Desh* already functioning separately under Amulya Sen, Kanai Chatterjee
- **1968** Split in CPM, Formation of AICCCR
  Several prominent leaders stay away from AICCCR
- **1969** Formation of CPI (ML) by Charu Mazumdar and others (April)
  Dakshin Desh renamed Maoist Communist Centre (MCC) in Bihar
- **1971** S.N. Sinha breaks away from CPI (ML) in Bihar to form CPI (ML-SNS)
- **1972** Charu Mazumdar dies in custody
- **1974** **CPI(ML-*Liberation*)** formed by Jauhar (Subrata Dutt)
- **1975** UCCRI (ML) formed by T. Nagi Reddy, D.V. Rao, Moni Guha and others. Vinod Mishra takes over CPI (ML-*Liberation*) after Jauhar's death, Nagbhusan Patnaik joins later
- **1977** CPI (ML-SNS) merges with CPI (ML-Unity Committee) to form **CPI (ML-Provisional Central Committee)** later joined by Santosh Rana

1980	People's War Group (PWG) formed under K. Sitaramaya
1983	CPI (ML-Party Unity) formed in Bihar
1988	**CPI (ML-New Democracy)** formed by Yatendra Kumar
	PWG squads move into Dandakaranya
1991	K. Sitaramaya expelled from PWG, Ganapathy takes over
1992	**CPI (ML-Janashakti)** formed after unity of six splinter groups
1998	CPI (ML-Party Unity) joins PWG to form CPI (ML-People's War)
2001	CPI (ML-People's War) launches PLGA in Dandakaranya
2004	CPI (ML-People's War) and MCC combine to form **CPI (Maoist)**
	Talks with state of Andhra fail
	Maoists begin to lose ground in Andhra
2005	Beginning of *Salwa Judum* campaign by Chhattisgarh state, Maoists almost wiped out from Andhra, consolidate in Jharkhand, Chhattisgarh
2009	Beginning of Operation Green Hunt by Govt. of India

CPI(Maoist) is a comparatively new organisation formed in 2004 when two naxalite factions Maoist Communist Centre (MCC) and CPI (ML-People's War) decided to join hands after fighting a bloody war for area control among themselves for close to two decades. By 2006, CPI(Maoist) was almost completely wiped out from Andhra after a presence there for close to forty years. They also lost major areas in Bihar. By then, the organisation had basically shifted to two of the most backward, tiny and newly formed states of Jharkhand and Chhatthisgarh (see Map 1 of India). In the past year, Maoists have lost considerable ground in Jharkhand and have been virtually driven out of the Saranda forest. Even in the Maoist hotbed in the state of Chhattisgarh, Maoists are significantly present only in the *forested areas* of just *five* of eighteen districts of the state: Bijapur, Narayanpur, (new) Bastar, Dantewada, and Kanker. See Map 2.[2]

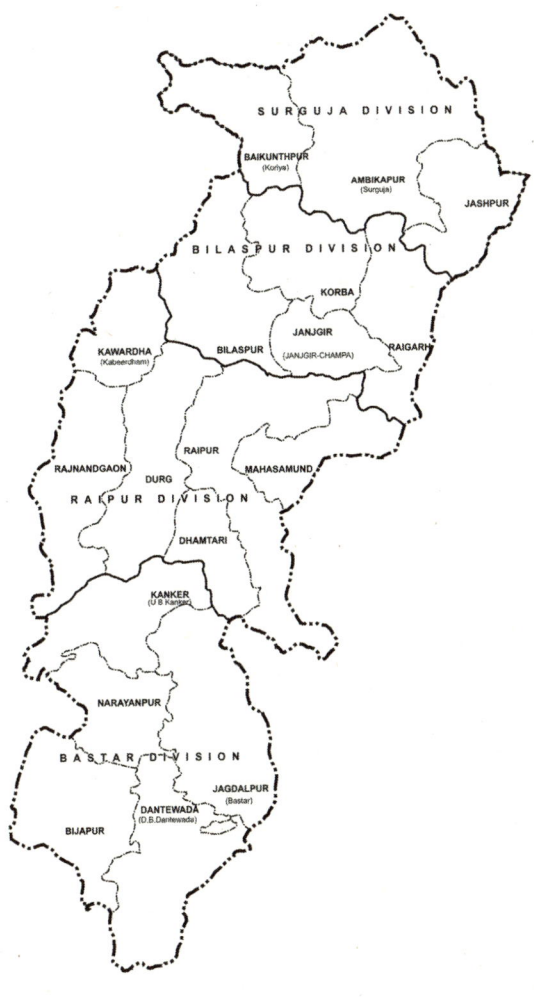

Map 2 Chhattisgarh

Chhattisgarh is a relatively small new state carved out of Madhya Pradesh. It had a population of 26 million according to the 2011 census; the current population of India being about 1.2 billion.³ The Chhattisgarh assembly has only 90 seats while Uttar Pradesh (UP) has over 400, West Bengal nearly 300, Tamilnadu and Bihar about 250 each and so on. Even the Union Territory of Delhi, a single city, has about seventy seats. The actual Maoist influence in Chhattisgarh is likely to cover about fifteen to twenty assembly segments. It is also one of the most backward regions in the country.

Maoist military headquarters are located in the Abujmaad hills of Dandakaranya, reportedly. In the jungles extending from their headquarters, they have also ostensibly developed hideouts and armed squads to create enough of a threat to mark their 'presence' in West Bengal, Odisha, Karnataka and elsewhere. However, they have essentially failed to emerge out of portions of forests of East-Central India after over four decades of campaign for this particular strand of MLM.

The organisation has no presence whatsoever in the vast agrarian and industrial terrains of the rest of the country. It has no national trade union and peasant organisation worth its name, no penetration in the Dalit, youth and women's movements. But its armed aggression seems to have captured the imagination of sections of the elite, urban and radical intelligentsia in Kolkata (previously Calcutta) and Delhi who have impressive connections with some Indian intellectuals settled in universities abroad (see Chapter Three).

'The only genuine alternative before the people' – as the general secretary of CPI(Maoist), Ganapathy, describes his party – was viewed as a 'terrorist party' by none other than the late legendary revolutionary Kanu Sanyal, who was one of the founder members of the original CPI(ML), and many currently active naxalites (see Chapter Five). As Sanyal (2010) put it, the original Maoist/naxalite organisation 'CPI(ML) was in name a communist party but in deed a terrorist party opposed to Marxism.' Clearly, Sanyal is referring to that faction of the CPI(ML) which he left early in the struggle. As noted, the current CPI(Maoist) is the only remaining strand of this faction of the original CPI(ML). As with other naxalite leaders of that era, Sanyal had used the 'terrorist' label for CPI(Maoist) as well. The basic reason why Sanyal called the CPI(Maoist) 'terrorists' is as follows.

Ever since its inception in 1969, this brand of Maoism rejected all classical forms of mass struggle and adopted the doctrine of the individual annihilation of 'class enemies', formulated by its leader Charu Mazumdar (see Chapter Three). 'Class enemies' typically consisted of hapless, poorly armed police constables, petty landlords and traders as also an assorted category of 'informers and traitors'. Most notably, the category of 'class enemies' also included grassroots cadres – not their leaders – of the parliamentary Left. In the states of West Bengal and Andhra, where this campaign originated, the parliamentary Left was largely the only organisation present at grassroots. The annihilation of these 'class enemies' – typically middle peasants, school teachers, party whole-timers etc. – effectively meant the capturing of areas already under the Left by means of guns and knives. To that end, the armed squads first targeted their own naxalite fraternity who refused to subscribe to their murderous politics. After the 'renegades' were silenced, the next target was cadres of CPM, CPI, etc. Several *current* instances of this practice are discussed in Chapter Five.

This 'red terror' basically led to the dismantling of democratic movements in the erstwhile red bastions. In West Bengal, a neo-fascist regime of the Congress party won the elections handsomely in 1972 and watched the mutual killings of the Left with glee. Once the task was accomplished, the government turned on

Maoists and the remaining Left with the consequence that white terror ruled West Bengal for five years. During the nightmare, all forms of democratic movements virtually disappeared from the state as lumpen youth accompanied by paramilitary forces roamed the streets.

In time, almost all of the initiators of this 'red terror', such as Kanu Sanyal, realised their grave mistakes and those who survived encounters, long imprisonment, and psychological collapse, returned to the classical mass line in a variety of forms including participation in elections. However, a fragment continued the murderous politics in the jungles of Andhra and Bihar in the form of two organisations, MCC and PWG, later unifying into CPI(Maoist), as noted.[4] With thousands of armed guerrillas and militia under their command, Maoists have been able to establish dozens of guerrilla zones and some guerrilla bases in the forests. In response, the Indian state has mounted a determined paramilitary offensive involving nearly one hundred thousand armed forces – Operation Green Hunt (OGH).

Caught in the crossfire are millions of poor, marginalised and historically isolated *adivasi*s. Their habitat, in which they have lived as forest-dwellers for thousands of years, is now heavily mined with hundreds of explosive devices planted by Maoists.[5] Maoists have occupied vast regions of the dense forests where their guerrilla zones and heavily guarded military headquarters are located. In response, state forces have set up hundreds of camps and have occupied school buildings to launch their attack. From these locations, the state forces invade *adivasi* habitations in search of Maoists, food and women. Plans are afoot to install a jungle warfare training school by the Indian Army close to the supposed Maoist headquarters in the hills of southern Chhattisgarh. Reportedly, military hardware such as Unarmed Aerial Vehicles

(UAV) and helicopter gunships have been deployed to keep track of insurgents.[6]

Hundreds of *adivasi*s have already lost their lives in the armed conflict and thousands are in jail, most of them on fake charges. Regarding the atrocious actions of the police on innocent *adivasi*s, the young and courageous reporter Javed Iqbal reports from Chhattisgarh:

> The now-released Jairam Khora joins countless *adivasi*s in Central India, to whom being 'abducted' and 'detained' by policemen is an event that takes place with frightening regularity. This is true especially for the thousands of people living in the interior forests of Bastar, who have given up on traveling to local markets, or traveling through police checkpoints, over risks of being interrogated, beaten or arrested simply by association.[7]

Further, several hundred villages have been looted and burnt by both state and Maoist forces, lakhs have fled their homes, hundreds of schools have closed down as state forces occupy them or Maoists blow them up, and malnutrition has reached sub-Saharan proportions. And violence from both sides is escalating.

Just to cite one recent incident out of many: In March 2011, three villages near Chintalnar in the Dantewada district of Chhattisgarh were reportedly raided and burnt by Central forces, SPOs and Koya commandos.[8] In Tarmetla village, 207 homes were burnt; in Morpalli, thiry-five homes were looted first and then burnt, two women were sexually abused and one person was killed; and in Timapuram, seventy-five houses were set on fire. Along with the houses, harvested paddy, which was stored in granaries was also burnt.[9]

A few months before this incident, Maoists 'mistakenly' exploded a civilian bus carrying fifty to sixty people. Nearly forty civilians and trainee SPOs, mostly *adivasis*, were killed by the explosion and the Maoists opened fire on the survivors. This is clearly a warning to the government of the shape of things to come if OGH continues.[10]

Further, as it usually happens with ill-grounded armed insurgencies, armed actions of Maoists and the state are already giving rise to ugly vigilante reactions from the same exhausted *adivasi* population: *adivasi*s killing, raping, looting other *adivasi*s. An (unpublished) official report (MRD, 2009) states that the vigilante campaign sponsored by Chhattisgarh state – called *Salwa Judum*, euphemistically meaning 'peace hunt' – was 'headed and peopled by (*adivasi*) Murias, some of them erstwhile cadre and local leaders of the Communist Party of India (Maoist) ... The first onslaught of the *Salwa Judum* was on Muria villagers who still owed allegiance to the Communist Party of India (Maoist). It turned out to be an open war between brothers'.

After earlier strictures by the Supreme Court of India on the illegality of state-sponsored vigilante campaign *Salwa Judum*, the 'war between brothers' continued unabated between those *adivasi*s who are with Maoists, one the one hand, and Koya commandos recruited by the state from the same *adivasi* population, on the other. With fresh strictures against the hiring of special police officers (SPO) and Koya commandos,[11] the 'war between brothers' is likely to assume newer, more clandestine, forms. *Adivasi*s will now be encouraged to 'spontaneously' attack other *adivasi*s owing allegiance to Maoists with the state acting behind the scenes; Maoists will retaliate in identical terms as they had done earlier with *Salwa Judum* 'relief camps'.

Also, the Chhattisgarh state is likely to induct more local *adivasi*s directly into police and paramilitary forces to compensate for the loss of low-cost SPOs and Koya commandos.[12] If the state could hire over 6,000 *adivasi* boys for a meagre salary of

3,000 rupees per month, they can surely hire three times more with regular police salaries. And money is not a problem with shining India; there are thousands of vacancies in Chhattisgarh police anyway. 'Few of the SPOs has ever been to school; hardly any has traveled beyond Bastar,' Jaideep Hardikar reports.[13] After talking to a twenty-year old *adivasi* youth Nandu, Hardikar writes: 'Nandu himself is an ex-Maoist: he was once a *dalam* (squad) member. He says he had never wanted to go with the rebels when he was a child. Now, he has no option but to join the police.'

Alternatively, some of the Koya commandos, 'disarmed' by the Supreme Court, may want to go back to Maoists for food, guns and shelter; a veiled invitation to that effect is already on offer. 'The government knows,' Hardikar explains, 'if Nandu doesn't fight for the State, he may have no choice but to fight for the enemy. One reason the administration has been so quick to decide to raise the new force is that immediately after the court order, Maoists had appealed to the SPOs to return to their villages.' There is no Supreme Court stricture on 'special Maoist officers'; Maoists operate outside the scope of law anyway. 'For the tribal, there is no third choice,' Hardikar observes. With no dearth of jobs with guns, the land of Chhattisgarh is full of opportunities for *adivasi* boys and girls if they are willing to die.

With the reported scale and sophistication of Maoist military preparations and the determination and the vast offensive resources available to the Indian state, the grim picture just sketched appears to be just the beginning. It does not require either deep political insight or insider's knowledge based on 'field-studies' to infer that, ultimately, Maoists cannot win this one since they have never secured mass acceptance with the people of India. In fact, if their history of four decades of armed operations is any indication, it is extremely unlikely that they will ever expand beyond the forests of Dandakaranya (south Chhattisgarh), Sarguja (north Chhattisgarh), and Saranda (Jharkhand), all clustered in East-Central India. These forests denote their only habitat and (final) burial (Guha, 2007). Even Maoist sympathisers seem to understand this: 'There is no doubt that Maoists' militarised politics makes it almost impossible for it to function in places where there is no forest cover' (Roy, 2010b). It is another matter that Maoist sympathisers continue to be under the illusion that this (four-decades-old) limitation is just a fleeting phenomenon that will be overcome as the movement expands. So, the 'radical' expectation is that the war will expand and cover even more of the impoverished sections of the population.

Nonetheless, given the special character of jungle warfare and the relative inaccessibility of their operational zones, Maoists have certainly developed the means to ward off Indian forces, including eventually the Indian Army, for years. A single forest brigand, Veerappan, accompanied by a few dozen armed men, was able to resist security forces for decades (Chakravarty, 2008). As with Veerappan and the LTTE in Sri Lanka, the security forces are likely to suffer relatively more damage in the initial stages due to the unfamiliar terrain in remote hills and jungles and lack of penetration in the local population.[14] The history of insurgency in the North-East shows that the Indian government will respond to the early setbacks with escalated violence (Bhatia, 2011b), perhaps armed with special laws such as Armed Forces Special Powers Act (AFSPA) which has been in operation in Kashmir and the North-East for decades.[15]

The state of Chhattisgarh has already enacted and put into operation the draconian Chhattisgarh Special Public Security Act (CSPSA) under which an untold number of hapless *adivasi*s have been incarcerated. An impressive international campaign – involving scores of Nobel laureates and other dignitaries – ensued when Dr Binayak Sen was jailed under this act. Dr Sen had left his plush job decades ago at the prestigious Vellore hospital to work in the villages of Chhattisgarh for *adivasi* healthcare. His 'crime' is that he protested against the atrocities committed by state-sponsored vigilante groups. It is a victory to democratic forces that Dr Sen has now been released. However, thousands of faceless *adivasi*s are still in jail as the campaign petered out once Dr Sen was granted bail.

Needless to say, the entire brunt of the projected 'protracted war' will be borne by *adivasi*s, while elite urban radicals become progressively stoned on the imaginary fumes of revolution emanating from Maoist guns. As the activist-political scientist Aditya Nigam (2010a) put it, 'We have a Maoist-aligned intelligentsia vicariously playing out their revolutionary fantasies through the lives of *adivasi*s, while the people actually dying in battle are almost all *adivasi*s.' Someone remarked recently that Maoists will make sure that the fight continues down to the last *adivasi*, and the Indian forces will not stop firing until Maoists do.

The primary culprit for the historical plight of *adivasi*s is, of course, the Indian state whose policies and actions have led to the widespread destitution of the people with the *adivasi*s at the very bottom (Guha, 2007; DCEAA, 2008). As we will soon see, the general condition of Indian people includes nearly two hundred thousand farmer suicides in the last decade, per capita income of less than twenty *rupee*s (less than half a US dollar) a day for seventy-five percent of the population at 2007 rates, extensive malnutrition, massive destruction of forests and rivers, atrocious violation of human rights, and a dismal record in each index on quality of life (Ghandy, 2011a).[16] However, it does not require either pronounced radicalism or scholarly skills to grasp the general condition of vast masses in India; the stench of outrageous poverty and indignity engulfs our senses daily.

The impoverished condition of the people had enabled Maoists and other secret forces to enter the scene with some apparent legitimacy (Sundar, 2006; Guha, 2007; Chakravarty, 2008). In turn, these armed upheavals have enabled the Indian state to respond with a massive paramilitary offensive. How do we understand this vicious conflict?

For now, I wish to focus on a single issue. Following the doctrines of MLM, let us assume that Maoists are essentially engaged in protecting the rights of *adivasi*s to just livelihood. What exactly is the rationale for initiating an armed struggle to achieve *this end*?

More specifically, consider the following list of Maoist actions: hijacking, derailment and burning of trains; blowing up railway stations, school buildings, and police stations; killing and occasional beheading of suspected informers; attacks on police armouries to loot hundreds of weapons and thousands of rounds of ammunition as in Nayagarh; looting of banks and treasuries; mass killing of security personnel in their camps as in Rani Bodili and Silda; ambush and killing of security personnel (and making of 'ambush' videos); recruiting children as young as twelve years old for indoctrination and guerrilla training; amassing thousands of guerrillas in People's Liberation Guerrilla Army (PLGA), armed to the teeth with AK series rifles, machine guns, rocket launchers, grenades and other explosives; recruiting several thousand village-level militias who wield anything from bows and arrows to guns; colluding with varieties of mafia and private contractors to raise funds for arms; and killing of political opponents, especially from the Left and often from depressed sections of society to grab control over an area.

No doubt these are 'standard' operations in many insurgencies across the world (Simeon, 2010; Mander, 2011). In each case though these atrocious operations need to be justified in respect of the proclaimed cause. As noted, there is at least some justification for Maoist uprisings in Nepal and the Philippines because in each case vast masses of poor people are trapped in a brutal state where peaceful resistance to secure welfare of people is hardly feasible. This criterion applies to many armed insurgencies of the non-Maoist kind as well such as the prolonged armed rebellion of FARC in Colombia. In the Maoist case in India, how do the listed actions relate to the welfare of *adivasi*s in Bastar? Who brought this war on these people? Could the war have been avoided while addressing the rights of *adivasi*s?

Unsurprisingly, the answer of the Indian state is that Maoists are squarely responsible for the war: Their armed control over a vast area has prevented the state from undertaking welfare measures for . The authority of the state is required for the development of *adivasi* areas. Hence, the war. For the purposes of this book, including its narrow textual basis, I will not examine the view of the state via documents of the state and its propagandists (Chenoy and Chenoy, 2010, for critical review).

Importantly, the 'propagandists' of the state consist of virtually all major political parties including the parliamentary Left. As noted, the parliamentary Left had militarily attacked the entire naxalite fraternity since its emergence in the late 1960s. Apart from police action in Naxalbari itself, followed by paramilitary operations elsewhere in the province, it has suppressed peasant uprisings by force in Singur and Nandigram, conducted a genocide of refugees from Bangladesh in the forests of Sunderban in Marichjhanpi, and has cooperated with the central government in launching a version of OGH in the state of West Bengal.

I simply assume that the state is what it is. It has a long history of conducting protracted wars, including economic wars, on people throughout the country. It is evident by now that each of its organs including the parliament, the government, various welfare commissions and the system of justice including the Supreme Court of India – all supposedly designed to serve the people – has essentially failed vast masses of people. After over half a century of 'welfare measures' for the people, the basic picture is that a small minority of elites have garnered most of the national wealth while a vast majority of people languish in increasing poverty and indignity.

The concentration of wealth and impoverishment of masses during the last two decades may be summarised as follows. Although GDP growth had indeed increased to about 6.7 percent per annum during the 1990s, employment growth rate has actually fallen from 2 percent in the mid-eighties to 0.98 percent in 2000.[17] Turning to other indicators, there has been a drastic fall in the off-take of subsidised grain by the poor from the Public Distribution System (Utsa Patnaik, 2007a; 2007b); further, between 1995–96 and 1998–99, a total of 60.84 lakh subscribers have ceased their memberships to the provident fund scheme.[18] The incidence of poverty actually increased in the next decade resulting in a per capita income of less than twenty rupees a day for over seventy-five percent of the population in 2007 (Sengupta et al., 2008; Sengupta, 2009), as noted, while the GDP increased to about nine percent throughout the same period. It is a national shame that the government itself had fixed the poverty line in India in 2011 at rupees thirty-two per day per person or a little over half-a-dollar a day.

So, who grew? During the earlier decade, 'the MNCs increased their sales by 322 percent and gross profit by 369 percent', and 'Indian corporates garnered an increase in gross profit of 336 percent and net sales by 303 percent', while their excise duty obligations increased by less than half of these figures.[19] While per capita income, boosted by rising GDP, showed substantial growth by Indian standards, massive poverty in rural India culminated in large-scale suicide of farmers across the country (Sainath, 2009). It is not difficult to understand how the effect of the noted growth was distributed. During this period of aggressive neo-liberal agenda which saw a number of Indian corporations enter the Fortune 500 club and a relatively affluent middle class – roughly twenty percent of the population – emerge, the rest of India essentially turned into what the noted economist Utsa Patnaik (2007a) has called the 'republic of hunger'.

So, it is at least questionable if this state has the moral authority to administer all areas under its titular control. In any case, insofar as the Bastar area is specifically concerned, except for occasional harassment by police and forest officials, *adivasi*s were completely ignored by the state before Maoists moved in (Sundar 2006; Guha, 2007; DCEAA 2008; Chenoy and Chenoy, 2010). As we will see, it is the Maoists who brought some measure of relief and dignity to people by their sustained efforts for over two decades. As to the character of those measures, more of that later (see Chapter Four).

Once the predatory role of the Indian state is understood, what are the viable forms of resistance to this state to ensure lasting welfare of people? Some influential authors such as Roy (2010b) suggest that, despite current limitations, Maoists belong to the spectrum of rising resistance; Maoists themselves believe of course that the Indian people will 'rise like a tornado' under the leadership of the party. I happen to believe that these suggestions are absolutely false: Maoists are not only the other culprit for the current plight of *adivasi*s, they are a danger to resistance itself.

Consider, for example, the almost complete absence of any alternative left, including other naxalites, in the areas in which CPI(Maoist) thrives while right-wing parties such as the Bharatiya Janata Party (BJP), Congress, Rashtriya Janata Dal, Jharkhand Mukti

Morcha, and now Trinamool Congress are able to operate freely and win elections. These parties are not likely to interfere with the Maoists' control of populations. Their armed command over remote areas – inhabited mostly by the poorest of the poor – will remain as long as Maoists enable these parties to win elections and continue with the loot of the treasury. Left organisations, in contrast, are likely to organise these destitutes on issues of livelihood since, devoid of gigantic money power, this is the only viable alternative for the Left to win elections.[20] In that sense, classical Left politics directly interferes with the Maoist agenda of exclusive control over land and people.

To cite just one crucial evidence among many, in the Maoist-dominated Bastar region itself, the right-wing BJP has eleven out of the twelve assembly seats, Congress has the other one.[21] In contrast, CPI which used to have significant presence among *adivasi*s and peasants in the Bastar area for many decades has virtually disintegrated with most of its local leaders and activists in prison.

No doubt, CPI(Maoist) is embedded in an *adivasi* population in a small section of the country. However, CPI(Maoist) is 'with' *adivasi*s in the restricted sense that it thrives in their destitution, just as Tehrik-e-Taliban thrives in the destitution of *adivasi*s in Waziristan in the North-West region of Pakistan, adjacent to Afghanistan. The Tehrik is evidently popular in those *adivasi* belts and it recruits its foot soldiers from them. The leadership of course rests with elite mullahs. It will be a travesty of political interpretation to claim, therefore, that the Tehrik is a people's (liberation) movement and that *adivasi*s of Waziristan have taken up arms as a form of resistance against the US hegemony, even if the US has given *adivasi*s of that region enough reasons to do so.

In the extreme, the destitution of *adivasi*s can reach a point where they can align with palpably fascist forces like Rashtriya

Swayamsevak Sangh (RSS) and Vishva Hindu Parishad (VHP) in Gujarat for whatever respite they can get from grinding poverty and abysmal neglect by the state. One can understand what scale of desperation lead to such destructive alliances, yet just a local support from historically marginalised people does not always lead to genuine resistance. Hence, the bare fact of local support does not necessarily reflect on the respectability of the political methods of the organisations themselves; even *khap panchayat*s have considerable local support. As a matter of fact, people who might offer temporary local support out of desperation, soon realise the long term political meaning of such alliances. Thus, when the Maoist leadership and guerrillas were driven out of Andhra Pradesh after over three decades of armed struggle, *adivasi*s and peasants failed to 'rise like a tornado', as the Supreme Commander expects the people to do on his party's behalf.[22]

In this perspective, when classical forms of democratic resistance based on militant mass movements collapse and reactionary forces begin to dominate political options, the cited militarism is likely to ensue in favourable pockets, as we will see in more detail in the next chapter. Although the militarism is launched in the name of people, its grossly sectarian and vigilante character not only restricts the scope of genuine mass action, it also enables the state to initiate wars on people with perfect moral authority to attack the remnants of civil resistance. The rise and fall of the LTTE in Sri Lanka is a classic case (see Chapter Three).

The tragedy in Bastar is that these *adivasi*s are losing lives basically for nothing. There is growing – sometimes spectacular – resistance across the country against the forcible occupation of land, mining operations and the destruction of rivers, forests and mountains. In one case among many, *adivasi*s and marginal peasants in the Niyamgiri region of Odisha, adjacent to Dandakaranya, organised a powerful resistance against the bauxite mining giant

Vedanta to the point that the government was forced to stop all operations and cancel all licenses. This saved the vast adjoining forests and the Niyamgiri hills worshipped by *adivasis*. The struggle went on for five years assisted by a variety of Left groups, but the village *panchayat*s were the basic organisational centre.[23] Maoists are nowhere in these peaceful but militant struggles (see Menon, 2009; Bhattacharya, 2010).

Moreover, the predatory character of the Indian state, sketched above, includes its overwhelming gun power to stifle resistance by force over vast areas inhabited by unarmed populations if it is given the opportunity. The response of the Indian state to freedom movements in Kashmir and the North-East are the most glaring current examples (Chenoy and Chenoy, 2010). Needless to say, when an attack begins, the unarmed poor are its immediate victims. It is the grave responsibility of organisers of resistance movements, then, to ensure that the opportunity of the state to unleash the full force of terror under its command is not allowed to mature until the point when the poor are able to defend themselves.

Resisting the autocratic, neo-fascist monarchial regime in Nepal, the Maoist movement there ensured this abiding principle by organising vast masses of people in the Nepalese countryside by adopting strategies, including protracted armed struggle, such that the Royal Nepalese Army was left virtually paralysed during most of that struggle. As noted, the armed struggle was given up as soon as the monarch was removed and a republic established. The Maoist party in Nepal proved its popularity by winning over forty percent of seats in parliamentary elections that followed.

In contrast, my own view is that resistance movements in Kashmir and the North-East essentially lie in ruins now – accompanied by immense suffering of people – precisely because arms were taken up, enabling the Indian state to expand its massive military intervention. It is important to note that, unlike the Maoist movement, these are freedom movements calling for separate nation-states at the borders of the Indian state. The demands are therefore on a different plane than the Maoist programme of seizure of power of the Indian state itself (see Chapter Six). In the separatist case, the Indian state was likely to respond with aggression from the very beginning, which it did. In Kashmir, for instance, the army moved in, armed with instruments such as the AFSPA, much before arms were actually taken up by resistance movements. Given the narrow democratic space for peaceful resistance, it is understandable – though not *justified* – why arms were taken up at a certain point. But the consequences are there for all to see.

In fact, despite severe setbacks, the freedom movement in Kashmir has survived to an extent due to the presence of organisations such as the Jammu and Kashmir Liberation Front (JKLF) who *gave up* arms many years ago. The movement has developed renewed vigour in recent years as the armed struggle faded away and impressive mass protests filled the streets.

The resistance in Manipur does not have the equivalent of JKLF to my knowledge, yet a solitary indefinite hunger strike by a woman, Irom Sharmila, and the women's organisations that have spawned around her, have kept resistance alive while dozens of 'liberation armies' – and drug syndicates – compete among themselves for area control. Irom Sharmila started a hunger strike over a decade ago for the repeal of the draconian AFSPA when a dozen unarmed civilians were gunned down by the army in an open market, yet no punitive action followed as the soldiers were protected by the Act. Irom Sharmila is under continuous arrest and is force-fed through her nose for all these years (Mehrotra, 2009). Contrary to Roy (2010a), Irom Sharmila has shown the world that, even in the middle of a vicious armed conflict, an action such as indefinite hunger strike is no laughing matter (unless, of course, you are in the company of trigger-happy guerrillas saturated with distaste for 'Gandhian humbug').

I am aware that a large number of well meaning individuals, groups and organisations in India – including non-statist Left comprising liberals, Gandhians, socialists and non-Maoist naxalites – are opposed to the Maoist militarism just sketched. Some of them will be documented as we proceed, especially in Chapter Five. But the ideological climate is such that people seem to find it difficult to articulate strong resistance to Maoists without feeling guilty of apparently siding with statist propaganda. It is another sign of a significant dent in the voices available in what is supposed to be a pluralist democracy. It is taken full advantage of by both the state and Maoists.

Thus, a well known Left intellectual in Delhi, belonging to one of the naxalite 'splinter groups', advised me that, whatever be the objections to CPI(Maoist), we must side with them publicly in their struggle against the state while criticising them 'internally'. The argument obviously is that the historical choice is binary in character: Either you are with the state or against it. And the underlying assumption is that those who are against the state are somehow 'with' the people. Since Maoists are (apparently) against the state, they must be viewed as 'with' the people, warts and all. In not siding with Maoists then, intellectuals opposed to Maoists are actually siding with the state, according to the doctrine.

Biswajit Roy (2011) illustrates the doctrine as follows: 'The human rights groups in Bengal never criticised Maoists for indiscriminately killing CPM and non-CPM leaders and their supporters suspecting them as police moles. ... Long divided on the question of legitimacy of non-state terror, particularly revolutionary violence, both individuals and their forums feared that their criticism of Maoist follies would strengthen the "enemies".' Almost the entire spectrum of political opinion, left-right-centre, seems to have adopted this doctrine in one form or another depending on their location on the spectrum.

The state certainly believes in the binary doctrine. The Union Home Minister P. Chidambaram* has characterised all 'civil society' forums that are strongly critical of his murderous approach to 'Maoist menace' as Maoist supporters since their criticism of the government is apparently helping Maoists. The doctrine was earlier put into actual official practice in Chhattisgarh when the state applied CSPSA against Dr Binayak Sen. As the world knows by now, Dr Sen was arrested under this draconian act because he publicly protested the homicidal *Salwa Judum* operations of the state; hence, he was viewed as a Maoist collaborator.

More recently, the doctrine was applied at the street level in Chhattisgarh when hordes of Congress and the right-wing BJP workers attacked the peace mission undertaken by Prof. Yash Pal, Swami Agnivesh, Narayan Desai, and others; they were characterised as *Maobadi*s (Maoists) since the peace mission appealed to both sides to stop violence. Gautam Navlakha and Sumanta Banerjee, noted democratic rights activists and writers, also adopted the doctrine from the other direction as they protested the same peace mission which asked Maoists to lay down arms. We are living in disturbing times when the voices of right-wing hoodlums and Left wing commentators unite in opposing a peace mission of citizens which was designed to bring some relief to the beleaguered *adivasi*s of Bastar.[24] The peace mission predictably collapsed.

The parliamentary Left, especially CPM, also seems to favour the doctrine under the circumstances. In private (and due to the unbearable burden of their Leftist credentials) they do complain about the 'security-centric' approach of the government and

---

* Sushil Kumar Shinde has since replaced P. Chidambaram as the Union Home Minister on 31st July, 2012.

have been somewhat critical of the *Salwa Judum* campaign, still they are not prepared to voice these concerns in public strongly because then they will be viewed by Chidambaram as anti-state; hence, pro-Maoist. They would rather be viewed as siding with Chidambaram than with Ganapathy as a version of OGH expands in the Marxist-ruled state of West Bengal (see Biswajit Roy, 2010).[25]

Maoists are also strong supporters of this doctrine, especially during 'war times'. A circular issued by the *Janatana Sarkar* (people's government) in Bastar (see Apoorvanand, 2010) very clearly forbids *adivasi*s from mixing with police, SPOs or Central Reserve Police Force (CRPF) inviting them to the village for any event, providing them food or shelter, giving any service to security persons, and travelling with them. *Adivasi*s are also advised to keep track of the number of policemen in their area and the arms they carry, and report to *Janatana Sarkar* their movement and destination. The message is clear: If any *adivasi* fails to obey these orders, the *adivasi* would be viewed as not supporting the 'revolution'; hence, the *adivasi* would be viewed as with the enemy. It is the Maoist version of UAPA;[26] it is designed to transform an entire population of *adivasi*s into 'Special Maoist Officers'.

As another grassroots worker – well known in Delhi – from another 'splinter group' told me, George Bush famously proclaimed, 'You are either with us or against us': Choose between Bush and Bin Laden. In that instance, the comrade reminded me, the civilised world denied Bush his binary choices. Should we then have to choose between Chidambaram as he deploys his terror forces around *adivasi* habitats and the Maoist leadership as they push thousands of starving *adivasi* children – dressed up as militias and guerrillas – to face Chidambaram's forces?

So far, barring a few feeble voices such as Gupta (2010) and Simeon (2011), there are no takers for this option. Thus, the simple logic for the third option is missed in the dark clouds of violence, cunning, cynicism, and insanity that have gathered over Dandakaranya.

2
FRAGILE DEMOCRACY

It does not require profound socio-political insight to understand that forms of extremism begin to obtain some acceptance with sections of people in contexts of massive civil strife when classical, peaceful and democratic options begin to lose their relevance. Before we examine the contemporary Maoist upheaval in India in detail, a brief look thus at the state of Indian democracy may be instructive. To prepare this background, I will hardly touch upon the Maoist issue in this chapter. Rather, I will elucidate some of the general features of Indian democracy whose progressive degeneration has created the fertile ground for the emergence of extremist and other non-state forces; the Maoist issue then becomes a special case of the general phenomenon.

At a critical point in Indian democracy, Noam Chomsky (in Mukherji 2005, xvii) observed: 'Indian democracy is one of the triumphs of the twentieth century, but a fragile one. The plant has to be protected and nurtured, or it can all too easily wither, with consequences that are sure to be grim'.

The point was critical in that the country had just emerged out of a regressive, right-wing government led by BJP which is generally characterised as a communal-fascist organisation in the Left and liberal circles in India. There are reasons to agree with this characterisation as we will see below. The critical point illustrated the 'fragility' of Indian democracy in that this force could come to power at all in the otherwise pluralist India through legitimate electoral means. Still, it was also a point of at least temporary 'triumph' that the people used the same electoral system to throw it out eventually. What explains the phenomenon? I will return to the issue of communal-fascism after surveying some of the other aspects where Indian democracy has developed fragile tendencies.

Indian democracy is a 'triumph' because there are reasons to be impressed by the form and content of the Constitution of India, an election system offering a rich variety of political choices, institutions such as Human Rights, Minorities and Women's Commissions, a vast network of public enterprises, a reasonably effective public distribution system, a politically conscious middle class, an impressive judiciary, a free press and a long history of democratic struggle of working people in enforcing social policy. The ideals of democracy and, to an extent, socialism have found deep acceptance in the system. Despite its poverty, illiteracy, treatment of women and Dalits, and massive violation of human rights, India happens to be one of the better examples of functioning democracies in the world.

In what follows I will focus primarily on the election system since it has an obvious primacy in a democratic order based on universal franchise. Other institutions of the state are designed to deliver justice, dignity and welfare to otherwise unempowered sections of the population precisely because the election system endows these sections with timely opportunity to dismantle ruling regimes. Elections make sure that regimes are compelled to care even if grudgingly.

Incidentally, Maoists do not believe in the empowering function of the election system which is perhaps the only sustainable instrument of empowerment people have (see Chapter Five). Since dismantling India's electoral democracy is central to Maoists' doctrines and practice, in effect Maoists wish to deny people their only instrument of power. Such doctrines will begin to penetrate the popular imagination just in case the election system begins to lose its appeal.

Among the institutions of democracy listed above, the election system in particular has formed significant roots not only in the cities but even in rural India and other remote parts of the country. The fact that a largely independent Election Commission is able to enforce – often with the use of muscle power – widespread free and fair elections across an extremely complex and ethnically diverse country, is a clear testimony to people's acceptance and approval of the process. This is in sharp contrast with openly manipulated elections in much of the developing world, including some of India's South-Asian neighbours.

Moreover, despite determined efforts which have begun to pay some dividends in recent years, the Indian elite have not been able to exercise complete authoritarian control over the process even after six decades. This is in sharp contrast to the electoral processes in almost the entire developed world where people have been forced to exercise their franchise under an extremely narrow set of choices: Tweedledee and Tweedledum.[1] In contrast, the Indian parliament consists of literally dozens of organisations representing a wide variety of political options. Apart from the usual lawyers, representatives of big business, feudal interests and dynastic politicians, the Indian parliament also contains genuine representations from a variety of Left and other social justice forums. In favourable cases, these representations have made significant contributions in directing social policy. More importantly, the system has enabled the people to repeatedly throw out unpopular regimes, sometimes with much surprise and discomfort for the elites. In that sense, the Indian election system has helped sustain at least a diffused form of class war (Mukherji, 2004). In the same sense, the system has empowered the people to have some access to state power.

But Chomsky also says that this democracy is 'a fragile one'. As noted, Chomsky made this remark in 2005 when the 'fragility' of Indian democracy reached almost a critical point. Focusing on the election system, the fragility of Indian democracy means that the system of electoral democracy is no longer able to ensure people's access to state power. Viewing electoral politics as a form of class war, the ruling order had made attempts to influence the electoral system throughout with increasing success. Especially in the neo-liberal economic order that was enforced on the people around the early 1990s, the electoral system has failed even more to generate a form of governance whose basic function is to construct and widen the scope of welfare institutions. As a result, the conception of the welfare state serving the interests of the population is beginning to lose appeal. Despite the continuance of the electoral system, therefore, it is increasingly questionable whether the system in fact empowers people. One can thus appreciate the emergence of Maoist and other anti-electoral doctrines of 'direct control' of the system of governance, in the name of the people, of course.

The relation between the state and the people is central to this problem. Given the wide disconnect just noted, it is natural to think of the state as a hindrance to popular aspirations. The thought is consistent with the Marxist-Leninist idea that the ultimate liberation of people lies in the elimination of the state and all its centralised governing institutions. So the visible disconnect between the people and the state may actually be welcome in a long term reorganisation of society. As people become wary of the state, they will rise to resist it to make way for its ultimate elimination.

What notion of state is under issue here? I will basically hold on to the commonsense idea that the state is a system of institutions which formulates a set of laws to be enforced over a given region. When the laws are fundamentally changed, the old state collapses and a new one comes into being as new institutions develop to form and enforce a new set of laws. This does raise the chicken-and-egg problem between the conception of the state and the laws it enforces; but any other notion of state does the same.

The definition leaves much room for gradual change in favourable cases. When the system of institutions is tightly woven together with some super-institution – such as monarchs, dictators and politbureaus – monitoring the tightness, there is very little room for gradual change. However, in a large setup of loosely structured institutions, each institution will enjoy a degree of autonomy and will accommodate some change without immediately affecting the functioning of other institutions. The degree and the quantum of autonomy will obviously depend on the 'distance' from other law-enforcing institutions. The Indian Supreme Court and the Election Commission illustrate such autonomy when other things are equal.

This conception of the state is consistent with the Marxist conception that the state represents the interests of the ruling classes. The laws which the state formulates and enforces via its system of institutions are such that, in the long run and on the whole, they are heavily tilted in favour of certain classes. So the Marxist picture also requires that the state be viewed primarily as a law-enforcing system, albeit serving the interests of specific interest groups – a 'welfare state' for the rich. Given that laws are enforced, and not obeyed out of love, some amount of lawlessness will always prevail depending upon the reach and the efficacy of the enforcing institutions; the state might even encourage certain forms of lawlessness especially if it directly serves the interests of the ruling classes. In a capitalist system, industrial tycoons are routinely allowed to get away without paying taxes while the judicial and police systems routinely harass the working masses.

But typically, laws (with their loopholes) are so framed as to achieve these ends in any case. It follows that massive lawlessness is not in the interest of the state, whatever be the specificity of that interest. If there is a massive failure of law and order, we ought to conclude, other things being equal, that the state is beginning to collapse. In this light, phenomena such as massive corruption eating into the daily lives of people, inability of wide sections of the population to access welfare schemes and institutions of justice despite progressive laws to that end, widespread criminalisation of electoral politics and the emergence of armed insurgencies unmistakenly point towards a gradual withdrawal of the state. Each of these phenomena is an instance of lawlessness beyond the control of the state.

Varieties of Marxists and Gandhians share the view that the state is an impediment to human freedom and justice. It is well known that this is also the central point of departure for the libertarian-anarchist tradition which otherwise differs significantly from the Marxist tradition. Elimination of the state is thus a favoured option for a very large spectrum of radical political opinion. I will question this opinion from within the radical tradition. I do not defend the viability of the state on statist grounds, but on grounds of radical demands on human welfare and justice themselves. I argue that current radical priorities *require* the state with all its glaring limitations so that people can access it. The elimination of the state, or even the overthrowing of the Indian state to install a new one, currently favours the anti-people forces of society. Specifically, the radical task is to uphold and expand the electoral system which I take to be the most fundamental institution of the Indian state.

In a conversation about fifteen years ago, Noam Chomsky (1996, 164) makes the apparently startling suggestion that the current task for radical democratic movements is to *uphold* the state. The suggestion is startling since it comes from an anarchist libertarian thinker who has devoted his life to resisting repression and other encroachments on freedom which are routinely justified for reasons of state (Chomsky 1996, 1998, 1999a, 1999b, etc.) and for whom the preferred model of human organisation has always been the autonomous small community free from any external control. What is the argument then for rechanelling radical priorities *for* reasons of state? To avoid unnecessary controversies, let me cite Chomsky's view on this matter in full:

> In the long term I think the centralised political power ought to be eliminated and dissolved and turned down ultimately to the local level, finally, with federalism and associations and so on. On the other hand, right now I'd like to strengthen the federal government. The reason is, we live in this world, not some other world. And in this world there happen to be huge concentrations of private power which are as close to tyranny and as close to totalitarian as anything humans have devised, and they have extraordinary power. They are unaccountable to the public. There's only one way of defending rights that have been attained or extending their scope in the face of these private powers, and that's to maintain the one

form of illegitimate power that happens to be somewhat responsive to the public and which the public can indeed influence. So you end up supporting centralized State power even though you oppose it. People who think there is a contradiction in that just aren't thinking very clearly. (Chomsky, 1996, 164)

Apart from Chomsky's personal history, the suggestion is *prima facie* surprising on other grounds as well. Those of us whose political opinion has been largely shaped by a combination of Marxist and Gandhian conceptions of social organisation have viewed the state as a system of institutions that favour certain interest groups; it thus formalises and enforces inequality among people. For any egalitarian goals then the state must go. Chomsky is suggesting that this issue be reexamined afresh: 'The reason is, we live in this world, not some other world'.

Let me try to develop a unified approach to this problem so that we do not get embroiled in partisan discourse. Marx and Gandhi differ quite radically about how this task of the elimination of the state is to be approached. They also differ substantially about much else: for example, they differ in their conceptions of the human individual and the concept of freedom to be embraced. I do not wish to enter these issues since they have been discussed at length by Marxist and Gandhian scholars.

Despite these differences, maybe there are deeper points of convergence between Marx and Gandhi which lie as yet submerged under partisan discourse and are hindering a unity of democratic forces. In my view, at least some of the disagreements between Marx and Gandhi may be traced to Marx's conception that the first step for the elimination of the state is to overpower the current state with alternative social forces, namely the proletariat. Is it in the interest of the proletariat that the state be eliminated once it has captured state power? The proletarian state seems to impose new forms of control on freedom and it actually inhibits any further process towards the elimination of the state. If the aim of radical democratic movement is to achieve freedom from all forms of control, why should one settle for an intermediate form of control as a necessary step towards that end? I am aware of complicated responses to this objection from within the framework of Marxist theory. Nevertheless, the historical experience has been that when a state is installed in the name of the proletariat, its form of control is typically far more and severe than the state it has just replaced, even if the proletarian state ensures higher forms of welfare in some sectors.

It stands to reason then that a democratic movement ought to directly aim for the elimination of the state as a form of control. For example, when Gandhi talks of the village as the ideal unit of social formation, he uses the village as a metaphor for free local formations in cooperative engagement with each other. The task for the democratic movement right now is to establish such villages – 'liberated zones' – all at once. This is an ideal the seeds of which Gandhi thought, perhaps erroneously, to be already available in the current state of the (Indian) village.

Chomsky would certainly endorse this picture, but under contextual qualifications as we saw. Ultimately, I think, Marx also would have endorsed this picture though he would have differed in his conception of the village given the eurocentric framework within which he was working. Maybe one could begin with this central and agreed opposition to the state between Marx, Gandhi, and unqualified Chomsky, and work from there. Apparently, Chomsky's current suggestion seems to postpone the very project. Still, in support of Chomsky, there are reasons to rethink the entire issue of the elimination of the state. In fact there are rather compelling reasons for the continuation of the state *so that resistance can be directed against it*.

As a starter, let me try to describe how we used to visualise the ideal unfolding of events which was supposed to lead to the elimination of the state. Democratic opposition to the state, we thought, will slowly weaken its institutions including, hopefully, its institutions of repression. This will create more space for larger and more intense opposition and set examples for the hitherto silent social groups. The state will have to react with a simultaneous programme of compromise with increasingly larger groups of opposition while diverting its resources to the institutions of repression to smash the most rebellious groups. As repression increases in selective sectors, pacifying institutions – collectively labelled 'welfare institutions' – begin to lose their credibility creating unrest among the social groups hitherto friendly to the state. Evidently, many of these features are rapidly emerging in the Indian scene. In the 'Maoist-infested' areas in general and Dandakaranya in particular, the state is both trying to dispense more welfare measures for *adivasi*s and sending in more paramilitary forces to attack those *adivasi*s who are somehow affiliated with the Maoist armed struggle.

At a certain point in this unsustainable cycle, the state begins to withdraw itself from what it takes to be the 'dispensable' sectors and new cooperative forms of organisation emerge there. This has a domino effect on the adjacent sectors: more sectors join the movement until the state diminishes beyond visibility. The picture can be improved with various details; but it does seem to capture, in a nutshell, the political imagination that underlies much radical thinking and activism. To the delight of Maoists, it would seem that the Indian state is already caught up in the no-win cycle just described.

If I understand Chomsky's cited position, there are serious problems with the picture just sketched. At least two underlying assumptions need to be questioned. First, the picture assumes that there is *an absence of a third party* in the sense that it is uncritically assumed that the real confrontation is between the state and the people. Second, the preparation of the withdrawal of the state from a given political space is assumed to be coterminous with the preparation of the resisting people to occupy that space. Both the assumptions hinge on the idea that it is in nobody's interest – except the people – that the state be eliminated.

Chomsky is arguing that there is a powerful element, distinct from the (formal) state and the people, whose current interests are also served with weakening and ultimate elimination of the state. Chomsky is reporting largely on conditions in the United States and parts of Western Europe. Summarising and simplifying lengthy empirical argumentation, the situation, according to Chomsky, is roughly as follows.

The growth of global capitalism over the last century has resulted in such a concentration of wealth and power that capitalism no longer needs the facade of the state to ensure its growth. Personal institutions of capitalism – the corporations, the private think tanks, the chambers of commerce etc. – are entirely totalitarian fiefdoms, not answerable to any public forum at all. By now, these institutions are so entrenched in the institutions of the state – primarily by installing its own personnel – that the state serves their interest to the hilt. Moreover, and perhaps more significantly, these institutions of capitalism have developed such enormous flexibility in their operations that they are not dependent on the machinery of *particular* states. This comes from their transnational ownership, offshore operations, global transfer of capital, and the like. In brief, they do not need to 'manufacture' consent anymore to push their activities through; they can push them either through sheer autocratic power or by a complete control over popular opinion-making. The classical state, with its layers of democratic institutions, is then largely expendable for global capitalism.

In fact, in many cases, the functions of the classical state, with its 'debating societies', is a clear hindrance. It is not surprising that even the remnant of the classical welfare state is portrayed as a 'nanny state' to justify 'rollback' of welfare measures. As Chomsky (1996, 28) explains,

> ... private tyrannies: spend billions of dollars a year on propaganda [not] for the fun of it. They do it with a purpose. For a long time the purpose was to resist and contain human rights and democracy and the whole welfare State framework, the social contract, that developed over the years. They wanted to contain it and limit it. Now they feel, in the current period, that they can really roll it back.'

Almost every form of public institution in which there is a semblance of democratic participation is an object of virulent ridicule in the mainstream corporate-controlled media. These include graphic reports on sexual and corrupt practices of the local council or to the apparently chaotic functioning of the UN General Assembly. In contrast, there is constant deification of the moguls of capitalism and those public institutions, such as the Pentagon and the Security Council, which directly serve its interests and are fiefdoms themselves. From all this, Chomsky concludes that the remnants of the institutions of the state are probably the last platforms for democratic participation of people. Hence, at least for now, the elimination of the (classical) state is *not* in the interest of the people.

Before I return to the Indian scene, I wish to highlight some general points of the argument to distinguish them from the features which are specific to the United States. First, although the modern democratic state continues to cater primarily to the interests of the elites, the state need not be *identified* with those interests; hence, the space – however tiny – for people's democratic participation. Rigid conceptions such as 'bourgeois state' miss this point. Second, since the modern state offers the *only* democratic space for the people by dint of its history of manufacturing consent, local organisations outside the state are likely to turn undemocratic when they are progressively controlled by essentially anti-people forces. In other words, local democratic organisations of people are not likely to be able to compete successfully for any political space outside the state. It is in the interests of the anti-people forces therefore to isolate – and thereby be in command of – local organisations of people. In the United States, this anti-people role is essentially played by the institutions of global capitalism in opposition to the state. In other regions, the identity of these forces may not be so historically scrutable.

I will now try to relate parts of this picture to the Indian scene. What follows is essentially a selective list of facts, which seem to throw light on the 'theoretical' issues just sketched. To that end, I will gradually develop a general pattern from these facts. Needless to say the selected facts are far from exhaustive. Some of what follows was written several years ago as an elaboration of Chomsky's thoughts just cited (Mukherji, 1999). Although there have been some changes in the Indian scene since, the broad picture, in my view, has not only remained the same, it has in fact sharpened with the emergence of communal-fascist forces, as we will see in the last section.

The people are by now almost irreversibly fragmented into a very large and complex collection of local, community-wide formations. The scale and the complexity of this phenomenon is only superficially captured in (a) the emergence of a plethora of political parties and organisations often exclusively centred around a single individual; and (b) a parallel and rapid disillusionment with hitherto centrist parties. While the inevitable jostling for limited political space mounts, there are signs of open hostility between these local formations themselves: *adivasi* against *adivasi*, Dalit against other backward castes, *adivasi* against Dalit, Dalit against women, women against Dalit, and so on.

So, in some ways, the first stage for the elimination of the monolithic state is indeed taking place in the very fragmentation of political space, thus allowing local formations to grow. No doubt there are new voices, new claims on history and, in general, a growing reassertion of human dignity. The question is whether it is necessarily leading to the fulfillment of the *democratic* aspirations of people in securing progressively more equality, justice and freedom. The answer, as I will attempt to document, is largely in the negative.

One, perhaps superficial, indicator of this deep problem is the dismal failure of successive United Front formations to sustain themselves on a national scale. For nearly three decades after India's independence from British rule, the Congress party of Gandhi-Nehru legacy ruled the country. By early 1970s, protest against this single-party rule was mounting. Having defeated her rivals in the Congress party and basking in the historic military victory over Pakistan that led to the creation of Bangladesh, the then Prime Minister Indira Gandhi sought to dispel the protests by clamping an internal emergency in 1975. The single-party rule finally ended when the Congress lost the general elections in 1977.

One would have thought that the rising local forces will forge a democratic unity among themselves and something like a United Front (UF) will represent this unity. The thought turned out to have weak foundations. The UF experiment with non-centrist parties was tried twice in recent decades: in 1977 and 1996. Each time the government collapsed much before the scheduled five-year term. Interestingly, however, despite the rise of the right-wing BJP in the 1990s and the current revival of the Congress, it is quite clear that the failure of UFs did not pave the way for single-party rule witnessed earlier. The political space thus remains fragmented. In other words, while the more genuine united fronts of a plethora of smaller parties — derisively called a *khichri* by major centrist parties — did not last long, the two major parties themselves had to contend with complex alliances with smaller parties — such as the National Democratic Alliance (NDA) headed by BJP during 1999–2004 and the United Progressive Alliance (UPA) headed by the Congress since 2004.[2] Moreover, the hegemony of a single centrist party dominating most of the provincial assemblies has also disappeared. The provinces are now governed mostly by regional formations often around a single individual even if they formally belong to a centrist party, as we will see.

The emergence of fragmentation has not led to a reassertion of what may be termed 'people's issues'; in fact, these issues are consistently sidelined as local formations apparently rise. I have in mind issues like land reform, judicial reform, health care, education and prices — particularly, land reform. Thus the main pillars of structured inequality not only remain stable, their removal is not even in the political agenda of the various local organisations that claim to represent local dignity.

For at least the last two decades there has been no widescale working class movement, no significant peasant uprising, nothing comparable to the food movement of the 1960s. This is not because there has been any amelioration on these accounts — just the opposite in fact; but because the very democratic basis for these movements has lost the power to unite. Whose interests does this loss of power serve?

The strikes are now seen only in the service sector: postal workers, nurses, teachers, *safai karmachari*s, and the like. Most of these fizzle out as soon as they begin with little or no gain in the limited economic demands they raise. This contrasts sharply with the strikes organised by big traders, transport owners, airline pilots etc. These strikes grow rapidly, affect the functioning of the state and of elite individual citizens at vital points, and are quickly rewarded.

It is still thought in some quarters that these facts only highlight the growth and the stranglehold of the 'bourgeois state' over people. Facts, however, seem to suggest just the opposite. We witnessed a rapid expansion of the state, say, up to the mid-1970s. A centrist party was in absolute power, the judicial and the electoral systems infiltrated much of the countryside, state-funded institutions including industrial, financial and educational institutions showed exponential growth, the police and the army expanded and spread. This was also the period when mass movements in various sectors increased both in depth and extent.

The period *since*, in contrast, may be viewed first in terms of the stagnancy and then as a progressive withdrawal of the state. The public sector, both industrial and financial, is a salient case. While there has been hardly any growth in this sector – except, for obvious reasons, in the telecommunication area – many public organisations have either disintegrated or have been passed on to the private sector. Roughly the same is true of healthcare and education. Even the repressive and bureaucratic arms of the state have shrunk. Obviously detailed empirical arguments need to be marshalled here; I am just sketching what seems to me to be the overall picture.

Thus we need to look at the actual numbers: yearly sector-wise ratio of employment in the public sector versus the private, the ratio of sector-wise investment, the increase in the diversification of the decreasing resources of the state to directly serve the elites in the private sector (e.g., the nature and growth of the telecom sector, the railways, airlines and other transportation sectors), the selective growth of financial services, the growth of the police and the military per designated unit of population, the diversion of limited and decreasing 'security services' to fewer people and thus to the elites, and so on. Supposing that these are some of the measures for deciding whether the classical welfare state is shrinking or expanding, it is assumed that these indices support the point made above.

Therefore, on the whole, the dissipation of democratic movements correlates at least with the halt of the state, *not* with its growth. Given the fractured and uncertain nature of governance in the last two decades, it would have been difficult for the state, other things being equal, to repress any large-scale democratic movement such as the rail strike of 1974. Yet there is a strong feeling that other things are not equal, that the conditions are such that nation-wide movements of working people cannot even be contemplated.

This brings us closer to Chomsky's point. The period in which we witness almost a simultaneous withdrawal of the state *and* of people's movements is also a period of unprecedented growth of private enterprise in almost every sector. Apart from industry, finance, real estate, communication and entertainment sectors, there has been a massive entry of private capital in the areas of health, school and technical education. Even higher education has not been spared. 'Trust'-based colleges and universities are appearing on a daily basis. Each of these is a fiefdom with no public accountability and many of them are directly linked to global capital. Alongside, there is the standard denunciation of public institutions and a deification of the private in the mainstream media.[3]

It will not be an exaggeration to suggest that once the state was used by the elites for several decades to create a market of roughly 400 million people, private capital has taken over much of the functions of the state for this market whence the rest of the 800 million people can simply be dispensed with. The utter failure of democratic movements to resist this phenomenon has allowed the phenomenon to acquire the current menacing character.

No doubt there has been a substantial growth in the civil rights movement over the past decades. Organisations such as PUCL, PUDR, APDR and others immediately come to mind. This has been one of the most promising developments in recent years: someone is trying bravely to occupy the vacant space *for* the people. In that sense, this movement is doing what the state ought to have done; that is, protecting people from structured but *unlawful* repression by upholding the laws of the state. A quick look at the location and the agents involved in this highly-fragmented democratic rights movement suggests that it offers at best a human face to the massive loss of people's freedom without any visible ability to either launch or link-up with large democratic movements. Moreover, it is well known that civil rights organisations are a 'fall back' refuge for many radical activists who have found themselves isolated from more direct democratic action otherwise. In that sense, the civil rights movement is a symptom of the absence of large scale mass movements. Roughly the same is true of movements geared to the environment.

In general then, the three dimensions of Chomsky's story are individually visible in the Indian scene as well:

- the weakening of the state and the creation of an empty space thereof
- people's inability to occupy that space
- the emergence and the ability of other elements to enter it.

Nevertheless, the extent of the picture sketched so far is restricted. Despite explosive growth, the political role of private capital, at least in direct and open institutional forms, is still fairly limited in India such that its survival and growth continues to be parasitical on the institutions of the state. Moreover, it is not at all clear how the growth of private capital in fact inhibits democratic movements although these links are fairly clear in the case of the United States. In the Indian context then, some further anti-people elements are needed to explain the shrinking political space for democratic movements. Also, it would seem that if forms of united resistance are able to emerge, the Indian people still have a democratic chance of enlarging — and engaging with — the welfare state.

This takes us back to the issue of 'fragility' mentioned earlier. Consider first the current election scene. Theoretically, the holding of elections and ensuring people's participation in it are paradigmatic functions of the state. In practice what happens is infinitely more complex. In a 'bourgeois state' such as the United States, the process is roughly clear: elections are really activities of the state to 'manufacture consent' in favour of the representatives of global capital. Hence, it was important to ensure participation of the people up to a point; it is no longer so important since consent need not be manufactured any more. The great mass of people realise this instinctively; hence they prefer to sit at home on election days. Elections in the United States are almost farcical, and I am saying this despite the euphoria around the election of Barack Obama.

In the Indian case, again at least up to the mid-1970s, which seems to me to be a watershed period in Indian politics critically marked by the imposition of Emergency in 1975, elections no doubt, served a similar purpose but there was ample space in the process for various progressive and radical forces to engage in it. This accounts for the significant presence, at all levels of legislature, of genuine representatives of the people, often from the Left – a phenomenon that is unthinkable in the case of the United States and most of Western Europe.

This situation has significantly changed over the last few decades. It is well known that elections are now determined largely at the local level. Except perhaps in some urban areas, national and even regional issues do not play any major role. Notwithstanding their propaganda, political parties understand this very well. The problem they face in each constituency is this: who is most capable of securing the votes of several hundred thousand people? The cynical answer that has emerged is: one who controls them. A guaranteed method of controlling several hundred thousand people is to control their economic lives. Two conditions need to be satisfied: (a) there be some homogeneity in their economic lives such that control over this zone ensures control over people; and (b) no other force is allowed to compete for the same zone.

It follows that fragmented formations of people – be it in the name of caste, tribe, creed, language, colour, habitat, festivals, icons, memories, whatever – supply exactly the domain of control insofar as these roughly coincide with homogenous economic lives. As a matter of fact, in much of the Indian context, they often *do* roughly coincide: for example, specific castes and tribes are often tied to specific economic activity. It follows as well that, since the state, in the absence of institutionalised private capital, represents about the only alternative force, much of the mechanisms of control needs to be developed outside and in opposition to the state.

I must hasten to add that the actual mechanisms of control are likely to be more complex. For example, it is not clear that fragmentations based on caste lines do actually coincide with homogenous economic activity. It is possible and indeed quite often the case that a given caste category may be distributed over heterogeneous economic spheres, while disjoint caste categories occupy a given economic zone. Then of course, the situation varies over a wide spectrum as regions change. Abstracting away from much of the complexity, let us draw attention to two central points:

(a) in a local context such as a village or a group of them, such identification can always be made even if tentatively and somewhat artificially; the local lords know how to exploit and give some ideological shape to the inherent inequalities in a village system.

(b) all one needs is to find categories which are *smaller* than the 'classical' categories of say, middle peasant, landless peasant, unskilled worker, bonded labour, women and the like, since these are essentially heterogeneous categories in the sense under discussion here.

Notice that both points are simultaneously satisfied by the fact that constant realliances are attempted on the basis of even finer and newer caste, creed or other subcategories.

It is natural then that the election system will increasingly depend on whoever is able to marshal the conditions just stated. Therefore, it is not at all surprising, given the primary fact of the withdrawal of the state, that massive unlawful organisations – essentially mafias controlling coal, sand, stone, wood, tendu leaf, land, road, sugar, rice and above all, arms and narcotics – are able to operate more or less freely. This is because these resources are often tied to the only economic activity of local populations divided under caste or tribe-lines.[4] Hence, as we go down the legislative structures from the national to the local, the prospective legislatures are either themselves leaders of the mafia or are closely linked with them.

This is the reason in many cases involving even the 'national' parties, local satraps determine the course of political events when differences arise with the more ideologically committed national leadership. To take some very recent cases among many, the CPM local leader Lakshman Seth is a muscleman in the Haldia-Nandigram area in West Bengal who controls both the local units of the party and much state-sponsored economic activity in the area that ensure the consolidation of his private fiefdom. It is well known that his autocratic methods were one of the major causes for the peasant uprising in Nandigram against the Left Front state government. Despite the huge loss of face for the Left government and the CPM party in Nandigram, the party failed to take any action against him. In fact, he was renominated by the party to contest a parliamentary seat in the 2009 elections. Needless to say, he lost the election comprehensively. His wife then was nominated to contest the assembly elections in 2011 which she lost.

Even more recently, the BJP leader from the *lingayat* community in Karnataka, Yeddyurappa, who was the chief minister of the state, was found to be in possession of astronomical illegal wealth probably accruing from favours granted to two of his minister-colleagues, the Reddy brothers, who were in jail at the time of going to press for engaging in massive illegal mining. As the BJP itself was campaigning against the ruling Congress party at the centre on the issue of vast corruption, Yeddyurappa's indictment came as a major embarrassment, and he was asked by the central leadership of BJP to resign immediately. In fact he had been asked to step down several months before when facts about the mining scam began to emerge from persistent investigations conducted by the provincial *Lokayukta* (ombudsman) Santosh Hegde. Yeddyurappa defied the command of the party throughout by claiming majority support from BJP legislatures who were obviously bought up by the Reddy brothers. When the situation reached boiling point in July 2011, Yeddyurappa finally agreed to resign only after a 'secret' ballot insisted by him installed his own choice as the next chief minister. After analysing the case, Suhas Palshikar observes, 'This development portends the death of the idea of a party and the survival of factions engaged in "democratic" fights over competitive extraction of public resources.'[5] If this is happening with 'disciplined' and cadre-based parties, it is easy to infer the state of affairs with other loose electoral formations that call themselves a political party.

In fact, the situation is even more complex and shifting. For example, I have largely ignored the role of various arms of the state itself – its executive, police, and lower judiciary – which help in the strengthening of these unlawful activities; thus they weaken or force withdrawal of the state by using it. As such, it may turn out that in certain regions what goes by the name of 'state' is already a conglomeration of mafia or, as in the case of various insurgencies, anti-state forces or both. Hence, the presence and use of parts of the erstwhile state machinery in these regions need not signal the presence of the classical law-enforcing state itself. Recall that the state is identified with a system of institutions enforcing laws. Therefore, if the machinery of the state is used to foster lawlessness, it follows either that a new state has come into being or that the old state is crumbling without creating a new one. It is obvious that only the second option is currently available.

The general point is already transparent: There is a close link between fragmentation and control of people, inefficacy and gradual withdrawal of the state, and widespread criminalisation of politics. The prime motivation for access to state power is to enlarge the bases of private fiefdoms and thus weaken the state itself. In this, the general picture matches that of the United States. The differences lie in the specificities of mechanism of control. Groups of people are mobilised and isolated from the rest on the basis of fragmented ideology – often called 'politics of identity' (Prabhat Patnaik, 2010). Then the isolation is linked to their livelihood. Then a combination of false leadership and sheer muscle power is used to drive them to the ballot box. The power so obtained is then used to both create and divert public resources for expanding private fiefdoms.

Once the process expands, it begins to cover vast regions – much larger than a single constituency – under suitable conditions of history and geography. The North-East, in my view, exhibits one extreme form of this expansion. In a dynamic in which gradual weakening of the state coincides with expanding control over people by non-state forces, there comes a point where the last vestiges of the state are no longer needed. In this scenario, the rule of the gun is able to exercise so much power that it aims at once to dissociate itself from the state and establish complete fiefdom in the garb of a rebellion (Mishra and Pandita, 2010).

It is quite likely that the process begins with genuine democratic aspirations of people, including the aspiration to secede from the coercive parent state and establish its own. Suitable conditions of history display largely the coercive face of the state, while suitable conditions of geography allow the scope for large-scale resistance. The North-East directly exhibits both on a vast scale. And so does Dandakaranya as we will see in Chapter Four.

Under genuine democratic leadership, this might in fact flower into a people's state. It all depends on how and on what basis the initial movement is formed. If it is based on land reform and popular control over habitat, some or other version of classical forms of resistance unfold up to a point before mechanisms of armed control over a population takeover. If it is based on ethnic categories, it is more likely to shake off its democratic character almost immediately. Faced with repression from the state, people rapidly fragment into subcategories and are brought under the complete control of various gun-toting leaders. Given the geography, the process gets linked as well to various transnational mafias, thus increasing its muscle power over the people and its ability to pursue a state in retreat. The original idea of a people's state vanishes into a conglomeration of fiefdoms at war with each other for 'competitive extraction of public resources,' as Palshikar observed.

In the states of Nagaland and Manipur, given the homogeneity of its people, the repressive institutions of the state have already become largely ineffective with the result that much of the remnants of the resources of the state actually feed into anti-state operations. Elections are a complete farce and parallel systems of administration, largely geared to collection of 'tax' from people, function openly. Given vast links to international smuggling channels for arms and drugs, a number of fiefdoms are in existence. There is large scale fragmentation of people along *adivasi*, religious and linguistic lines. Fiefdoms in the name of 'liberation armies' are rapidly forming with attendant enforcement of parallel governance.[6]

There has been a long concern about why the parliamentary Left in India failed to expand beyond its original locations mostly in eastern India and Kerala. In the academic circles, this failure is traced either to the 'obsolete' and 'hegemonistic' nature of Marxism to be replaced by 'subaltern narratives', or to some peculiarities of what is called 'Indian Culture'. In what we saw, we have a direct explanation of the phenomenon. If the Left is to function as a people's forum in opposition to the state, it must ideally force withdrawal of the state and occupy the resulting vacancy. In reality, there is no such vacancy outside their diminishing zones of influence; hence there is no occupation. Currently, therefore, as Chomsky has suggested, the only option for the Left movement is to help people consolidate their control over the *existing* democratic platforms of the state by resisting local, largely anti-people, fiefdoms.[7]

People, in their helpless isolation, generally get the point. They join local formations with the sole expectation that their access to the resources of the state will increase: jobs, education, health care, security, financial assistance, civil rights and so on. For well known historical reasons, the Indian state has failed to create institutions with sufficient reach where these expectations will be directly met. Hence the people are forced to congregate under a local label of caste, tribe, religion, language, ideology and so on. They are compelled to do this under a 'leader' or a central committee, who seem to have the only visible access to these resources, to bargain with the state for this assembled voice. Since the Left movement has failed to assume this leadership, it has passed on, sometimes with the collusion of the agents of the state itself, to forces outside the state. The sole task for the Left movement then is to bring the classical state back to the people.

These concerns about loss of democratic space took a rather severe form near the end of the last century. We recall that Chomsky warned about the 'fragility' of Indian democracy with possibly 'grim consequences' in the year 2005. At least since 1990s, there has been a phenomenal rise in numbers and political clout of communal-fascist *Hindutva* forces in India to the point where these forces were actually able to capture state power at the centre for the first time in independent India during 1999 to 2004, albeit in 'coalition' with smaller non-communal forces who played a minor role in the regime anyway. Furthermore, they were able to form governments in a number of major provinces in the northern and the western parts of the country. In that, they not only exercised prolonged control over the vast masses of people, they did so with legitimate electoral approval. What explains this phenomenon? Which deteriorating conditions of Indian democracy allowed these forces to come to power in the otherwise multi-religious, pluralist India?

It is implausible to think that this vast socio-political phenomenon could be traced to a single and decisive feature of Indian society. Social theory is not physics. Hence, the phenomenon has to be understood from a variety of directions, and in terms of interactions between them.

In a lecture in 2003 Utsa Patnaik traced the rise of communal-fascist forces in the country during the same period to the massive attack on agriculture.[8] Although the near collapse of the agricultural sector did create the necessary material basis for these forces to acquire strength, this condition by itself does not explain the specific form of fascism that emerged. For example, a very similar collapse of rural economy was witnessed in late 1950s to early 1960s with telling features of shrinkage in cultivated area, massive fall in productivity, exponential increase in unemployment, near-famine conditions, etc. Yet that period, instead of giving rise to fascism, led to one of the most impressive phases of people's movement in India that ultimately led to the consolidation of the public distribution system, rural credit, state control of agricultural pricing, and the like. An explanation of the current scene therefore needs some additional dimension missing from the economic dimension alone.

In an important article, Prabhat Patnaik (2002) traces the rise of communal-fascism to the loss of 'socialist vision' after the collapse of the socialist block. Again, without denying the international significance of this event, it is unclear if the rise of communal-fascism is necessarily linked to the collapse of 'socialist vision'. Two related phenomena immediately come to mind: the massive anti-war movements witnessed across the globe since

9/11 and the formation of the World Social Forum in 2001. Noticeably, much of the groundwork for these large movements was conducted over the last few decades independently of the socialist block – some would say, *in spite* of it, since the 'socialist block' had ceased to inspire 'socialist vision' decades ago (Nigam, 2010b). In any case, these movements took their current shapes at least a decade after the collapse of the block.

Prabhat Patnaik is careful to note both that, 'the triumph of the inegalitarian ideology predates the collapse of Soviet Union and hence requires a separate explanation,' and that 'the collapse of socialism does not per se explain the growth of communal fascism that has occurred.' According to him, one of the basic factors for 'the emergence of the inegalitarian ideology and the growth of fascism worldwide, including in our own country', is the emergence of 'international finance capital, based on the "globalisation of finance"' that 'undermines the capacity of the nation state to play any agency role, such as is enjoined upon it by all socialist and redistributivist visions.'

While we agree that much of the impoverishment of the masses and the concentration of wealth can be linked to new forms of international finance capital that gave rise to the current neo-liberal economic agenda, it is unclear if it necessarily leads to the loss of socialist vision on a grand scale, much as the rulers of the neo-liberal regime would want it to be. No other region of the world than Latin America has been subjected more to decades of direct enforcement of neo-liberal order, often backed by the power of gun. Except for Cuba, no country in that region could be viewed as belonging to the erstwhile socialist block. Yet, in recent elections in country after country – Venezuela, Bolivia and Brazil, for example – the neo-liberal order has been directly challenged by people's movements geared to 'redistributivist visions', as, interestingly, the Maoist leader Kobad Ghandy explains (See Chapter Five).

In India, despite the smaller (but growing) presence of neo-liberalism and sixty years of pluralist democracy, nothing comparable to the people's movements just mentioned has been seen for some decades; for example, popular protests against the Iraq war in the major metropolitan centres of India fell far short of what was achieved in small university campuses in the West. Robert McNamara was one of the principal architects of the Vietnam War. He visited India during the war. In contrast to the massive, nationwide protests against his presence in the country witnessed in the 1960s, the captains of the neo-liberal world order, including their representatives in the US government, are now given red-carpet treatment in their increasingly frequent visits to India with the Left watching quietly. The list includes Bill Gates, James Baker, Bill Clinton, Condoleezza Rice, Donald Rumsfeld, Colin Powell, Richard Armitage and others. Only when George Bush II himself visited the country in 2006 did the Left lead a moderately impressive protest.

These disturbing concerns took ominous shape in Gujarat. In early 2002, the simmering power of communal-fascism launched an open attack on the Muslim minority in Gujarat in perhaps the most savage communal pogrom in contemporary India.[9]

As Prabhat Patnaik rightly observes in his article: 'informed by honesty, integrity and a humaneness,' and 'with rare unanimity,' the mainstream secular media 'exposed the complicit role played by the state government in the attacks on the minority community and demanded the removal of the state Chief Minister.'[10]

Despite graphic and extensive coverage in the media, the pogroms went on for several months while the rest of the country more-or-less just watched. In fact, while the communal-fascist BJP had lost most of the provincial elections after coming to central power in 1999, it won handsomely in the elections that *followed* the pogroms in some major provinces. Subsequently, elections were also held in Gujarat itself where the BJP was returned to power with an overwhelming majority.

Part of the explanation for this phenomenon, no doubt, can be traced to 'Islamic terror'. As Basharat Peer (2003) observes, the victory of communal-fascist forces in Gujarat 'lengthened the shadow of Hindu religious violence and Islamic terror attacks that loomed over India throughout 2002. In Gujarat, the fear of Muslim-sponsored terrorism consolidated effectively the Hindu nationalist votes.' In the post-9/11 scenario, in the name of assisting the civilised world in its fight against terrorism, the BJP-led government of India sided with US military and economic interests with a straight face. Having thus appeased the US and its neo-liberal support in India, it returned to its basic communal-fundamentalist agenda in the atmosphere of unconcealed Islamophobia that engulfed the non-Muslim world after 9/11 (Nandy, 2001; Mamdani, 2003). What US aggression and accompanying propaganda machine enabled Sangh Parivar to do was to claim not only moral legitimacy, but also some form of international solidarity for its attacks on minorities, especially Muslims (Mukherji, 2002). Exploitation of this 'window of opportunity' paid handsome dividends for right wing, jingoist governments in both India and the US (Subramanian, 2004; Mukherji, 2005, Chapter 1).

However, the explanation essentially places the cart before the horse. The massive propaganda around 'islamic terror' could be launched and acted upon by BJP-led governments both at the Centre and in Gujarat precisely because people had already voted them to power. The Gujarat phenomenon, which includes impressive electoral successes for BJP, demonstrates the peak of that power; we need to explain how communal-fascist forces reached that peak. In other words, the ability of these forces to exploit the opportunity provided by 9/11 required that popular ground was already covered. The development of this popular ground for communal-fascist forces *is* the major concern here.

In the said article, Prabhat Patnaik suggests that 'what is true of the present situation, I think, is that people no longer have clear notions of "right" and "wrong" such that a degree of confusion, uncertainty and fuzziness has got introduced into the moral conceptions of the people.' As noted, Patnaik traces this state of moral confusion to, 'the collapse, for the time being at any rate, of all dreams of building a society that is not based on private aggrandisement.' Further, 'the recent inegalitarian thrust of social analysis, which has acquired credibility and hegemony, associated interalia with the collapse of the socialist project, has altered these long-held notions without substituting anything in its place'. It is natural therefore that the moral void 'forecloses the possibility of going beyond the existing authority class.'

It is at least debatable if the fairly definitive electoral verdicts across northern and western India and, more specifically, in such large provinces as Gujarat, Rajasthan, and Madhya Pradesh, can be explained in terms of a moral vacuum, rather than as an expression of a specific regressive moral choice. Furthermore, the case for a (recent) collapse of 'socialist vision' seems overstated since the Left had no penetration in the regions of the country under consideration. Hence it is difficult to understand what 'socialist vision' engaged the people in those regions prior to the rise of communal-fascism. If anything, explanation is needed as to why the Left movement with its 'socialist vision' failed to penetrate a greater part of India. In any case, Patnaik's suggestion explains at best the tilt towards authoritarianism – a phenomenon visible in the Indian scene long before the recent advent of communal-fascism. As mentioned, the rise of Indira Gandhi as the sole centre of power in the early 1970s and her act of imposing internal Emergency in 1975 clearly signalled the advent of authoritarianism in India. An explanation of the rise of the BJP thus requires an additional dimension to link the general rise of authoritarianism to one specifically of the communal-fascist kind.

The phenomenal rise of communal-fascist forces from the 1990s to the present day may be explained in terms of a combination of factors which emerged individually in the Indian scene independently of these forces. It is just that these forces were able to take advantage of the available regressive features of Indian democracy. First, the imposition of a neo-liberal order led to a gradual collapse of economic lives of people, especially in rural areas. Second, although this attack on people's lives gave rise to widespread discontent, it failed to find forums of democratic resistance in the absence of a 'socialist vision' typically propounded by the Left. Third, discontent found a natural voice in the existing and powerful religious identity. Fourth, in this case, religious identity happened to be a majoritarian one, namely, *Hindutva*. Fifth, the international context of islamophobia enabled the timely construction of the 'despicable other' required by fascism (Mukherji, 2007a). Finally, the convergence of these factors at that particular point in time enabled Sangh Parivar – which was waiting for nearly a century for these events to mature and converge – with the historical opportunity to unite large sections of *adivasi*s, Dalits, and middle class Hindus to attain state power.

It is important to note that, independently of their vulgar interpretation and use by communal forces, religious thought-systems do offer a range of sustainable practices. That is why communal forces are able to use them at suitable moments. For example, participants of religious practices typically experience that their lives are enriched by feelings of solidarity, altruism, egalitarianism, pacifism, domesticism,[11] spirituality and festivity (Mukherji, 2007a). One does not have to be communal to feel attracted to such a system of practices if religions provide them, especially when this is the *only* source available in an otherwise degrading human condition: 'Religion is the sigh of the oppressed creature, the heart of a heartless world, just as a spirit of a spiritless condition. It is the *opium* of the people,' as Karl Marx famously remarked.[12]

More significantly for our purposes, each of these practices is very much a part of progressive mass organisations. Those who have some acquaintance with people's movements – peasants, workers, teachers, youth, etc. – can amply testify to the festive character that almost spontaneously ensues when people gather under a cause. By parity of reason, the absence of broad, sustainable and democratic movements geared to the basic livelihood issues of people has left a wide vacuum in the political practice of the masses. It is not surprising that the masses have found those practices within religious systems since they are historically available in any case.

Keeping to the religious practices of the Hindu community, several million people take a dip in the ice-cold waters of the Ganges every day during *Kumbhmela*; millions throng the annual religious celebrations at Gangasagar, Puri and Dwarka; hundreds of thousands of people travel long distances to visit the temple at Tirupathi; despite heavy odds, several million travel to the shrines at Amarnath, Yamunotri, Gangotri, Kedarnath and Badrinath in the Himalayan high ranges every year. These are some of the more publicised events carried by the newspapers. Beyond these, there are hundreds of thousands of temples and other shrines scattered across the country which attract massive crowds for several days every year. Apart from these, there are local temples, gurus, assemblies, *akharas*, yoga centres and the like, where thousands of people gather on a daily basis. Most Hindu families actively worship statues or photographs of some or the other deity in their homes. Once we take a cumulative view of the total phenomenon, it is hard to see any significant section of the population – except urban, western educated, well-off sections of the intelligentsia – not taking part in some practice or other. The Left has largely ignored this massive fact.

In the last two decades – precisely the period of democratic deficit under consideration – the Sangh Parivar has been able to enter and fill that political space by adding an explicit religious dimension to their communal-fascist agenda. It is worth noting that the phenomenal growth of directly religious-communal forums such as Vishva Hindu Parishad and Bajrang Dal are more recent dimensions of the Parivar. By joining and thereby co-opting the religious lives of the masses, the Parivar has been able to marshal much of people's religious energy towards their sinister political agenda.

It is a well known human fact that when the positive penchant for the values of solidarity, altruism and the like, are satisfied, a certain sense of loyalty to institutions that offer them develops. As a result, participants may in fact ignore or downplay the negative features often associated with these institutions, especially when their personal act of participation can be viewed as essentially separated from the fall-out of such negative aspects: Most Hindus do not and will not take direct part in communal pogroms even if they are inclined to look away when these things happen. When the negative aspects begin to dominate, values of solidarity and domesticity tend to restrain the ability of participants to voice protest, generating thereby moral confusion among masses and allowing insidious forces to pursue their agenda.

This phenomenon is not restricted to communal-fascist programmes alone. The chequered, and often problematic, history of communist movement in the last century provides enough examples.

Given loyalty to 'infant socialism' and values associated in defending it, people essentially downplayed the outrages committed by ruling oligarchies in 'socialist' countries. When facts about mass pogroms, forced labour, wide scale repressions and secret operations began to attain a public face, people either recoiled in disbelief or lapsed into silence, while continuing to lend support to the regimes out of their historical loyalty to the basic cause.

In the Indian case, the absence of the Left – hence, of people's movements – across vast stretches of the country allowed Sangh Parivar not only to fill political space, as noted, but also to implement a massive propaganda almost at will since loyalty of people had already been secured through their entrenchment in religious machinery.

However, as with every repressive order, people ultimately withdraw their support when material conditions override binds of loyalty, and an alternative political space begins to open up. The general elections of 2004 testify in part to this phenomenon: class concerns superseded loyalties based on 'identity' (Mukherji, 2004). Thus, the phenomenon of the fragmentation of democratic space and the diminishing role of the welfare state, though alarming, is not yet absolute; it is not yet a defining feature of Indian democracy. As such, there is still much room for unified democratic resistance. The resurgence of impressive mass movements since about 2006 – for land and environment and against corruption and state repression – testify to the democratic spaces still available. It is unclear though if these largely scattered and local movements have the power to influence electoral politics. Also, salvaging the body politic from the clutches of communal-fascism was achieved only in part. Given the massive historical presence of religions and other forms of 'identity' in the consciousness of people, 'politics of identity' can always be used by anti-democratic forces if democratic alternatives fail to ameliorate the material conditions of the masses. It is no part of my argument that Maoists ought to be viewed at par with communal-fascist forces. Yet, in my view, the current Maoist upheaval needs to be understood as a part of the general phenomenon of democratic deficit.

3

ROLE OF INTELLECTUALS

The state of Indian democracy raises disturbing questions about people's growing inability to voice their protests about the state's authoritarian actions. Consider the imposition of the Prevention of Terrorism Act (POTA) in 2002, among other draconian acts such as AFSPA, MISA (Maintenance of Internal Security Act) TADA (Terrorist and Disruptive Activities Act), that the state has routinely invoked over the decades. No doubt, the country was faced with the difficult phenomenon of what was misleadingly called 'jehadi terror' at the beginning of this century. There were a series of attacks by alleged Islamic 'jehadists' on civilian targets resulting in much bloodshed.[1] However, except perhaps from some sections of the upper classes, there was no popular demand that something like an internal emergency be imposed as a response to the phenomenon.

Yet, the government proceeded to do just that in the form of POTA even as actual cases of terrorist attacks, frequently on innocent civilians, continued unabated. The chief minister of Tamil

Nadu, Jayalalithaa and that of Uttar Pradesh, Mayawati, targeted their political opponents and arrested some of their leaders under POTA. The Home Ministry used the opportunity to control democratic dissent in Kashmir by arresting dissident leaders and journalists. More importantly, hundreds of hapless individuals, typically poor Muslims, were picked up virtually at random on charges most of which subsequently failed legal scrutiny, but only after they suffered months and years of incarceration and torture, without protection from the law (Verma, 2004; Mukherji, 2005).

'The atrocities of 9/11,' Chomsky wrote in his letter to teachers of Delhi University,[2] 'were exploited in a vulgar way by governments all over the world, in some cases by escalating massive crimes on the pretext of "combating terrorism", in others by implementing repressive legislation to discipline their own citizens with no credible connection to preventing terrorist threats, in some cases by carrying out programmes that had not the remotest connection to terrorism and might even enhance it and that were opposed by the majority of the population.' In that sense, 'the authentic threat of terrorism' is sought to be exploited 'as a window of opportunity for intolerable actions.'

Except for valiant efforts by small groups of individuals working with democratic rights organisations such as the People's Union of Democratic rights (PUDR) and the People's Union of Civil Liberties (PUCL), the political order and the media not only stood and watched, but also frequently applauded the efficiency of security agencies for making so many arrests in such a short time.[3] No one complained as the budget for internal security was raised manifold while safety nets for common citizens, especially Dalits, workers and minorities, were progressively withdrawn, as the noted human rights activist Gautam Navlakha has repeatedly observed.

Why did the media and the Opposition fall in line on the issue of POTA? What is it that enabled an increasingly authoritarian state to impose its will on an otherwise pluralist society (Mukherji, 2001)? How could so much fear and prejudice be injected into the minds of the general population in such a short time? Why did the people of Gujarat repeatedly vote the BJP to power? Why did the nation not burst into massive rage as even the right to strike was progressively withdrawn by the courts from working people? Why did the people of India not come out in the streets to join anti-war demonstrations, while millions marched in hundreds of cities across the globe? Why did the formation of the evil US-Israel-India military axis go virtually unopposed?

In the previous chapter, I tried to find some general grip on these vexing questions. Nonetheless, it seems that the very asking of these questions suggests that the nation had already lost considerable democratic space in recent years, the loss accelerating as the Indian state exploited the window of opportunity created by US-sponsored 'war on terror', as we saw. Resistance therefore must accompany analysis if the residual democratic order – in fact, the human race – is to survive (Chomsky, 2003).

Given the role of the media and the official political order, who will assist the people to resist? This urgent question reopens the old issue of responsibility of the intelligentsia in interpreting and changing the world. In particular, intellectuals in academia and mainstream media – teachers, writers, journalists, and other managers of ideas – enjoy, perhaps, the maximum benefits of the combined effects of democracy, freedom of expression, globalisation of knowledge, and skewed economic development. By their very location, intellectuals are partly immune from the repressive mechanisms of the state: who will dare touch a university professor, a prominent writer or a high-profile columnist? As a community, intellectuals are still viewed with considerable respect by the rest of the general population. Most intellectuals in the developed and some developing countries such as India enjoy salaries and perks that match those of middle-level executives in private firms without being tied down to the totalitarian conditions of work suffered by private executives. Intellectuals have access to pillars of power, media, political and legal systems in the country, and institutions and agencies abroad. Most importantly, they have access to unlimited knowledge and are trained to disseminate it. In sum, they are in the most coveted position of being able to see through clouds of propaganda and prejudice as well as enjoy the freedom and the ability to do something about it.

By the same token, however, the community as a whole is not exactly the harbinger of real social change. Intellectuals cannot be so opulent in their priviledges in this obscenely unequal world order without developing some vested interest in its continuance: 'The history of intellectuals is written by intellectuals, so not surprisingly, they are portrayed as defenders of rights and justice, upholding the highest values and confronting power with admirable courage and integrity. The record reveals a rather different picture.' (Chomsky, 2010, *The Great Soul of Power*) In general, Chomsky observes that, 'the end of the last millennium was surely one of the low points in the generally dismal history of intellectuals ... most kept to conformist subservience to those in power.' (p.35)

Still, except for direct 'establishment' apparatchiks, intellectuals are usually located at some distance from real seats of power. While this endows intellectuals with some degree of autonomy, it also makes them at least partly vulnerable to the long arm of repression as an authoritarian state becomes increasingly belligerent. We need only recall the fate of intellectuals in Chile, Indonesia and in erstwhile East Pakistan. Intellectuals in India are still some stretch away from that stage, but current attacks on free expression, harassment of writers, artists and journalists and curtailment of autonomy as also the size of the university system are pointers of things to come if intellectuals do not intervene. It is up to intellectuals then to decide how best they face these conflicting currents of history in the intervening time.

The least intellectuals can do, once they have unmasked the propaganda of the state, is to tell the powers that the truth is out. Once the truth is uncovered and laid before the people, someone somewhere will pick up the thread and proceed to develop more sustainable forms of resistance. If intellectuals still have the energy and the courage, they can use their relative insularity from repression to help raise a protective wall around this resistance so that it can grow inside. So the moral is to protect resistance to protect truth.

In one of the more positive developments in an otherwise grim period, various groups of intellectuals in India have, in fact, taken up the task of protecting and expanding residual democratic spaces with forms of learned activism. I can briefly touch upon only a few of them to give a flavour of the uplifting phenomenon; also, I can only describe cases I am somewhat familiar with.

As mentioned repeatedly throughout this work, the principal agents of intellectual resistance are the courageous democratic and civil rights forums such as PUDR, PUCL, APDR (Association of People for Democratic Rights) and others that mostly consist of college and university teachers, intellectual activists, rights lawyers and writers. These organisations have meticulously documented and published innumerable cases of injustice as well as denial of rights to the poor and the marginalised, atrocious actions of state agencies such as the police and lack of adequate concern shown by responsible ministries as also national and regional human rights commissions.

With these measures, the democratic rights organisations have continuously exposed the character of an increasingly anti-people dispensation. In several cases, they have taken up cases before courts of law and have been able to reverse official action.

To mention some specific cases, APDR in West Bengal, in association with other democratic bodies and individuals, took up the case of Kaushik Ganguly, a young lecturer of chemistry at the University of Calcutta, who was arrested and tortured by the police of the Left Front regime in 2002. Ganguly was picked up because of his alleged Maoist affiliations; incidentally, the Maoist party was not banned in West Bengal at that point. Careful documentation that refuted the charges of the police, massive demonstrations and a range of petitions organised by rights groups compelled the government to release Ganguly after a few months. There are many such cases across the country. One of the most notable was the imprisonment of Dr Binayak Sen in Chhattisgarh, as noted. An international campaign organised by rights groups, especially those based in Delhi and Chhattisgarh, finally managed to secure his release after a two-year legal battle.

Turning to more direct interventions in the state's 'war on terror' mentioned earlier, a group of intellectuals comprising prominent writers, lawyers, and professors formed a committee to defend S.A.R. Gilani, a lecturer of Arabic at Delhi University who was falsely arrested by Delhi police as an accomplice in the attack on the Indian parliament on 13 December 2001. Soon, teachers of Delhi University also formed another defence committee for Gilani. It is important to note that these civil rights campaigns were launched during a period in which the mainstream media had so saturated the public mind with such hysterical – and patently false – coverage that the country was virtually baying for Gilani's blood (Mukherji, 2005).

After Gilani was acquitted of all charges by the Delhi High Court, the attention of intellectuals shifted to two other accused, both hapless traders from Kashmir: Mohammad Afzal and Shaukat Hussain. This time an even more high-profile committee of intellectuals was formed, not only to defend the accused but also to demand a full parliamentary inquiry into the whole episode. The campaign originated when the Supreme Court of India started hearing the appeals and *continued* even after the court awarded capital punishment to Mohammad Afzal while drastically reducing the sentence given earlier to Shaukat Hussain. It is worth mentioning that Professor Noam Chomsky supported these campaigns throughout, even if much of the mainstream Left in India, with admirable exceptions, stayed away for statist reasons and fear of losing Hindu votes. In 2004, the parliamentary Left, along with every other parliamentary party, supported the adoption of the draconian Unlawful Activities Prevention Act (UAPA) which formally replaced the even more draconian POTA.

As documented in various publications (Mukherji, 2006; 13 December 2006), a range of intellectuals boldly defied the possibility of contempt of court to challenge the most powerful institutions of the state, including its home ministry and the Supreme Court, to save the life of a Kashmiri Muslim. Afzal's only 'crime' was that he was trying to escape the horrors of Kashmir to begin a new chapter in Delhi with his young family. Mohammad Afzal has since been hanged at the Tihar Jail in Delhi on 9th February, 2013. But the fact that he was still alive six years after the Supreme Court confirmed his death sentence, despite regular campaigns by the Sangh Parivar for his blood, might have something to do with the international outrage raised by the intellectual campaign prompting the European Parliament to intervene to save his life.

The protest against 'war on terror' was taken up yet again

by a small but determined group of teachers from Delhi's Jamia Millia University, Jamia Teachers' Solidarity Association (JTSA), to expose the barbarism of Delhi Police as they killed two young Muslim students for their alleged involvement in serial blasts across the country. The spirit and determination of JTSA soon captured the imagination of scores of other intellectuals and activists across the country, joined by a significant section of the Muslim population of Delhi. By meticulous campaign and investigation, including high quality legal work, the group was able to obtain the postmortem report from the police through the National Human Rights Commission. The report proved conclusively that the students were shot at point-blank range while they were kneeling on the floor.[4]

In some cases, intellectual campaigns joined hands in solidarity with grassroots peoples' movements. The widespread and sustained movement to save the lives and land of *adivasi*s from the Sardar Sarovar Dam project on the river Narmada is a classic example. Under the auspices of the *Narmada Bachao Andolan* (Save Narmada Movement) led by Medha Patkar, hundreds of intellectual activists joined *adivasi*s stranded in the river basin to launch a sustained movement to restrict the extent of the dam and for meaningful rehabilitation of the displaced people. The decades-old movement still exists. It generated such energy and mass participation that the World Bank fled from the scene. It required sustained attacks by the state and a series of regressive proclamations by the Supreme Court of India for the project to increase the height of the dam. Some frustrated radicals in the country believe that the Narmada movement was thereby 'defeated'. On the contrary, even if the movement achieved limited success locally, it brought environment and *adivasi* issues to the centre of the peoples' struggle and changed the character of the peoples' movement in the country. For example, the Narmada movement gave rise to an impressive umbrella organisation of scores of movements: the National Alliance of People's Movements (NAPM).

More recently, intellectuals from Kolkata, joined later by writers and activists from across the country, stood in solidarity with peasant uprisings in Nandigram, Singur and Lalgarh in West Bengal as the Left Front regime attempted to acquire fertile agricultural land by force to pave the way for big business. As we will see in Chapter Five the sustained intellectual campaign was one of the catalysts for the turn of events that ultimately removed the Left regime from power in recent elections. Similarly, radical intellectuals in Andhra played a significant role in the massive defeat of the right-wing TDP government in 2004.

The ability to investigate the issues with intellectual diligence and honesty to expose the falsity propagated by ruling dispensations is a central aspect of the moral value and political success of these intellectual campaigns. The campaigns arose from a direct and sustained understanding of people's plights and their inability to voice them. The widespread harassment of Muslims in the name of 'war on terror' led to mass suffering of poor Muslim communities, but they were obviously not in a position to articulate their anger against an aggressive majoritarian rule. The intellectual campaigns not only brought out the truth, but also sought to give protection to these communities by voicing their despair. In that sense, the campaign for Afzal was in solidarity with the people in Kashmir; the campaign by JTSA was in solidarity with Muslim populations in Jamia Nagar in Delhi and Azamgarh in Uttar Pradesh;[5] the Narmada campaign was in solidarity with *adivasi*s, and so on. These campaigns have value because they stood with the people on the ground of truth. Intellectual campaigns degenerate into propaganda when these cardinal principles are disregarded.

Regrettably, these principles are sometimes violated to promote partisan politics. Political petitions asking people to support a cause sometimes exhibit this tendency. This is particularly serious when signatures are sought from distinguished individuals who are not likely to know the background well enough to give an informed consent. Very distinguished persons like Noam Chomsky are routinely asked to sign hundreds of petitions. In most cases, they are compelled to react in terms of prima facie plausibility based on quality of content, personal acquaintance, previous knowledge, and the likes. In some cases, it's just 'gut feeling'. But the bottom line is that once someone signs a petition, the signatory must take full responsibility for the contents of the petition. Hence, it is all the more crucial for the organisers of a petition to supply as much background information as possible to ward off uninformed consent and embarrassment to the signatories. Inadequate and distorted information, in fact, defeats the very cause a petition is designed to address. The point is illustrated by a fiasco over some statements on the struggle at Nandigram.

Nandigram is a village in the state of West Bengal. The state was governed for over three decades, 1977-2011, by an alliance of Left parties, the most prominent being the Communist Party of India (Marxist), (CPM). After over fifteen years of popular governance, the Left Front began to lose appeal as it alienated itself from its basic constituency of workers and peasants. It sought to compensate the loss by appealing to the rising middle classes in terms of neo-liberal policies that they failed to implement as well. (Mukherji, 2008a; 2009a) The discontent of the masses came to a breaking point when the government attempted to acquire fertile agricultural land by force to pave the way for multinational companies. Land was sought to be acquired in and around Nandigram for a massive fertiliser factory in the private sector. A significant peasant uprising took place.

When the Nandigram struggle erupted, the anti-CPM

activists approached Chomsky and others with their view of the uprising which did not include information regarding the growing involvement of Maoists, the right-wing Trinamool Congress, and the Muslim fundamentalist organisation Jamat-e-Islam in the movement. Their appeal also failed to mention the flow of arms from both sides in the area. Not knowing much about the issues, Chomsky offered his general solidarity in an e-mail in which he expressed his 'concern' at the worrying turn of events. This line about his 'concern' was flashed prominently in a big anti-government rally on 14 November 2007, addressed by Medha Patkar among others. To counter, a petition was drafted and circulated by a pro-CPM lobby consisting of noted Leftist intellectuals. The petition said almost nothing about killings by the police and the operations of CPM-controlled armed cadres. People like Chomsky, Tariq Ali, Susan George and a few others, who relied on the views and presentation of things by their Leftist friends, signed the petition. The CPM-led government, in turn, used this statement in various ways; CPM reproduced it in the party journal *People's Democracy*.

The storm that this petition created can be felt even today (Nigam, 2010a). In response, many individuals, including myself, protested to Chomsky and other signatories for endorsing this statement. These protests were directed principally at Chomsky, one of the signatories, because the opinion of Chomsky matters. In response, as the protests were going on, Chomsky and others decided to issue yet another (more balanced) statement. It was *not* signed by the earlier pro-CPM signatories. The statement was released via *The Hindu* on 4 December 2007. Very few people noticed this statement.[6] In the chaos generated by the earlier statement and counter-statement, mostly revolving around the name of Chomsky, the significant last word from Chomsky and others was lost to the struggle in Nandigram. Did it help the struggle in Nandigram? Also, one cannot fail to notice the deep embarrassment caused to our distinguished friends from abroad who depend entirely on what information we furnish concerning our struggles here.

A recent international intellectual campaign on OGH illustrates the point even more vividly. *Sanhati* is an online forum presumably run by some radical Indians from outside India. It is one of the most significant forums in recent years for radical opinion on a variety of peoples' struggles. It came into prominence during the struggle in Nandigram and Singur in West Bengal. A number of writers contributed important articles analysing these movements. The forum also carries news, reports and statements from the ground which are otherwise inaccessible to the general public. *Sanhati* is an asset for democratic struggle.[7] However, as I have repeatedly pointed out, the Maoist upsurge has caused much division within democratic opinion and movements. When OGH broke out in 2009, everyone in democratic circles immediately (and justly) saw it as an attack on *adivasi*s in Dandakaranya, the poorest of the poor. It was important, therefore, to protest this operation. Given the formidable *armed* presence of Maoists in the scene, what are the terms in which such a protest is to be framed?

Sanhati issued a statement in the form of a letter to the prime minister. Since I wish to criticise this statement at some length, I have placed the entire statement at Appendix II.

The statement was endorsed by hundreds of intellectuals from India and abroad.[8] International signatures – including Noam Chomsky, Howard Zinn, James Scott, Gayatri Spivak, Mahmood Mamdani, Abha Sur, Gilbert Acchar, and the likes – itself ran to several hundred. Interestingly, the organisers were able to obtain the signatures of a very large number of Indian academics associated with leading universities and institutions in the West. This suggests meticulous planning and networking by the organisers. The signatures from India also ran into several hundred, including well-known writers, social scientists, journalists and artists, as well as a large number of scientists, technocrats and lawyers from leading institutions. In terms of scale and quality of signatures, this was one of the most impressive intellectual efforts seemingly to protect 'the poorest and most vulnerable section of the Indian population.' Nonetheless, the statement was essentially a blatant distortion of reality – given the careful planning – it is unlikely that the distortion was accidental.

Three points raised in the statement are transparent, as we saw in the introduction in some detail: (a) the Indian government *is* planning a massive armed operation in *adivasi*-hilly areas in the East-Central parts of the country, especially in the Dandakaranya area of Chhattisgarh; (b) the poorest of the poor and the historically marginalised will suffer the most in terms of loss of lives, livelihood and habitat; and (c) for whatever its worth, an all-out campaign by democratic forces is needed to resist the armed invasion of people's habitat by *any* party.

To that extent, the statement does bring out the urgency of the matter. What is not so transparent from the statement is the condition that has brought about this state of affairs. It is said that large-scale neo-liberal policies – including formation of Special Economic Zones (SEZs) and encroachment of *adivasi* habitats for mining and other forms of exploitation – have led to mass impoverishment. So, in desperation, the poor have allegedly taken up arms to defend themselves.

This picture is wrong in (i) ascribing the armed struggle to the people on the false basis that 'political violence by the poor' has led to 'a civil war like situation'; and (ii) being silent about the *specific* source of the current aggression by the state, namely, the massive armed operations of CPI(Maoist).

In the statement, Maoists are mentioned exactly once almost passingly to plant the idea that the Government of India is using this 'shadow of an insurgency' as an excuse to 'hunt down the poorest of Indian citizens.' The huge arms build-up by Maoists is nowhere mentioned. Instead, there is an ill-concealed attempt to paint Maoists in terms of the 'desperate resistance of the local indigenous people.' Further, the area of armed operation of the state is now totally ambiguous, to suggest that OGH covers all the '*Adivasi-* populated regions of Andhra Pradesh, Chhattisgarh, Jharkhand, Maharashtra, Orissa and West Bengal.' There is no mention of the *specific* location of OGH in areas of the Dandakaranya forests – mostly in the greater Bastar area of Chhattisgarh – where Maoists have a formidable presence with sophisticated arms and well-concealed hideouts.

Let me elaborate on what other crucial facts are missing from the picture sketched in the *Sanhati* statement. Since most of the signatories, especially foreign signatories, are not likely to be aware of the complex history of the Maoist movement in India, it was the solemn responsibility of the organisers of the statement to furnish these facts before they sought wide-scale endorsements. As we will see, these glaring omissions effectively turned the *Sanhati* statement into a well-concealed Maoist document. Maoists of course have the right to construct and circulate such a document in their own name. The issue is whether an intellectual campaign, launched in the guise of protecting the poorest of the poor, can take such a partisan form. More importantly, it is certainly questionable if so many signatures would have been obtained if the statement was explicitly (and honestly) crafted with Maoists fully in view.

Hundreds of organisations working at the grassroots level across the country are engaged in a variety of struggles against state repression and the insidious economic policies of the government. This includes many Gandhians, liberal and Leftist organisations and individuals. Importantly, some of these – such as the organisations led by veteran activists Kanu Sanyal, Santosh Rana and Asim Chatterjee, among many others in Bengal, Andhra, Bihar, Odisha and elsewhere – also subscribe to Maoism and are known initiators of the original Naxalbari Movement (see Chapters One and Five). Thus, the labels 'Maoist' and 'naxalite' apply to a much wider category of organisations and individuals than CPI(Maoist). Needless to say, even the wider category of Maoists, not to mention just CPI(Maoist), forms a tiny fraction of the broad democratic resistance to the policies of the state. The current armed operations of the state are directed ostensibly against CPI(Maoist) in the areas under its control.

The state of course makes no such distinction in public; by identifying the wider category of naxalites with the narrower one of Maoists, it is constructing the opportunity to target the entire Left-democratic fraternity in due course. To put the point differently, although the undeclared target of the state covers the entirety of Left-democratic forces – as evidenced, for example, in the growing attacks on industrial workers especially in the private sector – the declared target currently consists of CPI(Maoist) and its areas of control. The significance of this specificity is wholly missing from the statement.

The identification of CPI(Maoist) with the entire resistance movement suits CPI(Maoist) as well (Menon, 2009). Its supreme commander, Ganapathy (2009), recently declared from his hideout from a guerrilla-controlled area: 'People, who are the makers of history, will rise up like a tornado under *our party's leadership* to wipe out the reactionary blood-sucking vampires ruling our country … our party's influence has grown stronger and *it* has now come to be recognised as the only genuine alternative before the people.' (emphasis added) The evaluation the factual content of this declaration is given below.

For now, it is interesting to note the character of the propaganda: somehow the propagandist interests of CPI(Maoist), the state and the corporate media suitably converge. The supreme commander's claim is grimly endorsed by the prime minister and home minister of India; according to them, the 'naxalite menace' is the greatest threat to internal security. It is also endorsed by the corporate media: The 'menace' is said to have spread in 15 of about 25 states, and 180 of about 600 districts of the country – the numbers keep accelerating each month to encourage the prospect of a 'civil war' soon across the country.

Newspaper reports and books on the Maoist issue routinely publish maps of India in which large swathes of provinces and districts are marked as naxal-dominated, naxal-influenced, naxal-affected, and the likes.[9] A whole province is marked as naxal-influenced even if there may be a few squads in the province hiding in some villages and urban settlements. And these provinces are typically larger than many European countries!

The Central Government frequently convenes high-profile meetings of chief ministers, secretaries and police chiefs of the country to meet the challenges posed by the 'menace'. Cutting-edge special forces, carved out of the paramilitary forces, are being constructed and deployed in 'naxal-infested' areas. In recent months, even the army and the air force are beginning to enter into the picture.

'Naxalite' actions – widespread arson, mass killings and the ability to take on the security forces – are prominently reported in the corporate media with ill-concealed awe. This strand of the naxalite movement never had it so big in its close to forty years of existence in hideouts in remote jungles.

Two recent – and contrasting – events in the neighbourhood throw significant light on the consequences of this brand of politics. In Sri Lanka, a vast freedom movement of Tamil nationalism arose about three decades ago. As the movement became progressively militant, it gave rise to a formidable militarist organisation under the leadership of Velupillai Prabhakaran: LTTE. The LTTE declared armed struggle, systematically eliminated all other groups advocating Tamil liberation, took to the jungles and launched a civil war.

There were several rounds of 'negotiations' between the government and the LTTE, often with international effort. LTTE refused to give up arms and join the democratic process; thus, it used each pause in the hostilities to consolidate its forces. After over twenty years of bloody war with Sri Lankan security forces, resulting in incalculable suffering of Tamil people, the LTTE was recently wiped out from Sri Lanka. The calamity facilitated the emergence of a neo-fascist regime in Colombo; it also left behind nearly a million hapless Tamil refugees at the mercy of this government. With all moderate forces from both sides eliminated from the scene, the Tamil freedom movement is now faced with a historical setback after over a hundred thousand deaths.

The Maoist Supreme Commander Ganapathy, whose organisation was trained in guerrilla warfare by former commandos of LTTE, agrees with the consequences: 'There is no doubt that the movement for a separate sovereign Tamil Eelam has suffered a severe setback with the defeat and considerable decimation of the LTTE. The Tamil people and the national liberation forces are now leaderless.' But he puts the blame elsewhere: 'The jingoistic rallies and celebrations organised by the government and Sinhala chauvinist parties all over Sri Lanka in the wake of Prabhakaran's death and the defeat of the LTTE show the national hatred for Tamils nurtured by Sinhala organisations and the extent to which the minds of ordinary Sinhalese are poisoned with such chauvinist frenzy'. (Ganapathy, 2009)

So, the problem is with 'the minds of ordinary Sinhalese,' not the blood-thirsty operations of LTTE that led to the creation of such minds. Nonetheless, Ganapathy hopes that 'the ground remains fertile for the resurgence of the Tamil liberation struggle. Even if it takes time, the war for a separate Tamil Eelam is certain to revive, taking lessons from the defeat of the LTTE.' Although he is prepared to learn – perhaps tactical – lessons, he does not seem to have any problems with the militarist, sectarian and exclusivist politics of LTTE.[10]

In sharp contrast, the Communist Party of Nepal (Maoist), CPN(M), also launched a civil war, after all democratic methods failed, in the early 1990s against a ruthless feudal monarchy protected by the Royal Nepalese Army. The war lasted nearly a decade with the CPN(M)-directed People's Liberation Army dominating vast terrains of the country with massive popular support. The basic point to note is that what CPN(M) strove for during the armed struggle – republic, constituent assembly, supremacy of the parliament created by universal franchise, etc. – India already has. Once that was achieved in Nepal within just a decade, a genuine armed struggle – far superior to anything Indian Maoists have ever envisaged – was immediately brought to a halt. CPN(M) proved its point by winning over forty percent of the seats in the interim parliament after the republic was established. With this mandate in hand, innovative, peaceful but militant processes were then adopted to broaden the democratic base even in a context in which the possibility of a counter-revolution orchestrated by the ousted monarch, the army and the ruling elites of India loomed large. To my knowledge, it is the only instance in which a vast Maoist insurgency is trying to adjust itself to parliamentary democracy.

This is not a determined opinion on Nepal; that is for the people of Nepal to decide. The point is that at every stage of the struggle, armed or unarmed, the CPN(M) built up impressive popular support and sought a course which ensured the least harm to non-combatants even at a grave risk to their organisation. This required courage, vision, statesmanship and magnificent humanity sorely missing from the current state of Left politics in India. Maoists in Nepal are still far away from all the republican institutions and state-policies India has. For example, one of the current issues in Nepal concerns the supremacy of the parliament over the army. As the leader of CPN(M) Prachanda pointed out, the democratic movement is at a crossroads due to this seminal conflict. Indian republicanism addressed and solved that problem sixty years ago. So, the struggle against the undoubtedly predatory state in India is of a different order altogether based on over six decades of republican experience; I didn't say 'democratic' experience. Given some of the impressive yet 'fragile' features of Indian democracy (see Chapter Two), people in India face higher democratic challenges, perhaps, unprecedented in history.

During the war in Nepal, the PWG – followed by CPI(Maoist) – maintained close contacts with CPN(M). But after the CPN(M) joined – in fact, established – the democratic process in Nepal, CPI(Maoist) does not find any lessons to be learned. This time the blame is on CPN(M). As the Supreme Commander puts it: 'It is indeed a great tragedy that the CPN(M) has chosen to abandon the path of protracted people's war and pursue a parliamentary path in spite of having de facto power in most of the countryside.' In a letter to CPN(M), CPI(Maoist) 'advised' the former not to give up armed struggle until the 'old order' is smashed and the CPN(M) is able to seize power all by itself to usher in a 'new democratic revolution'. However, the Supreme Commander remains optimistic since, 'given the great revolutionary traditions of the CPN(M), we hope that the inner-party struggle will repudiate the right opportunist line pursued by its leadership, give up revisionist stands and practices, and apply minds creatively to the concrete conditions of Nepal.' So, the Indian Maoists fondly hope that the complex, uncertain, but peaceful democratic process in Nepal will eventually collapse and the CPN(M) will return to the path of 'protracted war'.

Beyond the bluster, it is not difficult to discern that, no matter what, CPI(Maoist) is not prepared to give up its fatal policies. They are not open to any debates, no one can enter their 'liberated zones' without unconditional support to their line. Like Prabhakaran and his LTTE, having meticulously secured hideouts for themselves in 'impregnable' dense forests protected by squads armed with sophisticated weapons, they are prepared to carry on 'protracted war' for many years before their inevitable decimation. In the process, not only will *adivasi*s under their control suffer immensely, it will give the growingly authoritarian state a golden opportunity to smash whatever avenues of hard-won democratic resistance still remain in place.

As noted, CPI(Maoist) has exactly two channels of 'popular' support: *adivasi*s they control in some restricted forest areas and a section of radical, urban intelligentsia. It is the support of the latter that gives CPI(Maoist) significant propaganda mileage and a false impression of legitimacy and popular support. By posing the current military preparations of the state only as a state-versus-people conflict, the *Sanhati* statement effectively exonerates CPI(Maoist).

So, my complaint is that the *Sanhati* statement and its background note did not furnish crucial information on the very complex issue of OGH. In particular, it did not mention the operations of CPI(Maoist) in the concerned area for many years, and the government's plan to use OGH ostensibly to flush out the 'naxalites' in that area. In that sense, OGH itself has little to do directly with 'the widening levels of disparity and the continuing problems of social deprivation and structural violence.'

Now, whether this information is a determining parameter for the general protests to the general protests to the sinister OGH is something that can be debated. But the point is that the signatories to the petition, especially the foreign scholars, have not been given a chance to reflect on and participate in the debate.

As a non-partisan background, *Sanhati* could have attached the rather comprehensive and sensitive study of the Maoist issue in Shoma Chaudhury's (2009) piece which contains a very timely discussion of the views of K. Balagopal, a noted human rights advocate and an erstwhile sympathiser of the Maoist movement himself. In this case, what appears to be transparent turns opaque once the background is factored in. I wonder how many would have agreed to sign the one-sided petition with its sweeping, undocumented generalisations if the signatories were given the opportunity to examine the complexity of the issue.

The brief description regarding the history and politics of the Maoist movement must have been well known to the organisers of the petition; yet they decided to sit on this knowledge. The organisers do not have to agree with my analysis of Maoists; they just have to be aware that such an analysis is widely shared even by other strands of naxalites such as the legendary Kanu Sanyal, as noted. Unless an unlikely explanation is offered, it follows that the statement was essentially drafted to serve the Maoists' cause by their intellectual friends. Many hundreds of intellectuals across the world endorsed it essentially out of understandable ignorance. A petition from urban academics and other intellectuals would have been more truthful and morally valid if it simultaneously demanded: (a) stop all aggression by the state; (b) Maoists must disarm; and (c) direct all attention to the safety, dignity and welfare of *adivasi*s. This is where the statement failed: factually, morally and politically.[11]

Although a very large number of academicians working abroad and in India endorsed the *Sanhati* statement in good faith without being aware of the complexity of the issues involved, there were quite a few prominent intellectuals, mostly from India, who are obviously familiar with these issues due to their well known Left-of-CPM location in the radical spectrum. Without further evidence, it cannot be immediately inferred that all of them were thus consciously supporting the underlying exoneration of Maoists. Some might have signed because they thought that the attack by the state is more serious than Maoist armed operations. Others might have followed a (false) sense of solidarity with Maoists given the binary choices offered by the prevalent 'Bush' doctrine (see Chapter Three). Still others might simply not have given enough thought to the issues involved before joining in; they could have signed because their radical friends did. It is also possible that some of them regret having signed the *Sanhati* petition. We do not know. I set aside the issue of whether these are responsible intellectual actions in the face of immense calamity that has descended on *adivasi*s in Dandakaranya.

Yet, as subsequent events and publications revealed, we do know by now that at least some of the intellectuals who signed the petition, such as Roy (2010a) and Navlakha (2010), do wish to champion the Maoist movement as a genuine form of resistance to the Indian state. We will examine the factual and ideological bases of this claim in some detail as we proceed.

For now, keeping to the issue of intellectual responsibility, I will focus on the 'reconstruction' of Charu Mazumdar by a prominent public figure, Arundhati Roy (2010a). The focus is needed because, on the one hand, Charu Mazumdar, the original general secretary of the CPI(ML) in 1969, is perhaps the most reviled figure in the contemporary communist movement in India, *including* the broad naxalite movement sketched above. On the other hand, since he disappeared from the national scene after his death in 1972 and the original naxalite movement faded away, the general public is not likely to be aware of the disturbing history and politics of Charu Mazumdar. Especially come to mind, the upwardly mobile, young, Western-educated audience of the popular English magazine *Outlook* in which Roy's piece was published with much fanfare.

It is the intellectual's responsibility, then, to place this controversial figure in proper perspective to enable the ill-prepared reader to engage in a balanced review, even if the intellectual's prime and rightful motivation is to extol this figure. Suppose the current generation of young people in Cambodia is not aware of Pol Pot. Will it be an example of intellectual responsibility if an influential writer in Cambodia, who happens to be a Pol Pot admirer, presents Pol Pot in a sanitised form to this new generation? Is there a legitimate account of the Pol Pot regime without the killing fields?[12]

The memory of Charu Mazumdar entered public discourse recently, even if marginally, through an interview with the general secretary of CPI(Maoist). (Ganapathy, 2010a) In his opening remarks, Ganapathy remembered his, 'great beloved forefounder leaders and teachers, Comrades Charu Mazumdar and Kanhai Chatterji, who led an ideological and political struggle ceaselessly for a long time against revisionism and modern revisionism of Communist Party of India and CPI(Marxist).'

Soon after, there was a very influential article by a prominent writer, as noted, who describes Charu Mazumdar as a 'visionary', and the 'party he founded' as keeping the 'dream of revolution' alive in India: 'imagine a society without that dream' (Roy, 2010a). The spirit of Charu Mazumdar is here to stay, then, to enable us to inhabit the dream. No doubt, Roy agrees, the said 'visionary' and his party had a 'problematic past'; but so do the Congress party of another visionary Mahatma Gandhi and the African

National Congress (ANC) of Nelson Mandela. Benign mention of a 'problematic past' thus does no polemical harm to the image of the Maoist party while it enables the author to claim 'objectivity.' In any case, the party has by now 'evolved' out of that 'problematic past', Roy assures us.

It stands to reason that the political thoughts of an individual are likely to be influenced by many thinkers of the past. These influences shape the structure of the individual's thoughts in a general way. It does not follow that the individual 'owns' these influential thoughts. For example, it is a truism that, like almost any communist of his era, Charu Mazumdar subscribed to MLM.[13] These ideologies did shape his vision, but we cannot ascribe Charu Mazumdar's authorship to these aspects of his vision. We need to distinguish, therefore, between the influenced part and the original part of Charu Mazumdar's vision to understand which 'dream' the society has been invited to inhabit afresh.

Thus, Charu Mazumdar subscribed to Mao's vision that in a semi-feudal and semi-colonial condition, a society can be transformed by a protracted – primarily peasant – war to seize state power to establish a 'new democratic revolution'. This was one of Mao's original contributions to revolutionary theory and practice, as noted. As to the issue of whether the Indian condition is suitable for initiating a protracted peasant war, one of the founders of naxalbari movement, Kanu Sanyal (2010), observes that, 'while debating the party history it should be kept in mind that neither the CPI(ML) formed in 1969 was the forerunner of the armed agrarian struggle in the Indian context nor was it the first application of Mao Tse Tung Thought. Such a wrong conception is still persisting among the communist revolutionary ranks.' Sanyal's observation was supported by many revolutionaries, such as Sengupta (1970/1983), who were intimately connected with the Indian communist and naxalite movements.

So, what is original about Charu Mazumdar's ideas that can properly be called *his* 'vision'? Charu Mazumdar's *specific* thoughts are enshrined in detail in the following paragraphs from what is often viewed as a 'murder manual'. I am not denying that anarchist documents of the past might contain some of the 'methods' suggested in the paragraphs (Simeon, 2010; Mander, 2011). But the concrete adoption of these methods, with detailed application in the Indian context to launch a protracted peasant war, was certainly Charu Mazumdar's most original contribution – an 'addition' – to Mao's thoughts.

> The method of forming a guerrilla unit has to be wholly conspiratorial. No inkling ... should be given out even in the meetings of the political units of the Party. This conspiracy should be between individuals on a person-to-person basis. The petty-bourgeois intellectual comrade must take the initiative in this respect ... He should approach the poor peasant who, in his opinion, has the most revolutionary potentiality, and whisper in his ears: 'Don't you think it is a good thing to finish off such and such a jotedar'. ... We should not use any kind of firearms at this stage. The guerrilla unit must rely wholly on choppers, spears, javelins and sickles. ...The guerrillas should come from different directions pretending ... to be innocent persons and gather at a previously appointed place, wait for the enemy, and, when the opportune moment comes, spring at the enemy and kill him. ... The middle peasant cadre and the petty-bourgeois intellectual comrades should be removed (from the guerrilla unit) if possible. When guerrilla actions become more frequent we have to gradually bring in these willing fighters. In fact, a time will come when the battle cry will be: '*He*

who has not dipped his hand in the blood of class enemies can hardly be called a communist.[14]

Dipping one's hand in the blood of class enemies — that's his 'vision', take it or leave it. As Simeon (2010) put it, 'a man whose sole contribution to socialism consisted of elevating homicidal mania to a political principle has become an icon for the ultra-Left tradition. There is no sign of a change in the expendable status of human life for revolutionaries.' Anyone who is appealing to Charu Mazumdar's 'vision' now must be either recommending these methods or does not know what one is talking about.

Yet, except for vague references to an 'annihilation campaign', this crucial thought was never mentioned in the recent write-up on Charu Mazumdar, whereas the writer did not shy away from graphic depiction of individual rapes and killings by Indian security forces. So the writer's failure to describe Mazumdar's actual methods cannot be traced to her aesthetic aversion for gory detail. There is just one mention of Mazumdar's, 'abrasive rhetoric [that] fetishises violence, blood and martyrdom, and often employs a language so coarse as to be almost genocidal.' But the effect of this apparently critical remark is almost immediately transferred to an endearing romantic image: 'When he said that only 'an annihilation campaign' could produce 'the new man who will defy death and be free from all thought of self-interest' — could he have imagined that this ancient people, dancing into the night, would be the ones on whose shoulders his dreams would come to rest? (Roy, 2010a)

How do we interpret this rhetoric? Is it meant to be so veiled a criticism of the 'annihilation campaign' that its meaning is virtually lost? Or, is this meant to be an expression of ecstasy as the 'annihilation campaign' is now adopted by the 'ancient people dancing into the night' to produce 'new' men and women?

Once the discourse of annihilation is removed from its original context of slit throats, severed heads and gashed stomachs in dark alleys, the 'coarseness' of a 'genocidal language' in fact begins to acquire charming innocence in the sprawling wilderness inhabited by ancient people. In the subconscious of the elites who constitute the target audience of *Outlook*, these people carry the 'aboriginal' image anyway; so it is 'natural' for the ancient people, as they dance into the night, to be armed with bows, arrows, spears and sickles as recommended by Charu Mazumdar. With this transfer of agency, Charu Mazumdar's vision attains sublime legitimacy on the 'shoulders' of *adivasis*; in turn, Maoists, who are leading these ancient people, can now be viewed as vanguards of death-defying freedom.

The write-up does not mention the well-documented conspiracies and secret confabulations with which Mazumdar orchestrated the formation of the All India Coordination Committee of Communist Revolutionaries (AICCCR) and CPI(ML) by keeping only to the 'faithful' and sidelining a range of respected comrades long active in the movement (Mohanty, 1977).[15] To cite Sanyal (2010) again: 'Promode Sengupta, Satyananda Bhattacharya, Parimal Dasgupta were all thrown out in the name of differences. It is all the more a glaring example that Asit Sen who took a major lead to mobilise and organise the AICCCR throughout the country was not included in AICCCR and even he was thrown out on the eve of formation of the CPI(ML) ... The AICCCR under the leadership of Com. [Charu Mazumdar] played tricks of factionalism ... Thus AICCCR sealed the path of unity and created disunity among the revolutionaries.'

Despite such 'safeguards', there was so much dissent against Mazumdar within the central committee of the CPI(ML) within one year of its formation that, according to some judicious commentators familiar with the early history of naxalism,

Mazumdar stood virtually 'expelled' from the party. Commenting on Roy's bizarre reference to Charu Mazumdar as a 'visionary' who, 'kept the dream of revolution real and present in India,' noted political commentator Jairus Banaji (2010) observes: 'The fact is that the "annihilation" line had led to such disastrous results by the end of 1971 that the majority of his own Central Committee denounced him as a 'Trotskyite' and expelled him from the party! Indeed, the majority of a twenty-one member Central Committee had withdrawn support from him by November 1970, and Satya Narayan Singh, who was elected the new general secretary, described his line as 'individual terrorism.' Even when the AICCCR transformed itself into a party in April 1969, leading figures of the early Maoist movement in India were unhappy with the decision and many stayed out.'[16]

With respect to the 'annihilation campaign', there is no mention in Roy's article that it was widely applied in West Bengal and elsewhere during 1970–72 by Mazumdar's murderous gangs comprising mostly of urban lumpens. We have already noted the disastrous consequences of this politics for democratic resistance in those regions (see Introduction). The writer fails to inform her readers that the current Maoists have continued with the basic method of dipping one's hands in the blood of class enemies; it's almost official policy. In his interview to *The Hindu*, the Maoist spokesperson, Azad (2010a), says: 'When our comrades hear of these cold-blooded murders committed by the APSIB (Andhra Pradesh Special Intelligence Branch) or other officials of the state, it is natural that their blood would boil and they will not bat an eyelid to hack any of the perpetrators of these inhuman crimes, say a man from APSIB or Grey Hounds, to pieces if he fell into their hands.'

Geneva conventions on prisoners of war notwithstanding, Azad gives an idea of how the classic 'annihilation campaign' is now conducted by the 'ancient people'. As Rahul Pandita (2011) cites a 'senior Maoist leader' with apparent approval, 'Maoists end up killing people in such a gruesome fashion' because 'it serves a psychological purpose': 'when a tribal guerrilla kills his "class enemy" in this fashion, it gives him [or her] immense satisfaction.'

Roy (2010a) herself reports that Maoists make elaborate videos during ambushes of security forces, but she mentions the videos far away from where an 'annihilation campaign' was implanted in the flickering lights of the forest; so the two images remain disjointed. Here's one video:

> It starts with shots of Dandakaranya, rivers, waterfalls, the close-up of a bare branch of a tree, a brainfever bird calling. Then suddenly a comrade is wiring up an IED, concealing it with dry leaves. A cavalcade of motorcycles is blown up. There are mutilated bodies and burning bikes. The weapons are being snatched. Three policemen, looking shell-shocked, have been tied up.

These recordings of dismembered bodies and streams of blood, embedded in the serenity of pristine forests, are shown to the guerrillas as a form of enduring entertainment. One of these guerrillas, an *adivasi* woman named 'Kamla', aged seventeen, does not like regular movies at all, she only watches ambush videos: a 'new' woman, as envisioned by Charu Mazumdar.

A noted commentator and consistent champion of the naxalite movement himself, Sumanta Banerjee (2009) described the scene in Lalgarh area of West Bengal:[17] 'It is these militarist priorities and political expediencies that are eroding the ideological commitment of [CPI (Maoist)] cadres. They ... seem to be degenerating into roving gangs of paranoid revengeful killers recalling the dark days of the fratricidal warfare between the Naxalites and CPM youth cadres in the 1970s.' In one particularly gruesome incident among many, a local CPM activist was killed and his body was left to rot on the main road of the village for six days to set an example; no one was allowed to remove the body for cremation.

As Simeon pointed out, nothing seems to have changed for Maoists since the days of Charu Mazumdar regarding the 'expendable status of human life for revolutionaries'. A new breed of 'communists' continue to dip their hands in the blood of suspected informers, and of corpses of security forces when the 'revolutionaries' hack them to pieces and snatch the weapons. The only difference from the 'problematic past' is that these 'communists' are no longer 'petty-bourgeois intellectual comrades' but *adivasi* children with empty stomachs, as we will soon see.

Beyond these glaring omissions, the role of some radical intellectuals extends to disturbing acts of conveying misinformation as well. In explaining the origins of the current war, Maoist Supreme Commander Ganapathy asserts: 'In general, Maoist revolutionaries do not want violence or armed confrontation with anybody. In unavoidable condition only they take up arms and resist their enemies and they are waging liberation war by learning from the history' (Ganapathy, 2010a). So, what is the 'unavoidable condition' in Bastar that has compelled Maoists to take up arms as they learn from history?

In support of Maoists, some intellectuals have persistently claimed across the world in distinguished Left forums and very visible publications that the Indian state has forced this war on people to displace and decimate *adivasi* populations so that various national and transnational mining companies can exploit rich mineral resources of the area (see Roy, 2010a; Navlakha, 2010). Apparently, the state government has signed 'hundreds of MOUs' *in secret* with these companies. *Adivasi*s are obviously unwilling to part with their land and leave their ancient habitat. So, the

Indian state is applying brute force to drive them away so that the MOUs can be implemented. As we saw, this is basically the story uploaded by *Sanhati* to secure international endorsement. An extreme version of this thesis is that the war is *not* directed at Maoists at all; it is exclusively directed at *adivasi*s to pave the way for the corporations.

Roy (2010a) insists on a specific date when the attack was planned and initiated: a speech of the prime minister in April 2005 to the effect that Maoists were 'the gravest internal security threat'. Roy also proclaims a causal connection between this speech and two MOUs signed the same month in Chhattisgarh for setting up integrated steel plants, the terms of which apparently also remain secret. Thus, according to Roy, the 'first phase' of OGH was soon launched in June 2005 in the form of *Salwa Judum*: '*Salwa Judum* was a ground-clearing operation, meant to move people out of their villages into roadside camps, where they could be policed and controlled. In military terms, it's called Strategic Hamleting.' (Roy, 2010a) So far, Maoists and their arms are nowhere in the picture.

In the proposed narrative, Maoists entered the picture because, as Navlakha (2010) suggests, 'Maoists offer formidable resistance against the implementation of hundreds of MOU for mining and mineral-based industries in predominately *adivasi* India, where they enjoy considerable support. Without weakening this resistance, Government of India's mineral as well as FDI policy will remain unrealised.' Except for imaginary causal chains, insufficient evidence has been advanced so far to expose the Government of India's alleged mineral and FDI policies *as they relate to adivasis in Bastar* where the state forces are largely concentrated. Citing evidence of sinister mining operations in Karnataka (Roy, 2010a) is plainly irrelevant because Karnataka is hardly a Maoist territory and there is no OGH (Gopalakrishnan, 2010).

Pursuing this critique further, how do these writers know that there are 'hundreds' of signed MOUs if they are mostly secret? With the Right to Information Act in place for over four years, why have these MOUs continued to remain secret? What steps were taken to uncover them? Why is the alleged secrecy of MOUs continued to be used as a wildcard to divert attention from a massive arms build-up by Maoists? Although there are supposed to be 'hundreds' of MOUs designed to take over '*adivasi* India', Roy (2010a) is able to cite just two of them for Chhattisgarh, as noted, and these are steel plants! Even if we ignore the embarrassingly low number of MOUs for precipitating an armed struggle, have we — especially *adivasi*s — already reached a consensus that '*adivasi* India' cannot have steel plants?

In this connection, it is interesting to record some revelations due to *WikiLeaks*.[18] It is well-known that these revelations carry some credibility because US consuls are not likely to lie to their bosses in Washington in secret communication.[19] A report from the US consul in Mumbai says that 'NGOs and activists routinely claim that villages have been cleared to make way for major industrial projects in the resource-rich regions in Chhattisgarh, Odisha and other states.' The cable cites one journalist, who had travelled in the region, saying that 'NGO claims stem from a habit of 'expecting the worst' from the Indian state when matters of tribal land, resources, and big business collide in rural and remote areas.' The activists in Chhattisgarh, the cable continues, were unable to point to, 'any specific instances of land reallocation or forced resettlement by the state for industrial projects since June 2005.' In fact, 'a coal power project planned by the American company AES has been stalled for years to obtain the consent of tribal villagers in northeast Chhattisgarh to purchase their land.' The cable adds that, 'the Chhattisgarh Mining Development Corporation recently announced it will open a new bauxite mine in the Keshkal area of Bastar region, the fourth such project in Keshkal, but NGOs have not identified any illegal procedures used to obtain the land.'

More importantly, even if we concede the story of MOUs, is a widespread armed struggle immediately needed to address such long standing and controversial issues? Why did Maoists not use their alleged support-base in *adivasi* areas to launch an intense mass campaign to resist mining corporations as other radical groups have done, say – in Koraput, Niyamgiri – and other places? As a matter of fact, it is the state agencies – compelled to act due to rising popular non-violent protests and revelations through the RTI – that have exposed the widespread mining scams involving MOUs in Jharkhand and ex-Chief Minister Madhu Koda is in jail. The Supreme Court has intervened in the Bellary mines scam in Karnataka. After the report submitted by the Karnataka *Lokayukta*, Santosh Hegde, ex-Chief Minister Yeddyurappa and Bellary-mines owners, the Reddy brothers, were still in jail at the time of publication.[20] Did Maoists exhaust these options before they took to arms? Is the issue of MOUs a convenient afterthought of Maoist propaganda, cheerfully lapped up by elite intellectuals to divert attention from Maoist operations in that area for a quarter of a century? What is Maoists' record of resistance to aggressive neo-liberal policies of the state *before* the onset of *Salwa Judum*? These questions easily multiply; we will take them up as we proceed.

Nonetheless, having said all this, it is agreed that, delinked from the Maoist issue, the story of MOUs by itself could be partly true. This is because, though we can question the evidential basis of the concerned Maoist narrative, we are *not* ruling out that the (predatory) state is capable of murderous assault on people for profit. As mentioned earlier, the government's own 'secret' document is a pointer in that direction (MRD, 2009).

Even though the government commissioned the report, it was never placed before the public for obvious reasons. Here is what the report says about the complicity between the government, political parties, and big business to launch *Salwa Judum* and drive *adivasi* populations out of their villages:

> A new approach was necessary if the rich lodes of iron ore are to be mined. The new approach came about with the *Salwa Judum* ... Ironically the *Salwa Judum* was led by Mahendra Karma, elected on a Congress ticket and the Leader of the Opposition and supported whole heartedly by the BJP-led government ... Behind them are the traders, contractors and miners waiting for a successful result of their strategy. The first financiers of the *Salwa Judum* were Tata and the Essar in the quest for 'peace' ... 640 villages as per official statistics were laid bare, burnt to the ground and emptied with the force of the gun and the blessings of the State. 350,000 *adivasi*s, half the total population of Dantewada district, are displaced, their womenfolk raped, their daughters killed, and their youth maimed ... Villages sitting on tons of iron ore are effectively de-peopled and (made) available for the highest bidder. The latest information that is being circulated is that both Essar Steel and Tata Steel are willing to take over the empty landscape and manage the mines.

The empirical basis and the authorship of these ghastly findings can be questioned.[21] Still, even if this assessment is partly valid, it reveals a very grim situation which could only have worsened since the report was written. Suppose then that the monstrous *Salwa Judum* operation was designed to 'weaken' Maoist resistance to attain the twin ends of displacement of *adivasis* and entry of mining corporations. Given the scale of these operations, Maoists had no other option but to take up arms *around* 2005.[22] Such is the 'unavoidable condition' in which the armed struggle began.

To recapitulate, the suggested picture is that, as Maoists devoted themselves to *adivasi* welfare and empowerment for the first twenty five years, Dandakaranya was largely a land of peace and tranquility – *no arms and no armies* – except perhaps for occasional skirmishes with the police. The peace was rudely shattered by the ugly *Salwa Judum* campaign in the summer of 2005. Then all hell broke loose. Lakhs of *adivasis* were displaced in 'strategic hamlets' after the usual killing, looting, torture and rape. However, as Maoists retaliated with increasing gunpower, the campaign was forced to retreat and Maoist ranks swelled. Sensing 'grave threat' to 'internal security', the state initiated the 'second phase' of OGH involving tens of thousands of paramilitary forces. So, this is the picture: The speech of the prime minister ⟶ signing of MOUs ⟶ emergence of *Salwa Judum* ⟶ Maoists' taking up arms ⟶ Operation Green Hunt.

In this work, we will see in some detail that the Maoist narrative just sketched is more propaganda than assertion of truth. As a matter of fact, *armed operations of Maoists in Dandakaranya started not in 2005, but in 1988 when a substantial number of armed squads moved in from Andhra Pradesh to establish guerrilla zones and bases, and PLGA was formally installed in* 2001 (see Chapter Four). Based on his extensive travels in Maoist territory in the winter of 2001, Satnam (2010) reports in his very sympathetic account that guerrilla activity and control over areas was already widespread by then. So much for the alleged post-2005 grand causal chain.

The real story is markedly different. Ever since the dawn of the neo-liberal regime, every local working class and peasant uprising has been ruthlessly attacked by the state; these struggles are the real danger to the state as they challenge and redefine class and property structures. In contrast, CPI(Maoist) has been allowed to grow into monstrous proportions until their presence actually interfered with broader interests of the state. Let me explain.

It is now very well established that the major source of funding for Maoist war efforts comes from 'levies', 'royalties' and extortions from mining and other contractors (Chakravarty, 2008; Mishra and Pandita, 2010; Pandita, 2011). In Jharkhand, for example, Maoists have been demanding up to 25 percent 'cess' from dozens of middle-level and minor 'dig-and-decamp' mining operators for at least two decades.[23] The process had a devastating effect on *adivasi* villages, forests and rivers. Maoists and their intellectual supporters do not seem to care.

The situation in Dandakaranya appears to be different. Compared to Jharkhand, Odisha, Goa and Karnataka, very large-scale mining projects in Chhattisgarh is a relatively recent phenomenon.[24] Also, this is where the Maoist headquarters – in particular, the guerrilla base at Abujmaad in the Narayanpur area of greater Bastar – is reportedly located too close to the proposed mining operations for comfort. The anxiety of Maoists on this score was revealed in their policy document of 2009: 'The bigger conspiracy of the reactionary rulers to extend mining from Raoghat to the innumerable hills in Maad [Abujmaad] and to loot the natural mineral wealth of the region should be exposed and a broad-based movement should be built against displacement' ('Post-election Situation – Our Tasks', in Mishra and Pandita, 2010). The specific mention of Abujmaad illustrates what the real problem is for Maoists. It is hard to recall Maoist calls for 'broad-based movement' against similar 'conspiracies' that have continued for decades in Jharkhand, Odisha, Karnataka, Goa and other places. As noted, at least in the case of Jharkhand, Maoists themselves are directly engaged in this looting.

Most importantly, in contrast to sundry 'dig-and-decamp' operators, giant steel corporations like Tata and Essar have their eyes on the lodes of high-quality iron ore beneath the forests of Chhattisgarh. Revelations from WikiLeaks, cited above, suggest that the Essar group has been paying protection money to Maoists for their operations so far: 'A senior representative from Essar, a major industrial company with large mining and steel-related facilities in Chhattisgarh, told Congenoff that the company pays Maoists 'a significant amount' not to harm or interfere with their operations; when Maoists occasionally break this agreement and damage Essar property or threaten personnel, Essar sets different Maoist groups against each other to suppress the situation.'

The story of Essar paying large sums of protection money to Maoists exploded in the mainstream recently when two courageous *adivasi* activists Soni Sori and her nephew Lingaram Kodopi were arrested on the charge of being Maoist accomplices. The story is worth recounting as 'it captures the brutal chaos of India's "greatest internal security threat".' (Chaudhury, 2011)

The basic problem is that Sori and Kodopi come from a respectable and well-to-do *adivasi* family. Sori's father, Madru Ram Sori, a respected and kindly man, has been a *sarpanch* for fifteen years. Sori's uncle is a former Communist Party of India MLA. Unlike the usual stereotype of the dispossessed, stupefied and voiceless tribal, both Soni Sori and Lingaram Kodopi are decently educated and had decided to use their relative priviledge to help *adivasi*s in Chhattisgarh. That's the problem. According to CRPF commanders in the area, 'You have to take sides here, you have to be either with the police and the paramilitary forces or with the Naxals. You cannot try to be in the middle.' (cited in Chaudhury, 2011) 'Earlier,' one of the commanders continued, 'the tribals didn't have a voice, but these two people changed that. Lingaram becoming a journalist was a grave threat to them [the police] as he could expose them. They want to make sure there is no tribal voice.' As such, Sori and Kodopi are eyesores for both the police and Maoists. As the police keep slapping false but extremely serious charges against them, Maoists wanted them to appear before 'people's court' to explain why they are seen with the police so often. As Sori and Kodopi failed to oblige the rebels, Maoists shot Sori's father in the leg as a warning.

Working meticulously through this bizarre and complex story, Shoma Chaudhury (2011) reports that payments to Maoists by Essar is connected in a convoluted way with the arrest of Sori and Kodopi. The valid question many are raising is how can contractors and mining operations survive in the region unless the Maoists are allowing them to continue for a hefty price? For example, an influential contractor B.K. Lala was allowed by Maoists to repair an Essar pipeline they had blown up earlier. A senior officer in the security forces said, 'Lala reconstructed those pipes for Essar through deep jungles. It is impossible to imagine that a private contractor could do that without Maoist approval. It's a place where even the paramilitary do not tread. The police knew this and because he [Lala] didn't take care of their interest, they arrested him.' So, once the WikiLeaks disclosures came out, the police found the opportunity to arrest Lala because they were not getting their due share of Essar payments. However, in their First Information Report (FIR), they made it look as if Lala was paying the money, on behalf of Essar, to Lingaram, now an alleged Maoist conduit. The strategy is to kill several birds in one stroke: arrest Linga, then arrest Soni for not cooperating with the police to frame Linga and finally arrest Lala so that he or his bosses in Essar cough up the money for the police.

Given such experience, it stands to reason that Tata and Essar are not going to pay 'royalties' to armed groups after a point; they want the whole thing to themselves and the area of their operations totally secured and sealed. For example, for an integrated steel factory, there will be long conveyor belts or other mechanisms, running through the forests, from the mines to the processing area. The steel giants cannot leave this essential part of the system exposed to extremist attacks or blackmail, as the case may be. From this perspective, for both Maoists and the corporate giants, mining operations in that area basically pose problems of security. For them, *adivasi*s and the environment are of little concern.

Given a choice between Maoists and Tata-Essar, it is obvious which way the government is likely to tilt. We are quickly reminded of how, despite international protests, the US nurtured the Taliban in Afghanistan until the Taliban grew big and began to demand too high a price for the US to exploit natural gas in the region. By 1998, the talks between US and Taliban collapsed. As a consequence, erstwhile collaborators turned into the greatest threat to security and democracy for the US. The rest is history.

4

ARMS OVER PEOPLE

There is overwhelming evidence that the Maoist forces at the frontline – the militias and the guerrilla army – consist entirely of *adivasi* youth. While the orders for a specific action could be emanating from the essentially non-*adivasi* leadership hiding safely in their secured bases, it is *adivasis* on the ground that carry out the explosions and killings. According to reports, there are thousands of armed militias and guerrillas operating basically in the Bastar area; *all these people are young adivasis*. Maoists have been able to raise this huge force because a large section of *adivasis* in Bastar have sided with Maoists for reasons discussed below. The massive presence of *adivasis* in the Maoist scheme of things has led commentators such as Roy (2009) to conclude that there is no difference between *adivasis* and Maoists.[1] I will evaluate the factuality of this conclusion below.

For now, it is evident – yet systematically overlooked – that any armed operation to flush out Maoists will have *adivasis*, *armed or unarmed*, as the direct target (Singh, 2010; Bhatia, 2011a;

Mitra, 2011). Further, as the ill-fated and murderous *Salwa Judum* campaign showed, any attack on *adivasi*s not only results in immense calamity for them, it in fact helps increase the Maoist base of support including the expansion of guerrilla forces. The essentially non-*adivasi* veteran leadership from Andhra Pradesh and Bihar has carefully planned all this after many years of poring over maps and demographic profiles.

To understand why even the militias and the guerrillas – not to mention the millions of unarmed *adivasi*s who support them – ought to be viewed as victims requiring protection, we need to understand the real character of how the (upper class) Maoists, driven out from Andhra Pradesh and Bihar, went about constructing their base of support in Bastar. The Maoist spokesperson Azad (2010a) asserted that 'the welfare of the masses is the first priority for Maoist revolutionaries.' The politbureau member and media-savvy Kishenji (Koteshwar Rao) offered to talk to any party that 'worked for the common good of people' suggesting that Maoists had devoted themselves to the 'common good' of *adivasi*s in Bastar forests.[2] More specifically, their Supreme Commander Ganapathy (2009) claims that, 'The *Janatana Sarkar*s in Dandakaranya and the revolutionary people's committees in Jharkhand, Orissa and parts of some other states have become new models of genuine people's democracy and development.' Maoists had already entrenched themselves in these forests for about twenty five years before the first of the major attacks by the state began in 2005 in the form of the *Salwa Judum* campaign. So, what did Maoists accomplish for *adivasi*s in that quarter of a century? What is the real content of 'genuine people's democracy and development' in their control areas?

We now have five important documents in the public domain to study this issue. Two of these are based on recent travels inside Maoist territory by two public intellectuals from Delhi (Roy,

2010a; Navlakha, 2010); the others are detailed interviews of the general secretary of the Maoist party Ganapathy (2009; 2010a) and the Maoist spokesperson Azad (2010a). The last three are Maoist documents by definition.

As for the other two, it stands to reason that Maoists would not have allowed the intellectuals to travel extensively in their territory, accompanied by guerrilla forces, in times of war unless the intellectuals showed prior sympathy for the Maoist movement. It is beyond belief that Maoists would invite people, including other naxalites, who are opposed to them, to travel with the guerrillas for weeks, take photographs, make audio recordings, visit the headquarters at Abujmaad to interview the general secretary and inspect documents of Maoist administration (Navlakha, 2010).[3] As it turns out, there is not a single remark in the two (very) long pieces written by these intellectuals that questions the basic objectives of Maoist strategy.[4] Furthermore, each article is strewn with the political remarks of the authors themselves, some of which directly support basic Maoist goals and practices.

Occasionally, I have also used Satnam (2010) which is also a very sympathetic account of the Maoist movement. Satnam's account though is somewhat outdated as he reports on his extensive travels in Maoist territory in late 2001. Away from the propaganda of the Indian state, then, this chapter is based on pro-Maoist documents.[5] What picture of *adivasi*-welfare emerges from these documents?

The ability of an organisation to engage in the welfare of a given population is obviously a function of the influence of that organisation in the concerned area. As the writers report, Maoists from Andhra entered the Dandakaranya forests in small groups – two squads (Navlakha, 2010), seven squads (Roy, 2010a) – back in 1980.[6] (The puzzling issue of why they chose Dandakaranya of all places in this vast country will be taken up later.) Having secured the confidence of the local, predominantly *adivasi,* population, they set about organising them so that they can realise their rights – for example, rights of land and forest produce (Pandita, 2011, for some details). Needless to say, vested interests, such as *adivasi* chiefs in cahoots with the local police and forest officials, initially attempted feeble interventions.

There were more determined attempts in 1991 and 1997 perhaps because, after some relatively secured zones were established, one third of the entire armed Maoist forces in Andhra Pradesh were shifted to Dandakaranya in 1988. This formidable influx could have triggered bigger and more organised police action. In any case, these were easily dispelled because a large number of *adivasi*s had benefited from the movement by then: 'killing a few of the most notorious landlords did the job (Roy, 2010a). As remnants of state representatives were driven out of the area, things seem to have proceeded smoothly till about 2005.

During this period, Maoists were able to build up a substantial organisational base both in terms of the participation of people and the coverage of area. As Roy and Navlakha report probably from their Maoist sources, the peasant-worker front, Dandakaranya Adivasi Kisan Majdoor Sangh (DAKMS), currently has nearly 100,000 members. The women's front, Krantikari Adivasi Mahila Samity (KAMS), has nearly 90,000 members. Even the cultural front, Chetna Natya Manch, has over 10,000 members.

From 2001 onwards, parts of Dandakaranya is directly administered by Revolutionary People's Committees (*Janatana Sarkar*s, JS). Each JS is elected by a cluster of three to five villages whose combined population can range from 500 to 5,000. Fourteen to fifteen such JSs make up an area JS, and three to five area JSs go on to constitute a division. There are ten divisions in Dandakaranya. So, the general picture is that the party's authority 'now ranged across 60,000 square kilometres of forest, thousands of villages, and millions of people' (Roy 2010a). I must emphasise that these are Maoist numbers as told to the visiting intellectuals who seemed to have believed these figures as told. We can now ask what Maoists have achieved for these 'millions of people'.

The travelogues attempt to paint an impressive general picture of Dandakaranya. Away from the ugly inequalities of the rest of India, with its filthy towns and failed countryside, we get a picture of a land of pristine rivers and lush green forests. There lives a population of beautiful people in colourful attire going happily about their daily lives, armed with their newly found dignity and self-reliance in a largely egalitarian society. According to Vandana Shiva, peace and tranquility prevailed in Bastar before the Indian state attacked the people.[7] Despite grinding poverty and historical neglect by the state, *adivasi* areas usually present a sense of serenity on the surface. A very different and disturbing picture emerges when we scratch it.

Consider wages. On a seasonal basis, much of *adivasi* livelihood in the concerned area depends on collection of forest produce such as tendu leaves and bamboo culms, among other items. A bundle of fifty to seventy tendu leaves, according to Navlakha (2010); seventy-five, according to a Maoist document – fetched one rupee at the time of writing. To earn about thirty rupees, then, an *adivasi* has to collect and bundle nearly 2,000 tendu leaves per day! No doubt this is a substantial increase from a meagre three paise per bundle in 1981 (Roy, 2010a). Similarly, the wage for a bundle of twenty bamboo culms had raised from ten paise in 1981 to seven rupees at the time of writing. So, an *adivasi* has to cut, collect and bundle hundred bamboo culms to earn thrity-five rupees a day. These figures were roughly corroborated by the politbureau member Kobad Ghandy (2008), still in jail at time of going to press, who reported that daily wages have been raised three or four times from ten rupees some years ago.[8] I suggested the preceding figures basically to match Ghandy's estimates. Personally, I do not think that it is physically possible to collect nearly 2,000 leaves or hundred bamboo culms in a day.

It is difficult to compare wages on an absolute scale since they vary widely with respect to nature of work, location, caste, gender etc. It is well known that *adivasis* occupy the bottom rung of the economic ladder. Given their atrocious exploitation in the past by state and private operators, the wages sketched above signal 'huge achievements for *adivasi* people' (Roy, 2010a); the impoverished *adivasis* never knew anything better. The documents report, without furnishing data, that these wages – negotiated by Maoists with private contractors – are higher than those announced by the Chhattisgarh government. Maoists were also able to eliminate traditional social evils such as free first day labour for tilling the land of the village chief. These measures explain why *adivasis* feel indebted to Maoists.

Yet, the mere surpassing of highly exploitative wages announced by a particular state government to satisfy the greed of private contractors does not by itself qualify as an 'alternative development model' that others allegedly preach but the 'Maoists have been practicing for last thirty years among millions of Indians,' as Navlakha (2010) asserts.[9] Even if absolute comparisons are difficult, it is evident that these wages are much, much lower than the minimum wages enforced across the nation; *adivasis* in Bastar 'make just enough to stay alive until the next season.' (Roy, 2010a) For agricultural labour, minimum wages typically vary between 80 to 120 rupees a day in the rest of the country. In a 'high-wage' state like Kerala – perhaps one model Maoists would wish to compete with – wages under the rural employment guarantee scheme range up to 150 rupees a day. (Utsa Patnaik, personal communication)

The other side of this problematic picture is that, having negotiated what I consider to be merely subsistence wages for *adivasi*s, Maoists themselves collect 120 rupees per bag of tendu leaves from contractors (each bag contains 1,000 bundles), according to Roy (2010a); Bhattacharya (2010) reports that Maoists collect 135 rupees per bag. The contractors are allowed to collect up to 5,000 bags per season per contractor. This means that for a big contractor with 5,000 bags, the party makes about 600,000 rupees. Roy (2010a) reports that, at a conservative estimate, such a contractor makes about 5,500,000 rupees per season. The documents do not state how many contractors operate in the Dandakaranya area; in general, it is said that the tendu leaf business itself runs into hundreds of crores of rupees. A similar story obtains for bamboo culms, tamarind, honey, timber, *mahua*, resin and other forest products that generate 'royalties' for the party and huge profits for contractors.[10]

As for agriculture, Maoists did encourage *adivasi*s to grab about 300,000 acres of forest land which they had in any case been cultivating 'illegally' for generations. The task was relatively easy since there were no landlords from the outside and *adivasi* societies have an insignificant class structure. As Maoists realised, the issue was basically to grab forest land from the state at will since there was no real intervention of vested interests. In fact, something like a class-structure developed as *adivasi* chiefs and other elements with muscle power grabbed disproportionate portions of land. The problem was subsequently addressed by killing a few of the more notorious landlords, as noted. The net picture, it is claimed, is that 'there are no landless peasants in Dandakaranya'.

Maoists also organised *adivasi*s to construct some harvesting structures such as ponds, check dams and wells, and encouraged the nomadic *adivasi*s to learn proper cultivation techniques. There's an attempt to introduce multicrop and shifting cultivation. Navlakha (2010) presents some details about the grain and vegetable items cultivated, and their yields, as recorded in a given JS. There's some mention of using tractors and buffalos for ploughing in some areas in recent times. None of this sounds anything more than routine and primitive agricultural practice, even when compared with classically backward states such as Bihar, Rajasthan and Madhya Pradesh. In fact, these practices compare poorly with agricultural development in the non-forested areas of Chhattisgarh governed by the right-wing BJP.[11]

It is difficult to form a picture of the extent of these efforts and their role in improving the quality of life of *adivasi*s. Recall that we are talking about an area of 60,000 square kilometres and a time span of a quarter of a century, as proclaimed by Maoists and faithfully reported without any qualifications by their intellectual sympathisers. In general terms, Roy (2010a) writes: 'Only 2 percent of the land is irrigated. In Abujmaad, ploughing was unheard of until ten years ago. In Gadchiroli on the other hand, hybrid seeds and chemical pesticides are edging their way in [Gadchiroli is in adjacent Maharashtra].' 'We need urgent help in the agriculture department,' Comrade Vinod says, 'we need people who know about seeds, organic pesticides, permaculture.' Why is Comrade Vinod asking for these absolutely basic things now? And from whom? What have Maoists been doing for close to three decades?

A more concrete picture of the food situation emerges when we look at the health sector. There is no mention of even a single health centre with permanent structure initiated by Maoists in that vast area. All we are told repeatedly is that people have been advised to drink boiled water. Apparently, this has reduced infant mortality by fifty percent (Ghandy, 2008). Navlakha (2010) reports that lately the JSs have initiated a scheme of 'barefoot doctors' in which some *adivasi*s are trained to apply some medicines (distinguished by their colour) for afflictions such as malaria, cholera and elephantitis, the three most dreaded illnesses. Again, we do not know the extent of these efforts.

However, Roy (2010a) reports a doctor she met – a doctor who was visiting that area after many years. The doctor said that most of the people he had seen, including those in the guerrilla army, have a haemoglobin count between five and six (when the standard for Indian women is eleven). There is extensive tuberculosis caused by more than two years of chronic anaemia. Young children are suffering from Protein Energy Malnutrition Grade II. Apart from this, there is malaria, osteoporosis, tapeworm, severe ear and tooth infections and primary amenorrhea – malnutrition during puberty causing women's menstrual cycles to disappear or never appear in the first place. 'It's an epidemic here, like in Biafra,' the doctor said. 'There are no clinics in this forest apart from one or two in Gadchiroli. No doctors. No medicines.'

Notice that most of the severe conditions are caused by acute malnutrition – especially in women and children – suggesting what the 'alternative model' of agriculture and other efforts at Maoist 'development' has done to the people of Dandakaranya. Words like 'famine' and 'sub-Saharan condition' are frequently used in the documents under study. (Navlakha, 2010; Azad, 2010a) The words are of course polemically directed at the state: 'Look, what the Indian State has done to *adivasi*s.' Any index on quality of life certainly brings out what the Indian state has done to its people, not just *adivasi*s (Ghandy, 2011a). But the area at issue concerns essentially Maoists 'with a history of more than two decades where the party has been able to create an alternative structure, virtually uncontested.' (Navlakha, 2010)

As with an almost complete absence of health centres, the documents do not provide any evidence for any new and regular schools for *adivasi* children in the vast area. *The rare schools that exist are all provided for by the state.* By now, a large number of these impoverished schools have either been occupied by the security forces or blown up by Maoists to prevent the security forces from doing so. Lately, the JSs under Maoists have initiated a mobile school programme; there's also a mention of some evening schools operating in some areas. The mobile schools are 'in [the] nature of camps where children attend schools for anywhere between fifteen to thirty days, depending upon how tense the situation is in a particular area. Classes last for ninety minutes for each subject with four subjects taught in a day. There are between twenty-five and thirty students and three teachers. They have begun to employ certain teaching aids … globe, torchlights to CDs to teach history and science.' Again we do not know the extent of these efforts. In any case, beyond these rather primitive and grossly inadequate efforts, the documents do not explain why Maoists failed to introduce thousands of *regular* schools in the ten divisions supposedly under their control during at least two decades of *non-tense* situation. As to the real purpose behind the mobile schools, more later.

Insofar as *adivasi* welfare is concerned, could Maoists have done better on wages, agriculture, health and education? Given their vast command area with visible support from millions of *adivasi*s, it is not difficult to conceive of real alternatives to the measly 'development' programmes they initiated. With thousands of villages under their control, they could have dominated thousands of *gram sabha*s and hundreds of *panchayat*s in the Bastar area. The point is not restricted to Bastar alone. Mishra and Pandita (2010) report that, at one point, Maoists controlled over twelve hundred village *panchayat*s and more than thirty percent of electoral outcome in Jharkhand. Despite such domination, these areas of the province essentially lie in ruins as Maoists persistently attacked plans for enhancing health facilities, roads and the like.

Under the auspices of these *adivasi*-controlled *panchayats*, they could have formed hundreds of democratically constituted cooperatives to administer the livelihood of *adivasi*s (Sundar, 2006). For example, cooperatives devoted to forest produce such as tendu leaf could have competed – with massive popular support – for the tenders floated by the state each year. This way the system of greedy contractors would have been eliminated from the scene and the entire profits – after paying 'Kerala'-type wages – would have remained with the *adivasi*s. Similar efforts could have been directed at other forest produce and agricultural land.

Add to this the state funding that would have been allocated to these *panchayats* along with the ability to draw rural credit from local banks. One can only imagine what good could have been done for *adivasi*s with the public funds so available: schools, colleges, technical institutes, health centres, tractors, buffaloes, tubewells, irrigation canals from rivers and safe sources of drinking water. In time, these peoples' organisations could have made full use of national rural employment guarantee scheme, the forest rights act, the right to information, the education act and other schemes of the state.

There are other advantages to strong legal people's bodies. For example, it is mandatory for corporations to secure the consent of local people before they can start operations. To that end, Tata Steel authorities organised a public hearing for their planned steel plant on 12 October 2007. The corporation 'secured' the required consent by hiring an audience of about fifty people in a meeting far away from the concerned area; obviously, the war-like situation helped. It is doubtful if they would have dared to do so if vigilant peoples' committees, under the auspices of *panchayats*, were in place. Roy (2010a) reports on a wonderful initiative by the women's mass organisation, KAMS, in which members immediately surround a police station after someone is falsely arrested to get the person released before the police is able to file charges. One wonders if such initiatives can be expanded with legal peoples' forums in place.

None of this of course was going to be easy. The alternative just sketched would have required creative economic initiatives backed by democratic movements; it would have also involved legal battles with the state and the private operators, as every people's movement in the rest of the country knows. Nonetheless, in Dandakaranya, Maoists enjoyed unprecedented advantages, as noted, to pursue these democratic goals. There is no evidence that Maoists even contemplated these obvious steps.[12] Why not?

A disturbing answer emerges when we look at what else Maoists have done in the area during the same period. The basic idea, as General Secretary Ganapathy told his visitors is that 'it is important to guard against getting bogged down in legalism and economism and forget that masses have to be prepared for seizure of power.' (Ganapathy, 2010a) So, 'seizure of power', and not welfare of *adivasis*, is the central goal. In this light, it is seriously questionable if Maoists entered the forests of Dandakaranya three decades ago with *adivasi* welfare in mind at all. The documents suggest the following story.

After considerable setbacks to their armed struggle in Andhra Pradesh, Maoists of PWG decided to enter these forests way back in 1980, as noted. The basic goal was to 'build a standing army, for which it would need a base. Dandakaranya was to be that base, and those first squads were sent in to reconnoitre the area and begin the process of building guerrilla zones' (Roy, 2010a). Dandakaranya offered a variety of advantages. It was a vast densely forested area spanning across several provinces such that people can cross state boundaries through the forest itself. After the refugees from the erstwhile East Bengal left the area, it was inhabited almost entirely by *adivasi* communities who have been there for ages. The state had only a rudimentary presence in some areas and was almost totally absent in others. For example, land surveys had not been conducted in the hilly area of Abujmaad since the days of the Mughal emperors three hundred years ago. Also, as noted, 'there was a class society here, but due to *adivasi* traditions, unlike the plains, the Mukhia/Manji's [village chief] exploitation did not appear sharp' (Navlakha, 2010). Finally, due to their historical isolation and exploitation from outsiders, *adivasi* traditions have been compelled to acquire some degree of militancy to defend themselves. Well before Maoists entered the scene, *adivasi*s in Bastar had a history of resistance against the British, the landlords and the moneylenders (Guha, 2007; Mishra and Pandita, 2010). Dandakaranya was virtually a 'blank slate' on which Maoists decided to inscribe Charu Mazumdar's — and later, Kanhai Chatterji's — 'vision' .

The first task was to create enough guerrilla *zones*, and the second was to secure guerrilla *bases* in the guerrilla zones so created. Navlakha (2010) explains the distinction: 'Guerrilla zone is a fluid area in the sense that there is contention for control and the state is not entirely absent, even if only in the form of its police or armed forces. However, there are spots in these guerilla zones which are demarcated to ensure that some work can carry on relatively uninterrupted. These are 'bases' which are not easily penetrable or accessible.' The current plan is to 'intensify and expand guerilla war ... we have to utilise cleverly the tactics of hit and run basically' (Ganapathy, 2010b). Ultimately, however, 'we have to develop guerilla war into mobile war and guerilla army into a regular army' (Ibid.). That's the goal. *Adivasi*s are essentially cannon-fodder in this elaborate military strategy.[13]

To pursue it, one-third of the guerrilla forces of PWG were transferred to Dandakaranya from Telengana in Andhra back in

1988 after some support from *adivasi* population had been secured. The squads from Andhra started organising village militias from the very beginning. Militias consist of twenty to thirty young people armed with anything from bows and arrows, muzzle loaders, home-made pistols to genuine rifles and rocket launchers; ten percent of the used stock is distributed from the central army headquarters to the militias each year. Their basic task is to 'guard' a group of villages. Apparently, the best of the fighters from the militias are incorporated into more professional guerrilla squads whose members sport combat uniform and carry 'serious' weapons such as Insas rifles, AK-series rifles, self-loading rifles, pistols, revolvers, hand grenades and other forms of explosives; some carry light machine guns, mortars and rocket launchers. In December 2001, the PLGA was formally constituted. By now, the PLGA has 'moved from platoons to companies, and are now moving towards battalion formation' (Navlakha, 2010). The writers report that there are about 50,000 members in militias and 10,000 in PLGA.

Once guerrilla zones expanded and covered much of the area, the task of constructing guerrilla bases started in earnest in 2001. Two or three areas were selected for guerrilla bases in each division, and guerrilla bases were concentrated in around ten to twelve spots in these areas. Abujmaad forms the Central Guerrilla Base. To ensure that these bases are not 'easily penetrable or accessible', a complex system of landmines and IEDs punctuate every road, approach, landmark tree or rock formation throughout the forest areas. Needless to say, all of this requires an elaborate structure of informers, lookouts, technical experts, technical equipment for secure wireless communication, laptop computers, solar-charged batteries, electronic and other devices for triggering IEDs, vehicles such as hundreds of motorcycles and dozens of jeeps, well-concealed factories and workshops for the manufacture, repair and refitting of weapons and so on. Except for the supply of human power – young men and women – to the militias and PLGA (we return), *adivasis* are nowhere in the picture.

There is interesting evidential support to the preceding perspective in Satnam's (2010) very sympathetic account of his travels in Maoist territory in 2001. Satnam lived with the guerrillas for two months, much longer than the visits of either Roy or Navlakha. From what Satnam reports in detail, it is clear that the initial guerrilla zones were deliberately constructed in basically uninhabited areas so that complete secrecy can be maintained.

Unlike the plains, *adivasi* villages in the hills and jungles of Bastar are located in relative isolation from each other and are mostly thinly populated – just a cluster of huts in most cases.[14] Even then the guerrilla zones are located in the most inaccessible parts of the jungles away from the villages. Each camp is carefully hidden and an elaborate system of security posts guard these camps from any possible outside interference. Armed guards are spread widely over the jungles with rifles ready to fire if a leaf moves. The 'people's war' hardly involved the people except as cooks and helpers in the camps along with, of course, those as guerrillas carefully chosen from *adivasi* population, and kept under strict watch. For example, guard-duty is changed every two hours or so; permission is needed for every visit outside the camp, including for bathing in a river nearby. A search party is sent if someone is 'unduly' late in returning from morning ablutions; roll calls are made several times a day.[15] The guerrilla units are constantly on the move, splitting and rejoining frequently on the way, such that their location and personnel at any point of time is known only to a handful of seasoned commanders. Even with these precautions, scores of foot soldiers do desert the Maoist armed forces on a regular basis as the high number of Koya commandos illustrates.

The documents do not explain sufficiently where the money for this elaborate military structure comes from. Some weapons and related ammunition have been seized/stolen from police stations and armouries, some have been removed from the corpses of security personnel after ambushes. It is unclear if the total amount of these seizures explains almost battalion level weaponry. Navlakha (2010) does report, in general terms, the source of money: party membership fee, levy and contributions of people, confiscation of wealth and income sources of the enemy and taxes collected in guerrilla zones and base areas.

Presuming that most members are famine-stricken *adivasi*s themselves, party membership fees are not likely to amount to much. Later in the essay, Navlakha (2010) informs that 'revenue accruing from looting of bank or confiscation of wealth are far less' than the money collected from royalties on forest produce such as tendu leaf. So, it is really the royalties/levies from forest produce and taxes on contractors and companies that constitute the bulk of the funds.[16] It is anybody's guess how much money is so collected as well as how it is divided between military work and 'mass work'.

An apparently disjointed bit of information throws some light on the issue. Navlakha (2010) reports on the budget for 2009 of one area Revolutionary People's Committees [RPC] (recall that there are about fifty area RPCs in Dandakaranya). The income side showed about rupees eleven lakhs. It is interesting that, although the income includes about 3.6 lakh rupees from taxes on contractors, it does not directly mention the 'royalties' – the real money. Recall that the party makes about six lakh rupees per contractor from tendu leaf alone. Apart from tendu-leaves, there are other minor forest produce like tamarind, honey, bamboo, *mahua*, herbs and spices, etc. plus major produce like timber. So, these royalties must amount to many many crores of rupees. The budget says that about half of the income comes from allocation by the JS; it is unclear what it means. Does it mean that some of the other income, including royalties, is partly distributed by the divisional RPCs to area RPCs? Or does it mean that most of the real money remains with the party itself for military work?

Indirect evidence for the latter conclusion emerges when we look at the expenditure side of the budget. It is reasonable to expect that the income of a given RPC is primarily meant for development work in the concerned area. It turns out though that over fifty percent of the (meagre) reported income is allocated to 'defence', about 12 percent for agriculture, 9 percent for health, and 0.9 percent for education. It is important to note that 'defence' means providing just the kits for the militias and PLGA – three pairs of uniform, oil, soap, toothpaste, washing soap, comb, gunpowder, bows and arrows, along with food. The RPC budget does not pay for weapons and related military needs; so the astronomical money needed for that purpose must be controlled directly by the party itself. Is that where the rest of the money including the 'royalties' go?

The answer is likely to be in the positive since even most of the development money is diverted to military preparations that are euphemistically called 'defence'. Pandita (2011) reports, apparently from Maoist sources, that the military budget runs into sixty crores per year. Assuming this rather modest figure, it stands to reason that most of the royalties must be going for military work since other sources of income do not seem to amount to much. (Unfortunately, we have no direct means to examine the exact accounting of Maoist funds since democratic instruments such as RTI do not apply in the 'liberated zones', even if Maoists and their sympathisers insist that their 'enemy', the Indian state, should strictly follow the Constitution, the rule of law, the Geneva conventions on war and the like.)

Now that we have some idea of where the money from taxes, royalties and 'contributions from people' basically go, it is clear why the system of greedy and rich contractors – and similar characters – must continue to operate freely even in the 'liberated zones', while *adivasi*s continue to toil at subsistence wages to survive until the next season. In other words, these contractors and other concealed characters are allowed to cheat *adivasi*s all the way because they basically fund the war against the state for seizure of power.[17] One wonders if the 'rapacious plunder by the tiny parasitic class of blood-sucking leeches' that Maoists complain about (Azad, 2010a) includes these contractors who fund the Maoists' 'war of liberation'.

The preceding perspective also explains why Maoists never even contemplated alternative and genuine development plans based on *panchayat*s, cooperatives etc. For one, as noted, those plans would have driven the system of private contractors out of Dandakaranya resulting into a massive loss of revenue for the party. For another, those plans would have raised the condition of *adivasi*s from mere subsistence to the threshold of decent living. Having tasted decent living by their own cooperative enterprise, would *adivasi*s continue to clutch on to Maoists; most importantly, would they continue allowing their young people to join the militias and PLGA to die violent deaths at a young age?

Further, once real economic development with the associated democratic process unfolded, Dandakaranya would have abounded with state officials, other political parties, functionaries of banks and other funding agencies, agents of companies supplying a variety of goods, expansion of communication within the area etc. Dandakaranya would have opened up to the outside world. This would have seriously compromised the secrecy, security and inaccessibility of the network of guerrilla bases. Just to remind ourselves, this is the basic reason why Maoists are opposed to large-scale mining in the greater Bastar area. It is no wonder that Maoists *do not* allow development activities of the State in the areas they control (Navlakha, 2010; Sundar, 2006).[18] The ostensible reason given is that, in those areas, they themselves 'undertake reforms that benefit people'. By now we have a fair idea of the character of those 'reforms'.

Satnam (2010) cites one local commander Soma in Bastar who, recounting his prior experience in Warangal, Andhra Pradesh, observed that, in Warangal, 'the finger had to be kept constantly on the trigger'. In Bastar, in contrast, the conditions are better: 'There is no web of roads, no nexus with the market, no coming and going in and out of the jungle, no heavy patrolling by the enemy ... the guerrillas are trying to develop a self-sustained economy.' So, the very limited 'developmental' efforts like some fish in the ponds, introducing some grain and vegetable cultivation, etc., are also more directly designed to insulate the guerrilla zones from outside interference than with welfare of *adivasi*s.

In sum, then, *adivasi*s cannot be allowed to prosper beyond subsistence because it will interfere with the plans for seizure of power. Unsurprisingly, with gun-toting militants covering the ground, welfare dispensers like school teachers, doctors, and lower government officials are reluctant to enter these zones. Schools, primary health centres, and block-offices remain closed.[19] Then Maoist intellectuals point their fingers at the 'heartless' state.

It has been argued that one should not assess the impact of Maoists' work in Dandakaranya in terms of their contribution to the socio-economic welfare of *adivasi*s, because the war-like situation in which they have had to function leaves them little space to concentrate on health, education, agricultural improvement, etc. (Roy, 2010b).[20] Yet, if *adivasi* welfare was the first priority (as Azad and Kishenji claim as cited), then the struggle for better wages, education, health etc., could have started from the beginning, as with scores of movements around the country. If establishing guerrilla zones was the priority, then of course everything gets postponed; in fact, welfare measures cannot even be properly undertaken since you need money for arming guerrillas and that can only come from private operators, extortions etc. Twenty-five years is a long time to set up schools and health centres, achieve better wages etc., if armed struggle had not been the priority from the beginning.

The legendary activist Shankar Guha Neogi organised mine workers of Bailadila mines splendidly under the banner of *Chhattisgarh Mukti Morcha* (CMM) in nearby Rajnandgaon in the 1980s. Even after Neogi's murder, the CMM continues to organise worker's struggle in the area. It has resulted in one of the highest wages for mine workers in the country and an impressive network of housing, schools and hospitals for the families of workers. Maoists are nowhere in this promising scene.

Another repugnant aspect of the Maoists' protracted war is their use of children for warfare. Maoists complain justly, as we will see below, that the state uses 'school children as SPOs (Special Police Officers) and as police informers.' (Azad, 2010a) The state is what it is, as we keep saying. With their professed egalitarian 'alternative model' based on justice and dignity for the poor, what is Maoists' own record with respect to children?

Even if we set aside earlier reports of children being snatched away from *adivasi* families at gunpoint,[21] the documents provide a range of evidence about extensive involvement of children in the war. Roy (2010a) describes a young boy, Mangtu, who appears to be one of the conduits between nearby towns and the guerrilla army. Next, she describes another 'slightly older' person, Chandu with a 'village boy air', who actually belongs to a militia and can handle every kind of weapon except a light machine gun. Then, of course, there's this much talked about (and photographed) young woman, Kamla (see Chapter Three). At the time of reporting she is seventeen and is already a hardcore member of the PLGA with a revolver on her hip and a rifle slung over her shoulder. We can only guess about her age when she joined the armed forces. She had taken part in a number of ambushes; in fact, watching 'ambush videos' is her favourite form of entertainment. Yet she has a captivating smile; that's the human design of a seventeen-year-old, which even her addiction to ambush videos cannot disfigure.

These are not isolated examples. Roy's narrative and the accompanying photographs inadvertently furnish the distinct impression that most – if not all – of the people in the militias and PLGA are aged between mid-teens to early twenties. Most of these have been part of the armed forces for several years. Roy's motherly instinct wells up as she prepares to sleep in the forest amidst hundreds of armed guerrillas: 'I'm surrounded by these strange, beautiful children with their curious arsenal.'

Recruiting children for warfare seems to be an established practice in the Maoist scheme of things. Ganapathy explains the policy as follows in his open letter to the Independent Citizen's Initiative: [22]

> As regards training minors under 18 years in the use of arms, we wish to make it clear that our policy and the PLGA [People's Liberation Guerrilla Army] constitution stipulate that no one should be taken into the army without attaining 16 years of age. And this age limit is strictly followed while recruiting. In the specific conditions prevailing in the war zone [Dantewada and Bijapur districts of Chhattisgarh] children attain mental and political maturity by the time they complete 16 because they are directly or indirectly involved in the revolutionary activity from their very childhood. They receive basic

> education and political training early in their lives and have organisational experience as members of *bala sangam* (children's associations).... When the enemy [*Salwa Judum* and police] is erasing every norm of international law, the oppressed people have the full right to arm themselves and fight. Making a fuss over age makes no meaning in a situation where the enemies of the people are targeting children too without any mercy. If the boys and girls do not resist with arms they will be eliminated completely. The intellectuals of the civil society should understand this most inhumane and cruel situation created by the enemy and take the side of the people instead of pushing them more into defensive by raising all sorts of idealistic objections.

It seems that the Independent Citizen's Initiative and other 'intellectuals of the civil society' were duly convinced by the revolutionary force of Ganapathy's argument since I do not recall any further fuss – 'idealistic objections' – by anyone thereafter, including the union Ministry for Women and Child Welfare. It could be that the central government is reluctant to officially recognise this massive crime against humanity because of possible sanctions from the United Nations, as we will see. But this bureaucratic problem does not apply to the 'civil society', especially the human and democratic rights groups.

Even if children are not formally inducted in the PLGA until they attain the age of sixteen, children are recruited much earlier notwithstanding 'idealistic objections'. For example, comrade Madhav, who has now risen to be a commander of a PLGA platoon, joined Maoists at the age of nine in Warangal in Andhra Pradesh (Roy, 2010a). We now know that the politbureau member Kishenji joined the movement in his early teens. The entire thing is carefully organised. The mobile schools mentioned earlier (perhaps the only Maoist effort at education of *adivasi* children), are not meant to provide education to *adivasi* children in general. While the general *adivasi* child has no school to go to, these specialised schools, called Young Communist Mobile School (or Basic Communist Training School), host select groups of twenty-five to thirty children in the age group twelve to fifteen. These children receive intensive training for six months in a curriculum consisting of basic concepts of MLM, Hindi and English, maths, social science, *different types of weapons*, computers, etc., as Navlakha (2010) reports with ill-concealed admiration. Having learned Marxism-Leninism-Maoism at the age of twelve or so, 'they trail the PLGA squads, with stars in their eyes, like groupies of a rock band,' as Roy (2010a) reports with affection.

Navlakha (2010) also reports that, as with any regular army, recruitment drives are conducted with meetings and leaflets. One of the leaflets, directed specifically at 'unemployed boys and girls of Bastar' says, 'you will not get any salary but food, clothes, personal needs will be fulfilled and your families would be helped by the *Janatam Sarkar*.'[23] Elsewhere in the essay, Navlakha (2010) reports on the food supplied to the guerrillas: 'Breakfast can vary between *poha*, *khichri*, etc., mixed with peanuts and followed by tea. Lunch and dinner consists of rice with *daal* and *subzi*. Food is simple but nutritious. Once a week they get meat. Sometimes more than once if fish is available or there is pork, which is provided by the Revolutionary Peoples Committee.'[24] Even with this impressive food intake, most of the guerrillas, especially the women, have less than half of the normal count of haemoglobin, as noted. One can only imagine with horror the condition of these children when they joined the forces.

Are these children 'mentally and politically matured' to join 'revolutionary activity' voluntarily, as Ganapathy claims? With no schools to go to, no opportunities in hand and with sub-Saharan conditions prevailing in their families, which able-bodied *adivasi* child can resist the temptation of assured food, clothes, peer company and the ability to roam the forests with a rifle slung on shoulders (Sundar, 2006)? Naturally, when the state attacks and the economic lives of *adivasi*s are further disrupted, enrolment for militia and PLGA increases sharply. The more the repression by the state, the bigger the 'people's army' of starving children. Reportedly, children who cannot tell the difference, between the numerals '9' and '4', and are enthralled by the story of 'The Monkey and the Cats', are recruited as guerrillas and trained to fire at anything that moves (Satnam, 2010, 61).

As mentioned, the total strength of the militias and PLGA currently adds up to several thousand according to Maoist estimates with many more in the waiting. Assuming as above that most of them joined the forces when they were children, it follows that the Indian state and the Maoist leadership – consisting of Ganapathy, Koteshwar Rao, Kobad Ghandy, Ramakrishna, Narayan Sanyal, Pramod Mishra, Sabyasachi Panda and others in their politbureau and central committee – conspired to deny normal childhood to a vast number of *adivasi* children.

They never went to regular school, learned about life outside the forests, glimpsed the pluralistic complex of Indian society, acquired the skills to become a participating citizen – never allowed to make up their own mind. All they know is how to fashion an IED, to clean and fire a rifle, to ambush and to kill. They form the frontline – and get maimed and killed – when the police, the greyhounds, the CRPF and special operations forces encircle them. As for Kamla, 'if the police come across her, they'll kill her. They might rape her first. No questions will be asked.' (Roy, 2010a) Kamla won't be the only one. The Indian state and the Maoist leadership stand accused for willfully destroying the lives of thousands and thousands of hungry, hapless *adivasi* children in Bastar.

The issue of children of war received a grim human face when *The Hindu* posted the photograph of a person in its front page.[25] The person, Barsa Lakhma, is alleged to be a naxal 'leader', a 'commander' who is said to be involved in the gunning down of seventy-six security personnel. He along with five others – Oyam Hidma, Podiyami Hidma, Kawasi Budra, Oya Ganga, and Dura Joga – were in police custody after a 'major break-through'. After this report, Barsa Lakhma disappeared from news for sometime; the other five were subsequently released.

A recent short study based on 'interrogation reports' suggests that Barsa Lakhma is 'all of 25' although he joined the movement when he was 15.[26] The reassuring thing is that Barsa Lakhma seems to be alive. But do we know his real age? From his published photograph, he appears to be in his mid-teens. Incidentally, Chhattisgarh police have a profound anthropological view on this topic. The 'famous' Superintendent of Police Vishwa Ranjan states the phenomenon: 'There are many reports of underage SPOs but it's not true. Age is very difficult to assess. Tribal communities have a peculiar way of aging. They look very young even if they are not very young and then after a particular age, they begin to age very fast – so suddenly they look very old when they are actually not that old.' Also, 'we cannot go by their height and looks because the tribal build is different.'[27]

In a recent report,[28] the UN Secretary General Ban Ki Moon has commented extensively on the use of children in the 'long running Maoist conflict.' Bede Sheppard, Asia researcher on children's rights at Human Rights Watch, reports that the 'Secretary General Ban has brought international attention to the mistreatment of children in India's Maoist conflict.' The report says that 'both the security forces and Maoists in India are exploiting and harming children, destroying their chances at education and causing damage that will affect their entire lives.'

Specifically, 'having security forces occupy school grounds puts children and their education at unnecessary risk ... this practice is putting India's reputation on the world stage at risk.' Sheppard contends that 'the Security Council should be prepared to take action if the Indian government and Maoists do not act to better protect children.'

The issue is not new. An earlier Human Rights Watch report[29] observed that 'security forces – both police and paramilitary police – occupy school buildings as bases for anti-Maoist operations, sometimes only for a few days, but often for periods lasting several months and even years ... with students trying to carry on their studies in the remaining space, often under distracting and even frightening circumstances.' 'Girls,' the report continues, 'are especially likely to drop out following a partial occupation of a school because of harassment, or perceived harassment, by the security forces.' This aspect of the atrocities on children by the state has been justly and widely highlighted by the rights groups in India.

However, both the secretary general and Human Rights Watch proceed to a far more severe indictment of Maoists. The indictment has two parts. In the first – relatively 'benign' – part, 'the secretary-general's report describes how Maoists, particularly in Chhattisgarh State, have carried out systematic attacks on schools to damage and destroy government structures and to instill fear among local residents.' The Human Rights Watch report of 2009 'documented that at least 34 schools in Jharkhand and 16 schools in Bihar were attacked by Maoists during 2009. These do not include schools that were occupied by security forces at the time of attack. Most of the attacks occurred at night when students and teachers were not there.' This report does not cover the schools blown up by Maoists in Chhattisgarh. According to the home ministry's response in the Indian parliament, Maoists destroyed

258 school buildings between 2006 and 2011 with the following state-wise break-up: Chhattisgarh (131), Jharkhand (63), Bihar (46), Odisha (13), Maharashtra (4) and Andhra Pradesh (1).[30]

This aspect is sometimes taken up by rights groups but always with the proviso that it is the government which is the prime cause: if the security forces did not occupy these buildings, Maoists would have no need to blow them up. Thus, it is viewed as an 'excusable' deviance in times of 'war'.

The second aspect of the secretary general's indictment observes that Maoists 'are recruiting and using boys and girls in their ranks': the UN Security Council 'has stated repeatedly that it will consider targeted sanctions, including arms embargoes, against parties to armed conflict that do not end their use of child soldiers'. In the earlier report,[31] Human Rights Watch documented the use of children in the conflict in Chhattisgarh state. 'Maoists deploy children to gather intelligence, for sentry duty, to make and plant landmines and bombs, and to engage in hostilities against government forces. They organise children ages six to twelve into children's associations (*bal sangams*), indoctrinating, training, and using them as informers. Typically, children over the age of twelve are recruited into other Maoist ranks and trained in the use of rifles, landmines, and improvised explosive devices. Children in Maoist armed guerrilla squads (*dalams*) are involved in fighting with government security forces.' As we saw, this is just the tip of the iceberg. It is abundantly clear *from Maoist documents themselves* that Maoist armed forces — the militias and the guerrilla army — are almost wholly composed of people who joined the forces as children. The basic picture is that sub-Saharan conditions prevail in the Maoist-controlled areas in Chhattisgarh. In this condition, *adivasi* children are lured into the Maoist ranks — from lookouts, informers, militias to full-fledged guerrillas — with assurances of good food, clothing and protection to their families.

No doubt, some of the earlier batches of children have reached adulthood – and higher ranks in the armed forces – by now. *But there is no evidence at all that adivasi adults voluntarily joined Maoist ranks en masse*, unlike the radical students in West Bengal and Andhra Pradesh forty years ago. Again this raises uncomfortable questions about the character of the 'people's army' and 'people's war' planted in the public imagination by influential writers. The enormous fact is that Maoist militias and guerrilla forces currently add up to several thousands, with many more waiting and to emphasise, almost all of these joined the forces as children and a very large number still *are* children. And this has been going on for decades (Chenoy and Chenoy, 2010).

I am not aware of any sustained and significant voice from rights groups in India against this massive crime. Why isn't this issue at the centre stage of the raging debates on the 'Maoist problem'? Is it credible, for instance, that rights people didn't know about it? Writers affiliated to prominent rights groups have been visiting Bastar regularly (Sundar, 2006); some of them have travelled extensively – in the company of guerrilla forces – in Maoist territory (Roy, 2010a; Navlakha, 2010). It is an alarming reflection on our political culture that otherwise respected and well meaning intellectuals, who saw all this with their own eyes, continued to paint a picture of 'fervour and hope'.[32]

The police have been arresting and killing Barsa Lakhmas in droves over the years. Did they not have anything to report? What explains the silence? Could it be that the state prefers to remain silent because it will be both morally and legally difficult to unleash Cobras, Greyhounds, CRPF, Special Operations Forces, and the like on Maoist forces if it became common knowledge that Barsa Lakhma is the target, even if he carries a rifle? Does the Union Home Minister P. Chidambaram give more value to 'clearing' operations than the lives of children?

Could it be that rights groups such as PUDR, PUCL, APDR – not to mention direct Maoist sympathisers such as Roy (2010a) and Navlakha (2010) – prefer to remain silent because they know that the only humanitarian option is to initiate a massive process that will return these children safely to their families, in which case will Maoists be left with no forces at all? Are rights groups worried that any effective measure will lead to a 'defeat' of Maoists and, hence, a 'victory' for the state?

To recapitulate, the basic picture is abundantly clear from Maoist documents themselves. Taking advantage of the historical neglect and exploitation of *adivasi*s by the state, the Maoist leadership ensured the support of hapless *adivasi*s with token welfare measures while directing most of the attention secretly to construct guerrilla bases. In the process, they lured a large number of *adivasi* children with assurances of food and clothing. These children have now grown into formidable militia and guerrilla forces. After committing atrocious crimes in the name of 'revolutionary violence', these youth brigades are now facing the wrath of the mighty Indian state. It is reasonable to infer that a large number of *adivasi*s continue to side with Maoists largely because their children are with them (Satnam, 2010; Pandita, 2011).

5

FORMS OF RESISTANCE

The naxalite movement drew significant national and international attention in its heyday during the late 1960s to early 1970s, especially after the famous 'spring thunder' announcement from China. The movement virtually fizzled out with the arrest and killing of a large number of cadres and leaders; Charu Mazumdar, the general secretary of CPI(ML), was arrested pretty early during the counter offensive by the state. In a climate of deep suspicion, anguish and disillusionment, most leading (and surviving) participants of the original movement branched into many factions, each with its own critique of the original movement.[1]

It is not very well known outside inner and scholarly circles that the very formation of the original CPI(ML) – in fact, even the conspiratorial formation of the earlier All India Coordination Committee of Communist Revolutionaries, orchestrated by Charu Mazumdar – came under bitter criticism from various groups as the ideological content of the movement underwent progressive and drastic revision. I will look at the spread of this critical opinion below.

As noted in Chapters One and Three, two groups, People's War Group in Andhra and Maoist Communist Centre in Bihar, basically ignored this process of criticism and continued the murderous line advocated by Charu Mazumdar (Ganapathy, 2009). After fighting bloody battles for area control between themselves for nearly two decades, the two groups decided to join forces in 2004 to form CPI(Maoist) and concentrated on *adivasi*-inhabited Dandakaranya forests along with a less significant presence in neighbouring Andhra Pradesh, Bihar, Jharkhand and Odisha. They were almost completely wiped out in Andhra Pradesh by 2006, but their impressive preparations in Dandakaranya, conducted with extreme secrecy, remained mostly unaffected by the setbacks in Andhra; these preparations also remained pretty well unknown to the general public in the rest of the country. It is still a disturbing mystery, as noted, that the Indian state also appeared to be ignorant of their striking presence in Dandakaranya. Thus, the Maoist issue disappeared from the national scene for many years.

After decades of careful concealment by both the state and the Maoist party, the Maoist issue burst into the public domain first with the atrocious *Salwa Judum* campaign and then by the launch of OGH. The prime minister's 'gravest internal security threat' speech of 2005 contributed significantly to renewed interest in the Maoist movement. As a vast population of *adivasi*s became the primary victims of the resulting violence, an impressive variety of vigorous discourse ensued in both the print and electronic media, including several online forums that devoted significant space to the Maoist issue.

Unsurprisingly, much of the discourse is sharply critical of the Maoist party and is in favour of some form of military action against them. As we saw, the basic problem with this discourse is that it ignores the primary victims: If the state fires a bullet, it is likely to hit an *adivasi* even if she is wearing military fatigues. Bela Bhatia (2011a) says: 'Tribal combatants have been getting killed on both sides (as SPOs, tribal guerrillas and jan-militia), besides the many tribal non-combatants who are getting killed in this war.' Thus, the statist discourse, shared even by the parliamentary Left, lends at least indirect support to the atrocious violence of the state.

In that sense, this discourse imparts at least indirect moral credibility to the opposing Maoist discourse in the noted climate of binary choices. The Maoist discourse has a general two-part structure:

1. The discourse begins with a just and trenchant critique of the predatory Indian state, highlights aspects of crony capitalism imposed on the people and reports on the resulting widespread impoverishment and oppression of vast sections of the population.
2. The discourse ends with varying degrees of support of the Maoist programme.

Before I proceed to examine the discourse, it is interesting to note its more prominent authors. They obviously include Maoist spokespersons such as Ganapathy and (the late) Azad, and some of their intellectual sympathisers such as Amit Bhattacharya, Saroj Giri, Jesse Ross Knutson, Jan Myrdal, Gautam Navlakha, Varavar Rao and Arundhati Roy among others. Although these are powerful pro-people voices from the intelligentsia, none is known for direct and sustained grassroots work with the masses. Interestingly in contrast, the discourse does not find approval with a range of naxalite authors some of whom have a record of sustained participation in the original movement, have spent years in jungles and impoverished villages. They have suffered long imprisonment. Some respectable Left wing journals not given to state propaganda – *Economic and Political Weekly*, *Seminar*, and (the Bengali journal) *Aneek* – recently published special issues on the Maoist upheaval. Many authors belonging to the non-parliamentary Left and sympathetic to the original naxalite movement, contributed to these issues. As we will see below, they agree with the first part of the Maoist discourse while rejecting the second.

Unsurprisingly, the most direct and aggressive form of this discourse ensues from Maoist leaders themselves. Kobad Ghandy, in prison at time of going to press, is an interesting exception. Ghandy (2011a) is one of the most illuminating brief expositions of the first step of the discourse. Yet, despite being a politbureau member of CPI (Maoist), Ghandy refrains from articulating the second step, suggesting instead the 'urgent need for discussion of various models and policies being put forward' possibly in a 'future dialogue between the government and Maoists which is an urgent necessity'. We discuss the prospects for this 'dialogue' in the next chapter.

To substantiate the first part of the discourse, the Maoist spokesperson the late Chemkuri Rajkumar (Azad, 2010b) responded to the veteran journalist B.G. Verghese in these words,

> In which part of India is the [Indian] Constitution prevailing, Mr Verghese? In Dantewada, Bijapur, Kanker, Narayanpur, Rajnandgaon? In Jharkhand, Orissa? In Lalgarh, Jangalmahal? In the Kashmir Valley? Manipur? Where was your Constitution hiding for 25 long years after thousands of Sikhs were massacred? When thousands of Muslims were decimated? When lakhs of peasants are compelled to commit suicides? When thousands of people are murdered by state-sponsored *Salwa Judum* gangs? When

adivasi women are gangraped? When people are simply abducted by uniformed goons? Your Constitution is a piece of paper that does not even have the value of a toilet paper for the vast majority of the Indian people.

Needless to say, this is only a partial depiction of the Indian state. One could easily add grim facts about widespread malnutrition with sub-Saharan conditions prevailing in some parts of the country, the abject condition of women and children, massive youth unemployment, inhuman wages for agricultural and casual labour, plunder of natural resources, and so on. Hence, the General Secretary Ganapathy (2009) articulates the second part as follows:

> No fascist regime or military dictator in history could succeed in suppressing forever the just and democratic struggles of the people through brute force, but were, on the contrary, swept away by the high tide of people's resistance. People, who are the makers of history, will rise up like a tornado under our party's leadership to wipe out the reactionary blood-sucking vampires ruling our country.

In an earlier interview, Azad (2010a) was a bit more specific about the character of 'people's resistance':

> Let us suppose the men sent by Chidambaram are combing an area. When we come to know of it, we will carry out an offensive, annihilate as many forces as possible in the given circumstances, and seize arms and ammunition. We will also take prisoners of war where that is possible. Likewise, we may have to attack ordnance depots, trucks carrying explosives, guards at installations such as NMDC, RPF personnel and even outposts and stations far beyond our areas to seize arms, as in Nayagarh, for instance.

According to the strongest version of the Maoist discourse, therefore, resistance to the state means immediate armed struggle under the leadership of the Maoist party which is 'a revolutionary political party which represents the vast masses and which would lead the government that would be completely responsible for this country after we come to power' (Ganapathy, 2010b). No doubt, 'friendly' invitations are often issued to other groups and organisations that are resisting the state to form a 'united front', but with the ill-concealed proviso that the Maoist party will determine the course of events:

> We are appealing to all revolutionary and democratic forces in the country to unite to fight back the fascist offensive ... By building the broadest fighting front, and by adopting appropriate tactics of combining the militant mass political movement with armed resistance of the people and our PLGA (People's Liberation Guerilla Army), we will defeat the massive offensive by the Central-state forces. (Ganapathy, 2009)

Some of the writers mentioned above seem to support the exclusivist position of the Maoist party. While Jesse Ross Knutson[2] holds that the Indian state should immediately surrender to Maoists, Gautam Navlakha advocates that the armed struggle ought to continue until the Maoist party is in a position to dictate terms of peace with the Indian state.[3] As we will see in the next chapter, the security expert K.P.S. Gill advocates the same view from the opposite direction: the fight should continue until the state has the upper hand. As with his opposition to the peace mission (see Chapter 1), the views of Navlakha and the state form two sides of the same militarist coin.

Other writers such as Roy (2010a; 2010b) seem to advocate a milder view for now. According to them, Maoists are not the only ones resisting the state, but they form the most militant and organised part of a broad spectrum of (assorted, unorganised) resistance. The implicit (pious) hope is that Maoists will adjust themselves to a pluralist form as resistance expands. Perhaps the expectation is that Maoists will take lessons from Nelson Mandela and the African National Congress one of whose factions in fact advocated armed struggle for sometime before joining a rainbow coalition of over 600 groups. Alternatively, the assortment of other naxalites, break-away groups of parliamentary Left, radical liberals, enraged individuals, Gandhians, socialists, environmentalists, *dalit* forums, women's organisations, animal rights groups, NGOs etc., will be progressively organised under the overall umbrella furnished by Maoists.[4]

I will argue that even this milder view is unacceptable: CPI (Maoist) is no ANC. CPI(Maoist) simply does not have the moral, political and popular mandate of the ANC which represented the majority black population in South Africa and fought against the minority apartheid regime bolstered by Western military and economic might. The critique can take one of two forms: (a) a strong critique that denies that Maoists constitute a force of resistance at all, and (b) a weak critique that, even if we view Maoists as a (genuine) force of resistance in its motivation on paper, this form of resistance is inconsistent with broader democratic struggles leading to genuine welfare and empowerment of Indian people.

There is much to recommend the strong critique. As we saw in some detail in the previous chapters, Maoist practices in Dandakaranya and elsewhere raise grave doubts as to whether the Maoist party is genuinely concerned with welfare of people. To recapitulate quickly, we saw that the Maoist party has no history of struggle outside jungles, no history of participation in broad resistance movements, clear complicity with mafia and reactionary forces, little concern about abject conditions of the people in control areas; also, they have deployed a large number of children for warfare.

The cumulative evidence will be enough for some to conclude that, notwithstanding revolutionary proclamations, the Maoist party in practice is an undemocratic – perhaps even anti-people – force whose sole aim is to seize state power by hook or crook to bring the masses under the control of the leadership of the party.

If only for the sake of argument, suppose we take a softer view of Maoists. Suppose then that they are able to improve on their dismal record on welfare and human rights in their areas of control, stop the use of children, use arms only to defend themselves strictly in accordance with international conventions, avoid contacts with the mafia, develop a friendly attitude towards other radical groups etc. *without giving up on their programmes of secret organisation, armed struggle and protracted war.* The highlighted condition is crucial since, without it, the Maoist party will cease to be what it is.

Given their history and current practice, is the Maoist party capable of actually mending its ways? From what we saw earlier, there seem to be intrinsic connections between the various strands of Maoist practice. A secret armed struggle requires money and foot soldiers. Since a secret organisation impedes open interactions with people to secure their voluntary participation, recruiting children becomes an easier alternative. Similar and well known causal sequences obtain for their dealings with mafia and private contractors, authoritarian control over cadres and people, killing of suspected informers and the like. To sum up, it is hard to see how the Maoist party, with their basic strategy and goals in place, can form a part of a broader resistance at all.

Some of Noam Chomsky's recent remarks (2010) are instructive on this point. As noted, Maoists, with approval from authors under discussion, often reject the politics of other Left groups, including other naxalites and the parliamentary Left, as reformist and not genuinely revolutionary: 'contrary to the parliamentary parties and all kinds of reformist organisations, CPI(Maoist) which is based on a cadre that has unflinching faith in their aim, a sacrificing nature and dedication is shining like a bright sun, lighting up all the darkness surrounding our country. Indian people want revolution' (Ganapathy, 2010b).

Chomsky holds that a reformist is someone, 'who cares about the conditions of life for suffering people and works to improve them'. 'Reformists' in this sense support 'measures to improve safety in the workplace, to ensure adequate food and health care and potable water for everyone, and so on.' 'To accuse someone of being a reformist,' he continues, 'is to accuse him or her of being a minimally decent human being.' For Chomsky, anyone 'who is even worth talking to is a reformist.'

As the history of human struggle shows, even basic reformist measures to improve safety in the workplace and to ensure adequate food, healthcare and potable water require prolonged resistance to exploitative forces. What forms of resistance are viable to ensure these minimum measures? Chomsky holds that 'if we are committed to certain goals, whatever they are, we would seek to attain them peacefully, by persuasion and consensus, if possible – at least if we are sane and accept the most minimal moral standards. That is true no matter how revolutionary our goals.' In his prolific political writings over six decades, Chomsky has not discounted the tenability of armed struggle in certain contexts and contingencies. For example, his support to the armed resistance by Hezbollah against the Israeli military offensive in Lebanon is well known. Still, he insists that the issue of armed struggle is entirely contextual and must 'meet the minimum moral standards'.

It is deeply questionable, if in the current Indian context, Maoists have met either condition. More of this later.

As to the form of an organisation carrying out resistance to ensure welfare for the people, there is no ideal form in advance that is guaranteed to 'avoid pitfalls', yet, Chomsky holds, 'there is good reason to believe that more democratic and participatory forms of organisation can overcome the pitfalls that are inherent to the Central Committee or the tyrannical workplace or other forms of illegitimate hierarchy and domination.'

To illustrate the point, it is interesting that Chomsky cites the Sandinista movement in Nicaragua – not any other obviously authoritarian rule such as the communist regimes in Eastern Europe or the dictatorships in Africa and West Asia. It is well known that Chomsky himself was deeply associated with the Nicaraguan resistance led by the Sandinistas. He was one of the principal authors who exposed the vicious contra war launched by the Reagan administration to uproot the democratically elected government in Nicaragua. As they took on the might of the Pentagon and CIA, the Sandinista movement was a shining example of resistance throughout Latin America. However, after few years of valiant struggle, the movement collapsed and the Sandinistas lost the elections.

Chomsky interprets these events as follows. 'Anyone familiar with what was happening in Nicaragua,' he remarks, 'knows full well that the Sandinista's authoritarian practices contributed to undermining popular support that might have overcome the terror, and these were also exploited effectively by supporters of Washington's terrorist war to undermine solidarity movements in the United States and Europe.' Chomsky is drawing attention to familiarity with the movement because, unlike the communist regimes in Europe and dictatorships in West Asia, the Sandinista movement was vastly popular and was generally not known to be authoritarian in character. So, Chomsky's point is that even a vestige of authoritarianism in an otherwise popular movement can ruin it irrepairably;[5] in turn, it creates grounds for repressive forces to crush it completely.[6]

What means are available to achieve a non-authoritarian, reformist, and popular form of resistance? On this issue, the Maoist party had always rejected the salience of every form of electoral politics, including *panchayat* elections at the local level. According to them, 'this dictatorial and bourgeois parliament and State machinery ... would serve none else than [the ruling] classes. They may be sacred for those classes but they are a big menace for the people. So it is their birth right to pull them down ... They should establish a genuine democratic political system which constitutes new legislative bodies and a new constitution' (Ganapathy, 2010b) under the dictatorship of the Maoist party of course.

As we saw (in Chapter Two), electoral politics has lost much of its initial shine over the decades. Especially in the neo-liberal era, electoral politics has degenerated to the point where even liberal thinkers are beginning to express exasperation with it; this explains the problematic but spectacular growth of non-electoral activism. We will return to this topic shortly.

Chomsky agrees that 'the neo-liberal onslaught against democracy — its primary thrust — has imposed even narrower limits on functioning democracy, as intended.' Yet, it does not follow that 'the attack on democracy cannot be beaten back.' 'Electoral politics,' he asserts, 'has in the past achieved gains in human welfare that are by no means insignificant, as the great mass of the population understands very well.' Following Chomsky, then, an outright rejection of electoral politics - especially in the (rare) contexts such as India where it has 'achieved gains in human welfare' in the past — signals the Maoists' basic disconnect with the 'great mass of the population.'

It is also most instructive that Chomsky's views are matched, almost point by point, by the views of Santosh Rana. Santosh Rana is no internationally acclaimed public intellectual with a connection to the Massachusetts Institute of Technology. As he reported during a lengthy interview to the journal *Seminar* recently, he was one of the original participants in the naxalite movement. (Rana, 2010) He joined the CPI(ML) led by Charu Mazumdar, went underground and spent years in the now famous Jangalmahal area organising a peasant uprising. In the process, the party 'eliminated' about 120 landlords in that area as part of its 'annihilation campaign'. As the movement broke up under severe state repression, Rana – with other leaders of those times such as Kanu Sanyal, Jangal Santhal and Asim Chatterjee – was arrested, while others were killed in encounters, fake or real. Charu Mazumdar himself died a 'natural death' in prison, according to the police. (Mukhopadhyay, 2006)

After spending years in jail and undergoing torture, Rana was finally released under the general amnesty scheme for political prisoners announced by the just elected Left Front government in West Bengal in 1977. Almost immediately, he returned to his location of struggle in Jangalmahal and began to reorganise the deeply fragmented movement. He is *still there* working among peasants, *adivasi*s, Dalits, and other backward communities. His organisation is called Provisional Central Committee, Communist Party of India, Marxist-Leninist (PCC, CPI (ML). He is also one of the principal organisers of a mass front in the area known as *Jharkhand Andolan Samanway Manch*, JASM (Jharkhand Unity Forum), comprising a variety of radical groups and *adivasi* organisations.

Rana agrees with the first part of the Maoist discourse. 'Since early nineties,' he says, 'the regimes both at the Centre and the states have been spreading the tentacles of neo-liberal global economy across the country that resulted into the concentration of wealth in the hands of twenty-seven super-rich families. This concentration of wealth has been reflected in the country's politics also. Never before have Indian parliaments so many *crorepatis* [multimillionaires] as its members.' Linking this class character of the Indian Parliament with the repressive anti-people policies of the state, Rana contends that 'it was hardly unexpected that none of the 540 MPs had opposed the draconian Unlawful Activities Prevention Act (UAPA) ... this has only reduced the democratic space with the parliamentary system.'

But this reduction of the parliamentary space does not lend credibility to the programme of the Maoist party since 'in reality, both the state and the so-called Maoists are taking complementary roles in shriveling the democratic space.' His (strong) criticism of the Maoist party involves several steps.

First, he holds that 'we have to understand that no revolution in our age will be successful without addressing the question of democracy.' He illustrates the point with several historical examples: imposition of one-party state was the main reason for the Soviet debacle; 'proletarian dictatorship' in China has now degenerated into a capitalist haven because the party dictatorship was consolidated in the name of people's democracy. Rosa Luxemburg, Rana points out, was 'one of those few revolutionary thinkers who foresaw the dangers posed to the Russian revolution because of the denial of democracy.' In general, 'there is no reason to believe any more that the rule of the communist party is synonymous with working class rule.'

Second, the Indian case contrasts sharply with that of Russia and China because there 'the people had accepted the party rule in the name of the class since bourgeois parliamentary democracy was rudimentary or non-existent in pre-revolutionary Russia and China.' In India, 'parliamentary democracy, despite all its travesties [as above], has taken roots down to the villages'. Thus, 'revolutionaries have to move ahead in India not by shrinking the parliamentary democracy but by expanding it. For us, the basic question should be more and more power to the people in order to make the democracy meaningful in the lives of the millions.'

This is where the Maoist party has failed Indian people since 'there is no democracy in the so-called people's committees and people's courts ... Maoists' squads dictate everything in the name of people. Any dissenters will risk beating, even killing.' In the name of developing a people's movement, 'they are forcing people to join their rally, extracting tax from them, compelling the supporters of CPM and other political parties to give undertaking at the point of gun.' Referring to the bitterly-contested Lalgarh area in Jangalmahal where he himself works, Rana reports that Maoists 'have turned the people of Lalgarh into cannon-fodder' (see also Hensman, 2010).

Third, as I suggested earlier (Chapter Three), Rana also finds deep parallels between the operations of LTTE and the Maoist party. He says that Maoists are 'in fact following not only the LTTE military line but also its political line. Prabhakaran had exterminated all other Tamil groups. In the end, he got exterminated.' In fact, both the mass front Jharkhand Unity Forum, PCC, CPI(ML) have issued a series of appeals and statements to highlight this point. These have been entirely ignored by the mainstream media. Here are some excerpts from an appeal to intellectuals and other democratic forces issued by the forum on 25 August 2009:

> Maoists who were in the leadership of the movement in Lalgarh and Belpahari resorted to the method of resolving all contradictions with other forces participating in the movement with the use of force .... A virtual ban was imposed on activities of all other political parties ... It is

a matter of regret that Maoists are attacking the activists and supporters of Jharkhand movement. Nearly a dozen of Jharkhand supporters including Sudhir Mandi, Sarna Bara Besra, Manik Mandi, Rampada Mandal, Sankar Tudu, Kaliram Singh, Gopal Sardar, Karan Murmu, Lal Murmu have been killed by Maoist squads. All of them are poor *dalit*s and *adivasi*s. Moreover, more than 70 supporters of the CPM and some supporters of PCPA (People's Committee Against Police Atrocities) have also been killed. They, too, are all poor *dalit*s and *adivasi*s. We condemn all these killings .... We want an environment where any political party can propagate its line and organise the masses and where every individual may freely follow or not follow any political party.

More recently, another naxalite organisation, Central Committee, CPI(ML), issued an 'appeal to democrats' on the murder of *adivasi* leader Kendruka Arjun. The late Kanu Sanyal, mentioned earlier, was the general secretary of this organisation until his recent death. Some excerpts:

The leader of Andhra-Orissa border area *adivasi* movement and district secretary of *Chasi Muliya Adivasi Sangh* (CMAS), Comrade Kendruka Arjun was waylaid and shot dead today (9-8-2010) by Maoists when he was going on a bicycle along with his wife to hospital for treatment .... Comrade Kendruka Arjun, born in a poor *adivasi* family, [was] working in the movement for the last 15 years. He united *adivasi*s and non-*Adivasi* poor in the Koraput-Bandugaon area under the banner of CMAS and stood in the forefront in many struggles waged against forest officials, liquor mafia and landlords .... As *adivasi* movement in Andhra-Orissa border area is advancing under the leadership of CMAS, the leaders of Maoists several times tried to obstruct the activities and sent warnings to the leaders of CMAS including Comrade Arjun .... We are appealing to the democrats, progressive forces and intellectuals to take up this brutal murder and condemn the terrorist politics of Maoists who time and again are resorting to the murder of leaders of people's movement.[7]

Over the years, there are many instances of Maoists killing grassroots activists, including other naxalites and *adivasi*s. A more recent example is the killing of Niyamat Ansari on 2 March 2011 in Jharkhand. According to one fact finding report, Ansari was deeply engaged in a variety of peaceful struggles against the state – especially the widespread corruption in the implementation of pro-people projects such as NREGA; he was also a close associate of the economist Jean Dreze. According to this report, Maoists, some state officials and contractors joined hands in this murder.

Jean Dreze, Aruna Roy, Swami Agnivesh and others did formally protest this murder even if they chose to remain silent over dozens of similar cases earlier. As a response, Maoists claimed that 'Ansari had collected [rupees] 13 lakh from villagers and [was] involved in child sacrifice.' When these allegations were disproved by a fact-finding committee, Maoists issued the following warnings, among others:

> The death of Niyamat Ansari is just the beginning, members of *Gram Swaraj Abhiyan* [village self-rule campaign] are next; take back all the false cases against innocents implicated in the Niyamat Ansari case; punish Jean Dreze, Aruna Roy, Gokul Vasant and Nand Lal Singh in a *Jan Adalat* [people's court] for claiming Niyamat Ansari is innocent; Sonia Gandhi's agent Jean Dreze, come to your senses.[8]

Prolonged silence on 'armed struggle' by a 'people's army' is coming home to roost. In a letter to Jean Dreze (15 April 2011), Santosh Rana wrote (excerpts):

> I heard about the murder of NREGA activist Niyamat Ansari in Latehar by a Maoist squad .... This murder, along with many other murders committed by Maoists in Jharkhand, Lalgarh and other areas is the inevitable culmination of a line followed by Maoists – the line of establishing exclusive control over any area by physically eliminating not only their opponents but any activism which is different from them .... From the beginning of the movement in Lalgarh we have steadfastly supported the people's agitation against police repression and for autonomy of Jangalmahal .... Most significant was the participation of *Bharat Jakat Majhi Marwa*, a social organisation of *Santhals*. But Maoists destroyed the people's unity by killing Sudhir Mandi in the end of November 2008. Sudhir was a leader of *Majhi Marwa* .... His only offence was that he refused to act according to orders of the Maoist squads .... I drew the attention of a team of intellectuals from Delhi (led by Amit Bhaduri and Gautam Navlakha) who visited Lalgarh in early 2009 to this incident .... But nobody bothered about it. During 2009 and 2010, more than 400 people have been killed by Maoists in Jangalmahal, most of them have been *adibasi*s, *dalit*s and other poor people .... Now, on the eve of the Assembly election they are hand in glove with the Trinanmool Congress and are helping them to win the seats in the Jangalmahal.

Finally, as I detailed earlier (Chapter Four), Rana holds that 'the Maoist experiments in alternative development are all sham.

They are not interested in these schools, health centres or road-buildings. These are basically ideas of some city-based sympathizers, attempted half-heartedly.' These comments are a response to the widespread view propagated by some intellectuals in West Bengal that Maoists had initiated novel developmental schemes in the Lalgarh area. The actual story is the opposite. As Nigam (2009b) points out, organisations of people in that area did initiate some cooperative methods based on democratic participation. These efforts collapsed as Maoists entered the scene to impose rule of the gun (see also Sarkar and Sarkar, 2009).

Following extensive citations from Maoist documents, Menon (2009) summarises their strategy as follows: 'take over existing mass organisations when you cannot set them up, work towards subverting their existing processes by producing propaganda about those who are influential in it, always utilise movements towards a secret end, which, if revealed, very few will be with you.' The murder and the subsequent defamation of Kendruka Arjun is a case in point. In Maoist official parlance, this is called 'fractional work'. [9]

Other authors from the broad naxalite spectrum share many of these criticisms of the Maoist party. I can only cite a few remarks from a substantial literature by now. This literature is generally unknown in the mainstream which is essentially saturated with state propaganda and the views of Maoist-aligned intellectuals. The late K. Balagopal was an eminent civil rights lawyer, an activist and a respected author. He was a courageous supporter of the naxalite movement, including the People's War Group in its early stages, during the dark days of extreme state repression in Andhra.

In a sensitive piece (Balagopal, 2006), he wrote that 'a blanket condonation of the use of violence by a group that lives by its own norms, which are enforceable only by itself is no doubt unacceptable in any society, even when it is declared to be for the good of the oppressed.' When the violence of the rebels lacked mass approval from its social base, the inevitable 'upshot was heavy repression on the naxalite movement, in particular the rural poor who were part of the movement or its social base.' Moreover, in the face of heavy repression, the movement develops viscious authoritarian tendencies. Balagopal points out that authoritarian control over movements is often justified to preserve the 'purity' and 'integrity' of movements. In reality, the enforced insulation of resistance movements from broad popular bases in fact enables the state to infiltrate these movements (see also Banerjee, 2009a).

In this connection, Balagopal points out 'the invariant law of the sociology of armed insurgencies': as the state infiltrates the movement, the rebels 'kill or otherwise injure agents and informers and thereby antagonise more of their own mass base, in turn enabling the state to have more agents and informers. Without exception, all militant movements have killed more people of their own social base than their purported enemy classes.' Thus, as an alternative, Balagopal asks, 'What would have been the result if Maoists had decided to concentrate on exposing the anti-poor bias of the government and extend their mass activity to a point that would have given their aspiration for State power a solid mass base.'

Noted democratic rights activist and author Sumanta Banerjee has been closely associated with the naxalite movement since its beginning; he is also the author of one of the classic studies on the naxalite movement (Banerjee, 1980). In Banerjee (2006), he surveys the Maoist movement with much sympathy and hope. Still, he points out two grave issues that could lead to the collapse of the movement unless Maoists mend their ways.

First, he cautions Maoists that 'in India, a parliamentary republic, despite large-scale corruption and criminality, still enjoys democratic legitimacy among wide sections of the people and the major contending social groups who find the multi-party democracy useful for ends that make sense to them. The system apparently has not yet exhausted all its potentialities of exploiting the hopes and aspirations of the Indian poor and underprivileged sections.' Second, regarding the 'annihilation campaign' devised by Charu Mazumdar, Banerjee is concerned that 'the heinous practice still lingers on. Village *patwari*s, *panchayat pradhan*s, school teachers – and even poor *adivasi* people branded as police informers – have been targets of Maoists in their guerrilla zones in Bastar, Jharkhand and parts of Andhra Pradesh.' Banerjee seems to think of this practice as mere aberration, but, as Balagopal pointed out, these are inevitable consequences of a secret armed struggle without mass participation of the people.

In a later essay, Banerjee (2009a) uses harsher words against Maoist tactics that border on terrorism: 'Maoist armed struggle which is motivated by the egalitarian ideology of socialism is dangerously inching towards resentful terroristic outbursts as a knee-jerk reaction to the State's dragnet that is closing in to besiege their narrow base .... They are replicating the same methods of secrecy, conspiracy and terrorism that the state's underground apparatus adopts. The dark and diabolical debasement of the 'non-state' underground – whether of the Left or the religious/ethnic variety – is alienating its once popular support base.' A few months later, Banerjee (2009b) is furious: 'It is these militarist priorities and political expediencies that are eroding the ideological commitment of their cadres. The latter (in West Bengal today in particular) seem to be degenerating into roving gangs of paranoid revengeful killers recalling the dark days of the fratricidal warfare between the Naxalites and CPM youth cadres in the 1970s.'

I have much disagreement with some of Banerjee's analysis and understanding of the Maoist movement. For example, he suggests without citing independent evidence that Maoists 'have organised the poor on demands for higher wages, redistribution of land and other economic demands, as well as helped them in obtaining education, health facilities and essential services.' We saw that, beyond perfunctory measures, this is simply false of the Dandakaranya area. If Banerjee is referring exclusively to some efforts of the early phase of PWG in Andhra in 1980s, the contexts should have been made clear since, in his recent essays, he is primarily concerned with the current state of the Maoist movement. In a later essay in Bengali, Banerjee (2010) mentions travelogues by Arundhati Roy, Gautam Navlakha, etc., to suggest that Maoists have constructed small 'islands' of welfare in Dandakaranya. In Chapter Four, we saw what really follows from the information conveyed by the travelogues.[10]

Adopting a strictly Leninist perspective on strategies for drastic social change, the noted Marxist author Ratan Khasnabis (2010), like Sumanta Banerjee, does not rule out the relevance of armed struggle at some stage of resistance even in the Indian context. However, he contends that 'wherever a parliamentary system is available alongwith institutions of decentralised power at different levels (state assemblies, district councils, *panchayat*s, and municipal councils), radical organisations might use these effectively to prepare the grounds for revolution such that the masses are increasingly aware of an alternative socialist system.' By raising 'the choice between armed struggle and parliamentary path as mutually exclusive,' Maoists have turned 'possible friends in the working class into enemies.' This led to the 'boycott of trade unions, peasant organisations, student councils, teachers' associations, employees' associations and the like. Only armed squads remained whose 'membership required skills for slitting throats.'

Dipankar Bhattacharya is the general secretary of CPI(ML) Liberation group, perhaps the largest naxalite organisation (excluding Maoists) with significant mass support in several areas of the country. As with most naxalite groups, it was part of the original CPI(ML) led by Charu Mazumdar and it continued with Mazumdar's politics until the late 1970s. As the movement fragmented, the group formed its own identity ultimately under the leadership of Vinod Mishra, especially in the state of Bihar. After decades of armed peasant struggle in the face of relentless attacks by the state, by the state's ill-concealed vigilante army called the *Ranvir Sena*, and often by Maoists, the group progressively adopted a more balanced mass line including participation in the electoral process. In his piece, therefore, Bhattacharya (2010) has many polemical axes to grind to highlight the programmatic salience of his own organisation.

As for elections, Bhattacharya reports interestingly that in vast stretches in the state of Bihar, especially the rural poor were unable to cast the vote freely as the entire machinery was completely under the control of feudal landlords and their hired mafia. Creating conditions for people to vote freely, thus, required militant class struggle, often with arms! In Bihar, establishing meaningful electoral politics itself was an advanced form of resistance.

In this connection, Bhattacharya complains that Maoists have not only failed the people by shunning electoral politics, they have actually been absent from the most militant and sustained theaters of people's struggle. Thus, widespread movements are currently unfolding against SEZs, forceful acquisition of land via an ancient colonial act, eviction of people from their habitat, etc. These movements have taken particularly popular forms in Raigarh in Maharashtra, Barnala in Punjab, Dadri in Uttar Pradesh, Jagatsingpur-Paradip in Odisha, Singur and Nandigram in West Bengal, Kalinganagar, Kashipur and others. None of these were either initiated or led by Maoists even if they have tried to infiltrate some of them once popular uprisings took place. In fact,

Bhattacharya reports, in Maoists' own territory in Dandakaranya, exploitation and loot continues unabated; contractors still make a profit of ₹1200 per bag of tendu leaf, after paying a 'commission' of ₹135 per bag to the party.

K.N. Ramachandran is the general secretary of yet another radical organisation, CPI(ML) Red Star, which also has a tortuous history of splitting and rejoining a variety of naxalite groups and individuals. The organisation is mostly active in some parts of southern India including Andhra Pradesh and Kerala. As a general secretary of an organisation, Ramachandran, like Bhattacharya, has many axes to grind with other Left organisations. As a devout Marxist-Leninist, Ramachandran (2010) favours armed struggle as the ultimate weapon to establish the dictatorship of the proletariat. Nonetheless, noting vast historical differences between imperial Russia and feudal China on the one hand and the conditions prevailing in contemporary India, he is deeply critical of the Maoist view that armed struggle is the only method particularly in the context in which the world communist movement is yet to recover from the severe jolt of the disintegration of the Soviet Union. In this context, 'Maoist nihilism is only helping the reactionary rulers to repress isolated incidents of people's uprising and sparks of revolution.' In fact, 'even if we agree with their claim that they have liberated 60,000 square kilometers of forest area, the pathetic condition of *adivasi*s in this area is very far from what Edgar Snow described of liberated Yenan.'[11]

In a later statement for some intellectuals, such as Jean Dreze and Aruna Roy, on the murder of activist Niyamat Ansari, Ramachandran elaborated on the 'Yenan' aspect as follows (12 March 2011, excerpts):

> In Chaibasa under the *Krantikari adivasi Mahasabha* [Revolutionary Tribal Association], a major struggle is going on against ACC Cements management and Tatas

who are looting the mineral resources of the area. Instead of supporting it, the Maoist squads in the area take money and protect the mining mafias .... Unfortunately intellectuals like you do not take pains to understand why even after so called Maoist dominance in Dantewada, people in that region are the poorest when after the Red Army's presence in Yenan for three years in China, as Edgar Snow had written, the Communist-influenced area became the most advanced rural area in China as they were not blasting the existing schools and hospitals, but constructing more and more. Whether in Chhattisgarh or in Jharkhand *adivasi*s and other poor sections are not getting even the minimum wages and are more backward than many other rural areas because Maoists take money from the contractors and allow them to plunder the people .... My request to people like you is to recognize that the killing of Ansari is not an isolated action .... It is a repetition of the activities of LTTE and ULFA [United Liberation Front of Assam] and other terrorist outfits.

From a firebrand student leader in the 1960s, Asim Chatterjee – popularly known as *Kaka* [uncle] in radical circles – matured into one of the founding members of the original CPI(ML) under the leadership of Charu Mazumdar. Like Rana and many others, he went underground and joined armed peasant uprisings at various places in West Bengal. After his arrest and long incarceration he was also released by the first Left Front government under a near-universal amnesty for political prisoners. Since then Chatterjee has moved from one organisation to another, trying to regroup old comrades; in the process, he has also become a noted author in Bangla.

Chatterjee's short piece (2010) is interesting because, among the naxalite authors cited so far, he voices perhaps the most aggressive support for the Maoist party.[12] Keeping entirely to the writings of Mao, Chatterjee argues for the right of both the downtrodden to take up arms and the party to organise the masses in this direction. His primary argument is that 'every political organisation believes that genuine welfare of people requires access to power'; otherwise 'political parties will be reduced to voluntary organisations.' When the electoral method of gaining power fails, armed struggle becomes the only option. Focusing on the Jangalmahal area, where he had worked as a naxalite activist in the past, he is full of admiration for the commitment, sacrifice, and resilience of Maoist leaders and cadres for their ability to sustain armed struggle under most adverse circumstances.

However, in as friendly a tone as possible, Chatterjee is also deeply critical of many aspects of the Maoist movement. I have covered most of these through other authors; for example, the Indian condition satisfies *none* of the specific conditions of Chinese revolution. In addition, Chatterjee makes two interesting points. With regard to the form of armed struggle, Chatterjee reminds Maoists that 'Charu Mazumdar rejected the option of armed struggle with modern weapons in the vast Sunderban forests on the ground that too much dependence on jungles or firearms impedes dependence on the masses.' As we saw, Maoist operations have been restricted entirely to the forests, especially the uninhabited areas, for decades; we also saw that their weaponry – Insas, AK-series and self-loading rifles, pistols, revolvers, hand grenades and other forms of explosives, light machine guns, mortars and rocket launchers – is currently more sophisticated than the poorly armed police forces they typically ambush. Chatterjee fails to mention that Mazumdar's insistence on 'primitive' weapons – such as bows and arrows, spears, axes, sickles and knives – is intrinsically linked to the policy of individual 'annihilation' as we saw earlier. (Chapter Three) Maoist weaponry, in contrast, is more suitable for mass annihilation. Charu Mazumdar did not live to see this 'higher form' of armed struggle.

Chatterjee also reminds Maoists of the significance of electoral democracy: 'A lesson from history is that, while elections have never led to fundamental social change, there has never been a revolution in a country with parliamentary democracy.' By rejecting elections, Maoists are 'rejecting the masses themselves by a rejection of their aspirations;' as a consequence, perhaps the 'revolutionary war is turning into the party's war.'

By now, the broad naxalite movement has formed such a complex phylogenic tree that it is difficult to reach definitive general conclusions from the naxalite voices just cited. Current naxalite groups branched out from the original source at different points of time under different — often traumatic — circumstances. As such, there is a marked tendency in each group to defend its own history from that point onwards. Much of that history, we saw, involved some degree of armed struggle somewhere as most of the groups are still led by veterans of the original movement; there is also the issue of identity to distinguish themselves from the parliamentary Left. So, except perhaps for Santosh Rana and a few others, it is psychologically and publicly difficult for them to advocate essentially non-violent means for achieving a just society.

The MLM organisation CPI (ML-Liberation) typically illustrates this problem of 'necessity of the past.' As noted, it is one of the more significant MLM organisations in the country with impressive mass penetration in various regions and sectors such as peasants, workers, youth and women. About two decades ago, it decided to function basically as an open organisation and take vigorous part in the electoral process. Undoubtedly, these decisions led to fairly rapid mass penetration in the decades that followed. Despite its MLM tag, its current practices have little resemblance with those of the original CPI(ML); if anything, they bring back memories of militant parliamentarianism of the undivided Communist Pary of India of the 1950s when the communist movement swept across the country. Yet, as noted, CPI(ML-Liberation) originated from one of the very few MLM factions that continued with the 'politics' of Charu Mazumdar, including his policy of 'annihilation' till the late-1970s.

Thus, in its first party congress assembled by Jauhar in 1974, it was declared that 'class struggle, i.e., annihilation will solve all our problems.' Given this past, its next general secretary Vinod Mishra was compelled to state as late as in 1982 that 'it is because of this glorious tradition that Charu Mazumdar remains alive in the hearts of millions of oppressed people of India, that his line is taken to symbolise the only revolutionary line in India.' But then he enters into a tortuous and wholly unconvincing exercise to escape this past by (a) trying to give as 'revolutionary' an interpretation to 'annihilation' as he could muster; (b) shifting the blame for the 'distorted' form of this 'revolutionary' line on other people such as Mahadeb Mukherjee; and (c) declaring without any documentation that Mazumdar 'realised that annihilation had been taken too far and that, in most cases, it could not be properly combined with mass struggles.'[13] The 'problematic past' continues to haunt other less significant MLM groups as well.

Further, since each of them somehow belonged to the original tree, they all share a rather rigid and doctrinaire form of Marxism-Leninism-Maoism, MLM; the entire naxalite family has basically ignored the 'new Left' and social justice movements and ideas that have dominated Western radical thinking since the 1960s, and have penetrated political movements in Latin America and Europe as well (Nigam, 2009a; 2010b). In fact, there has been no effort at all to understand the views – and wide mass acceptance — of Gandhi, Ambedkar, Lohia and other radical political thinkers in twentieth-century India. Thus, any real criticism of Lenin, Stalin and Mao, along with a liberal-humanistic interpretation of Marx, is starkly missing in the naxalite discourse. As Partha Chatterjee (1983) puts it: 'Political debates are still conducted on the Indian Left in terms that would be wholly familiar to members of the Bolshevik Party at the time of the October Revolution' in 1917 without, unfortunately, the intense analytical resources deployed in the writings of Lenin, Bukharin, Trotsky and others.[14] In that sense, naxalite criticism of Maoists is compelled to work within a rather restricted set of polemical and ideological choices.

For example, consider the very early critique of CPI(ML) and Charu Mazumdar by Promode Sengupta (1970/1983), who himself was a veteran revolutionary of many battles including the Spanish civil war and the *Azad Hind* movement led by Subhas Chandra Bose. Sengupta complains that, by adopting either 'revisionist' (CPM) or 'Left adventurist' (CPI(ML)) politics, the Left movement in India suffered from deviations from the 'correct' path. The 'correct' path and the 'deviations' of course are to be understood only in MLM terms, suitably reinterpreted with selective uses of one liners from MLM literature, such as 'Don't forget class struggle' (Mao). As Chatterjee (1983) observed, Sengupta was 'arguing for a new revolutionary politics, but entirely within the discursive ambit occupied by the old.' 'Within that discursive tradition,' Chatterjee explained, 'Sengupta had no recourse to any independent criteria by which he could support his claim about the "correctness" of his interpretation.'

Unsurprisingly, each MLM group uses the same strategy against other MLM groups; that is, for each MLM group, other MLM groups exhibit either 'Left adventurism' or 'revisionism'. It is no wonder then, that, in their review of the history of the naxalite movement, Maoists also adopt the same strategy of highlighting the 'essence':

> In this period of setback [1971–80] three distinct trends developed within the CPI (ML). The first was a continuation of the Left line of 'annihilation of class enemies' which was represented by some pro-Lin Piao groups like the Second CC [Central Committee] and the Mahadev Mukherjee group, also the CPI (ML) led by Jouhar in Bihar and CPI (ML) led by Kannamani in Tamilnadu. The second trend was composed of those who swung to the right, by criticising the entire tactical line of the CPI (ML) and once again sought participation in elections. This was particularly [so for] the CPI (ML) faction led by Satyanarayan Singh. Others like Kanu Sanyal, Ashim Chatterjee, Souren Bose swung even further to the right finally veering towards the CPI (M). The third trend was particularly represented by the COC (Central Organising Committee) which upheld the essence of the CPI (ML) line but sought to rectify the Left errors.[15]

COC was a motley group of isolated revolutionaries, predominantly in Andhra, during the said 'period of setback'. Needless to say, Maoists (PWG) trace their 'correct' revolutionary politics to the line adopted by the Central Organising Committee.

It is interesting to analyse briefly the 'politics' deployed in the passage just cited. Employing the strategy of flogging left and right deviations, Maoists seek to gain legitimacy by distancing themselves from the discredited 'left line of "annihilation of class enemies"' even if the practice of *de facto* 'annihilation' continues unabated in the name of 'revolutionary violence' (see Chapter Three). Also, there was the compulsion to target the 'pro-Lin Piao' groups since by then Lin Piao was characterised by Chairman Mao as one of the 'Gang of Four'. The COC of course was 'free' of all these 'deviations' and so was PWG by inheritance! The politics is viewed as won as the 'line of annihilation' is now hooked up with 'pro-Lin Piao' deviations of post-Mazumdar individuals. Such cleansing enables the legacy of Charu Mazumdar to continue to shine so that Maoists can claim continuity with the naxalbari uprising. It is hard to see how the discursive tradition adopted by critiques such as Promode Sengupta – and later by CPI(ML-Liberation) and others – can be used to defeat Maoist reinterpretations framed within the same tradition.

Finally, there is the lingering 'Bush' doctrine that prohibits the outright rejection of Maoist politics even when one points out fundamental flaws with the form and content of the Maoist movement, as Chatterjee's 'apologetic' critique illustrates. In my view, these factors combine to partly diminish the clarity of political options advocated by non-Maoist naxalites. As a result, their criticism of Maoists sounds too arcane to carry actionable political meaning, more so because Maoists can flaunt numbers, including numbers of guns, which other naxalite groups do not have. In the absence of moral and political clarity, numbers begin to play the determining role.

Still, even if the prospect of a distant armed struggle is raised as a flag of identity to mark naxalite politics, a non-doctrinaire conception of Indian reality seems to be emerging as well. As we saw, there are two related aspects to this conception: (a) Greater appreciation of electoral politics as one of the salient reformist means to ensure welfare for the people in India; and (b) growing realisation that armed struggle is problematic in the impressive diversity and development of the Indian context. What is not yet fully appreciated is that armed struggle is actually inconsistent with electoral politics in the Indian context, perhaps in any context if the first option is available at all.[16]

This is what Maoists in Nepal realised once a widespread armed struggle created the conditions for establishing a republic based on universal franchise, and the institutions supporting these basic means emerged. In other words, once the first option was made available *through armed struggle*, armed struggle itself became obsolete as a political instrument. My own sense from the extensive citations above is that, except for Maoists, naxalites in India are very close to appreciate the primacy of electoral politics over armed struggle even if it is difficult to give up a dogma that has sustained much revolutionary enthusiasm for many decades since the uprising in Telengana in the 1940s. In turn, it opens up the prospect of broad coalition between non-Maoist naxalites, the sweep of the parliamentary Left, and other socialist-secular forces, if essentially verbal disputes and historical hostilities (often based on complex personal suspicions) can be overcome in the interest of the struggling people. As ever, radical intellectuals have a role to play.

Insofar as the Maoist party is concerned, I hope to have shown with some clarity and detail by now that almost every aspect of their undemocratic — often demonic — character, including the inability to form a mass base anywhere except in areas of near-absolute destitution such as the shrinking *adivasi* belts, can be traced to the adoption of armed struggle. The essentially undemocratic character of their armed struggle leads to other aspects of moral and political degeneration.

Interestingly, not all Maoist leaders hold identical views on the supremacy of armed struggle and of the Maoist party. The Maoist ideologue and politbureau member Kobad Ghandy, still lodged in Delhi's Tihar jail at time of publication, seems to advocate a much broader perspective. In a 2008 interview Ghandy dismissed the question of arms as a 'non-issue' and concentrated on what I have characterised as the first part of the Maoist discourse. In two subsequent write-ups sent from prison (Ghandy, 2011b; 2011c), he reviews the world-situation with incisive analysis that stands out from the otherwise trite MLM literature in India. After surveying the general economic collapse of the capitalist countries in the Western hemisphere, he turns to remedial options. In his 2011c article, he applauds some recent developments in Latin America.

> In Latin America, from Ecuador to Brazil, Bolivia to Argentina, elected leaders have turned away from the IMF and US, taken back resources from corporate control, boosted regional integration and carried out independent (of the US) alliances around the world. In Venezuela Chavez has cut poverty rates by half, tripled social spending and rapidly expanded health care and education.[17]

He does not reject these bold initiatives as 'revisionist' and 'reformist' and does not denounce the fact that these regimes assumed power after massively popular elections.[18] In his 2011a article, Ghandy holds that one way to ensure the welfare of people is to hold sustained dialogue between alternative models of development. The Maoist model, partly penned by Ghandy himself I guess, is of course one of them, but he agrees that the model proposed by the National Advisory Council, constituted by the Indian parliament and chaired by the Congress president Sonia Gandhi, is an equal contender. In general, although he urges that a 'pro-people government should divert huge sums of money for the real welfare of the people rather than for war games of the big powers,' the need for protracted war to achieve this end is nowhere mentioned.

To say this is not to rule out the prospect of armed struggle as a political principle. It is quite possible that all other efforts of ensuring genuine welfare for the poor and unempowered ultimately fail. But then armed struggle will become a necessity *demanded by the poor out of their own understanding* of that failed context. The historical fact is that, otherwise, it is always the poor who are asked to take up arms either for the state or for non-state forces; in either case, the poor are just expected to obey, not *decide*. Until that point, once a workable electoral system is grudgingly made available to the people by the ruling dispensations, it cannot be an *a priori* intellectual goal in advance to prepare for an armed struggle. As Chatterjee pointed out perceptively, 'there has never been a revolution in a country with parliamentary democracy'.

No doubt, Chatterjee also pointed out that 'elections have never led to fundamental social change'; they fail to shape a new society. But then what does Chatterjee mean by 'fundamental social change'? If *adivasi*s in Bastar are able to earn Kerala-type wages, have access to safe drinking water and reliable medical facilities, if their children have decent and free school education and so on, won't that be a 'fundamental social change' *at this point* from what we saw? Of course, there is no suggestion here that *adivasi* welfare is to be restricted to this minimal list. Yet isn't it then the right of the safe and well-nourished *adivasi* to formulate a more advanced list after exhausting the scope of the first, as the Dalits are beginning to articulate in Bihar and Uttar Pradesh after much success in Tamil Nadu? Or is there an intellectual blueprint formulated in advance of the wishes of the people?

The radical concern about 'shaping a new society' is appreciated. But the historical experience is that, after some initial populist measures to consolidate the rule of the elites, welfare measures are often progressively withdrawn as the 'new' societies get old. Thus, withdrawal of welfarist measures happened not only in US, Europe and now in neo-liberal India, but also in

Russia, China, Vietnam, Sandinista's Nicaragua, Mandela's South Africa and the like which were 'shaped' with promises of 'new society'. Thus, resistance ought to be unbounded without any expectations of a permanent shape. The state and the resistance to it are a (continuous) process in that sense everywhere. Any programme of political action that dismantles the possibility of such resistance even temporarily is to be rejected outright: no excuses for infantile socialism, unsettled new democratic revolution, fragile democracy, etc. As long as societies are unable to formulate the shape of a new society with people genuinely at the centre and *with their mass approval*, the only route is to resist injustice and indignity wherever they show up. What shape the collection of such resistance – 'million mutinies' – will take is not for any 'vanguard' to articulate in advance.

The perspective of continuous resistance just sketched is directly linked to the value of elections since elections seem to be the only method available to sustain the perspective. As Dipankar Bhattacharya pointed out, local armed resistance is sometimes required to enable people to vote freely. In this light, we can view the Nepal uprising as a country-wide articulation of the point; the armed struggle by Maoists in Nepal essentially made free vote available to every citizen. The availability of a free vote then assumes something of an absolute value. No doubt, elections are extremely complex: There are too many issues, conflicting interests and aspirations, too much dust and grime, and far too many compromises on the ground. Perhaps the overriding problem is the increasingly palpable disobedience on the faces of the poor when the elites seek their votes with folded hands. Although elections lack the pristine character of an unfolding blueprint directed at an assenting audience so that their consciousness is 'raised' in prescribed stages, they are direct expressions of people's power *for that reason*.

In contrast, community-based people's movements, direct actions ensuing from the grassroots, and related forms of resistance look attractive because the meaning of these actions can be typically captured in terms of neat blueprints. I am not rejecting the immense value of these grassroots resistance movements, with or without intellectual participation.[19] They are an essential ingredient, forever, for forcing an issue, increasing the cost for the state, and raising the bar for the electoral process. In that sense, the uprising in Nandigram was essential for the 2011 vote as we will shortly see; but then Nandigram would have remained just a singular un-empowering event without the subsequent vote. The range of popular movements by themselves never ensured any lasting empowerment and welfare of the people, not even for the communities from which they arose, until they are able to enforce redistribution of power. In that sense, empowerment requires access to power; in this case, access to state power (see Chapter Two). An electoral democracy, if it is available, is the only non-catastrophic method of ensuring progressive empowerment and welfare of people known to the current state of civilisation.

Extremists, elites and big business, with considerable ideological overlap between them,[20] are historically uncomfortable with universal franchise in any case. Harnessing the beast is a cumbersome enterprise, and it eats into direct control and profits. Yet the other side of the picture is that, after six decades of operation, the Indian electoral process has deteriorated considerably. With over 300 very rich people (called *crorepatis*) in the Indian Parliament, forced voting orchestrated by criminal politicians, massive flow of money, liquor, and other 'goodies', the alarming phenomenon of 'paid news', and the increasing rule of the gun (Chapter Two), there are reasons to feel frustrated with electoral politics.[21]

It is natural in these circumstances that otherwise democratic individuals and groups have started to blink and advocate 'direct democracy' outside the parliamentary system, including subliminal support to Maoists. According to Aditya Nigam (2009a), 'Maoists of course have been around for a long time without many takers for their kind of politics'. What has made them attractive recently is 'the violence of the law'. Thus, 'it is not for nothing that well-known Gandhians have of late been adopting tactical silence – if not an openly welcoming stance – towards Maoists.'

As Chomsky observed, the great mass of people seem to think otherwise as results in election after election show, especially during some of the worst phases of Indian democracy. Two of these immediately come to mind: the general parliamentary elections of 1977 and 2004. In each case, the elections followed massive misrule by palpably authoritarian regimes enforcing an internal emergency in the first case and a communal-fascist order in the second. Both the regimes were decisively thrown out by massive voter turnout. In each case, the elections were followed by some years of the most people-friendly governance seen in the country. For example, the 2004 elections gave a substantial mandate to the parliamentary Left such that, even with less than fifteen percent of the seats, it could bargain for progressive measures such as the rural employment guarantee scheme, right to information act, forest rights act and the like. But, as Rana pointed out, this parliament also unanimously passed the draconian UAPA with full support of the Left as soon as the new government assumed office: fragility accompanied triumph.

From an interesting direction, the 2011 assembly elections in West Bengal is another impressive affirmation of the essential salience of electoral politics. After thirty-four years of rule (a world record), the Left Front government in the state of West Bengal in India lost the elections decisively winning just 61 of 294 assembly seats. Except for die-hard supporters of the Left, the writing on the wall was loud and clear for several years. The people had warned the Left massively and repeatedly over the last three years through *panchayat*, parliamentary and civic elections. The fact that the Left was unable to change course and win back the support of the people despite these warnings showed the depth of the rot that had set in after three decades of uninterrupted power. It was clearly beyond the Left to enforce drastic organisational restructuring, alter character of governance, and win elections at the same time. The election apparatus – consisting of expert commissars, corrupt cadres, gangsters, feudal apparatchiks, and promoters – was inconsistent with any attempt at basic reforms (Mukherji, 2009a). The only way for the Left to redeem itself was to face near-extinction (Banerjee, 2011). The people of West Bengal made sure that was the case.

Throughout the thirty-four years of rule, the Left managed to secure about forty-nine percent of votes at its peak and the opposition vote was fragmented. In fact, there was considerable anxiety in the Left Front about the prospect of losing the election before the 2006 assembly elections as well. The government was already widely unpopular by then and the election commission was determined to weed out forced voting, 'scientific' rigging, and the like. It so happened that the forty-nine percent was eventually retained and the front won handsomely. In general, the voters remembered the first fifteen years of Left rule when the front functioned not only as a genuine welfare-dispenser, it also acted as a force of resistance against the neo-liberal onslaught and the war on terror within the obvious limits of provincial state power. It is important to remember that, in the first two decades of Left rule, reactionary and extremist elements disappeared from the scene and most naxalites were reduced to human rights activities which are in any case required under any dispensation of the state.

After the first fifteen years, the voters continued to support the Front, albeit increasingly grudgingly until the breaking point reached with Singur and Nandigram, and the front was fully unmasked. There was significant opposition to the authoritarian Left rule by the intelligentsia comprising writers such as Mahasweta Devi, university teachers, democratic rights organisations like APDR, theatre and film personalities and others, during the turbulent period between 2007 and 2010. The prime trigger for this impressive vocal opposition was the atrocious police action on peasants who were protesting against forcible acquisition of land for big business. The intellectual protest virtually died out in its overt form by 2010 after a combination of determined attack and conciliatory gestures by the state. It was the voters then who threw the Left out of power in 2011, not meetings of intellectuals in Kolkata Press Club and elsewhere.

The basic political difference this time was that Trinamool-Congress, a breakaway group from the original Congress of the 1990s, not only forged a durable alliance with the Congress, its firebrand leader, Mamata Bannerjee, was able to tap the rising anger of the people by joining people's movements in Singur, Nandigram, and elsewhere. In the earlier elections, the Trinamool not only failed to forge unity with Congress, it opportunistically aligned itself with the right-wing BJP which was then in power at the centre. The politically conscious people of West Bengal rejected such politics. From 2008 onwards, the Trinamool corrected itself by shunning BJP and aligning with Congress. The joint Trinamool Congress force routed the Left Front in election after election, as noted.

However, in the elections of 2011, there was an interesting variation on this familiar theme in the bitterly contested Jangalmahal area, comprising of about forty assembly segments. In the rest of West Bengal, the choice was overwhelmingly binary between the Left and the Trinamool Congress alliance. Except for the Gorkha areas, this explains the virtual elimination of third-party options from the state. In Jangalmahal, there was no major third party, but there was a major third factor: a significant presence of Maoist ideology in terms of a combination of Maoist squads, frequent interventions by some urban Maoist-aligned intellectuals, and the Maoist-backed popular organisation, PCPA – led by Chatradhar Mahato – currently in prison.

To cut a long story short, the Jangalmahal, spanning the forested areas of the districts of West Midnapore, Purulia and Bankura, had been a traditional stronghold for the Left. As the Left Front government brutally messed up in Singur and Nandigram and people's anger finally came out into the open, the Lalgarh area of Jangalmahal became an epicentre of protest leading to the formation of PCPA. As the Left government responded with further police assault, Maoists moved in from the adjacent Jharkhand forests and were soon in control of the movement.[22]

These developments did not have much electoral significance earlier since Maoists advocated and enforced poll-boycott in their pockets of influence (Ganapathy, 2009). As a significant section of *adivasi*s and other downtrodden people stayed away from elections year after year, the Left was able to retain its electoral strength through committed voting managed by its cadres. Even in the 2009 parliamentary elections in which the Left was severely mauled by the rising Trinamool Congress wave elsewhere in the state, the Left secured leads in thirty-one out of forty assembly segments of Jangalmahal.

This time (2011) as well, as the campaign for the elections was heating up, Maoists propagated vote boycott in the earlier stage. However, two developments altered the scene. First, following the huge outcry on the Netai massacre,[23] the Left government was forced to shut down the armed camps of CPM cadres. Second, the Election Commission enforced unprecedented security arrangements throughout the region, including especially the Maoist-dominated areas. With the removal of rule of the gun, people began to breathe freely for the first time in many years.

Sensing the mood of the people midway through the campaign, Maoists proclaimed that, although they continued to reject the electoral system, they will not object if people wanted to vote on their own. This was as clear an admission as we can get that, in the previous elections, Maoists had in fact physically prevented people from voting. In the final stages of the campaign, Maoists changed course again and directly asked people to vote for the Trinamool Congress in specific areas where the left still held some sway, the *Indian Express* reports.[24]

On the election day, nearly ninety percent of the voters showed up across Jangalmahal, including Maoist-controlled areas, walking for miles under scorching sun in some cases. The result was equally spectacular and uplifting. With negligible organisational presence, the Trinamool secured twenty-six of the forty seats mostly with impressive margins. As one commentator put it, the poor, marginalised and brutalised people of Jangalmahal joined the rest of West Bengal in voting out the rule of tyranny. Given just a marginal window of freedom, people grabbed it with both hands; the Maoist ideology of poll-boycott was comprehensively ignored.

More interestingly, although the Left was severely mauled, it was not routed in Jangalmahal. Jangalmahal itself returned fourteen Left candidates (with depleted margins) out of the sixty-one for the Left in the entire state. In other words, while the success rate for the Left is thirty-five percent in Jangalmahal, it is less than nineteen percent for the rest of the state; the Left did not win a single seat in erstwhile Left strongholds in several districts. District-wise breakups suggest that most of these fourteen seats for the Left have come from the West Midnapore part of

Jangalmahal alone comprising of Maoist and PCPA-dominated areas of Nayagram, Lalgarh, Gopiballavpur, and Salboni; so, in the West Midnapore segment of Jangalmahal, the Left's success rate is considerably higher than the thirty-five percent for the whole of Jangalmahal. Chatradhar Mahato, the earlier charismatic leader of PCPA, contested from jail and did manage to secure about 20,000 votes in the Jhargram assembly constituency; but he lost to the Trinamool rival by nearly 50,000 votes.

There are several aspects to this vote. First, people in Jangalmahal have been subjected to the poll-boycott politics of Maoists for years, as noted. Yet, given a free (and safe) choice, they exercised their right to vote in magnificent numbers. Second, the *mahatos* are not *adivasis*; they belong to the category of other backward castes (OBC) which has a substantial presence in Jhargram. It is most likely then that most of the (trifling) 20,000 votes for the ill-concealed Maoist representative Chatradhar Mahato came from the *mahato* community, rather than from *adivasis*.

Third and most importantly, as Santosh Rana pointed out, the mostly *adivasi* and Dalit cadres of CPM were engaged in a deadly battle with Maoists in the West Midnapur area of Jangalmahal; hundreds of them lost their lives. Unlike the rest of West Bengal where the CPM was largely identified in terms of shady feudal elements and corrupt party apparatchiks, the people in Jangalmahal saw with their own eyes the desperate struggle put up by ordinary cadres of CPM to resist the gun-wielding Maoists attempting to grab control of CPM-dominated areas by force. In essence, at a crucial moment of freedom, the people of Jangalmahal, while expressing their anger at the tyranny of Left rule, rejected Maoists as well.

6

QUEST FOR PEACE

The Maoist upheaval is qualitatively different from other insurgencies that happen in the country. The insurgencies in Kashmir and the North-East, including the Bodoland movement in Assam and Gorkhaland movement in West Bengal, are all separatist movements in that the resistance groups want varying degrees of self-governance either detached from or within the Indian state. While Bodo and Gorkha movements demand separate provinces for their people within the Indian state, people in Kashmir, Nagaland, and Manipur demand separation from the Indian state itself. Although every state, including erstwhile 'socialist' ones, adopts arrogant and non-negotiable notions of sovereignty and integrity, demands for autonomy, even separation, are intrinsically democratic if they are supported by historical facts and overwhelming popular aspirations, which seem to be case with the cited insurgencies (Mukherji, 2007b).

These separatist struggles fall into the penumbra of negotiability. The very demand for separation from a state is *prima facie* non-negotiable from the point of view of the state as noted. Thus, typically, the state provides no platforms for addressing the demand from within the existing forums of the state. For example, one cannot raise the demand for separation as an election issue; neither can the insurgent groups themselves organise a referendum of people to be officially recognised by the state. How then can people raise the legitimate democratic demand for autonomy or separation if the democratic conditions, as above, have been met?

It is not difficult to comprehend that the usual peaceful methods will not carry much weight in these cases due to the essential non-negotiability of the demand. The only options then are *unusual* peaceful methods such as prolonged satyagraha as advocated by Gandhi or armed resistance. As we saw, armed resistance has its own severe undemocratic consequences such as enabling the state to escalate attack on the people from an apparently high moral ground. The brutal attack by the Indian state, with the use of the army and AFSPA, has no doubt led to the fragmentation of the armed side of these insurgencies, as noted. At the same time, state repression has enhanced the real moral and the political cause of these movements, as Irom Sharmila's spectacular resistance illustrates.

It stands to reason, therefore, that talks are held between the state and the insurgent groups in an atmosphere of ceasefire to find a peaceful solution. Such talks do often take place leading to some peace in some cases, as with the earlier insurgency in Mizoram. Currently, much hope is placed on the interventions by civil 'interlocutors' appointed by the government in the long-standing Kashmir issue. It is reported that the decades-old talks with Naga insurgent groups has made some progress recently.[1] One reason why talks have a chance in these cases, despite the apparent non-negotiability, is that separatism comes in layers and degrees: there are numerous real points between complete separation and total subjugation, at least in a progressive federal structure (Chenoy and Chenoy, 2010). If the popular movements are able to raise the cost of the state — say, by internationalising the just demand or by interrupting some crucial economic activity of the state — the state may be willing to settle for one of these viable intermediate points if the state's attempt to prolong negotiations do not exhaust the energy of the movement.

None of these conditions apply to the Maoist upheaval primarily because the Maoist movement is not a separatist movement. Maoists demand seizure of state power by their party. This by itself has neither moral nor political value unless it is linked to some salient cause, involving wide sections of the people, which cannot be addressed within the forums available in the state. As we saw, the genuine cause of empowering and ensuring welfare for vast sections of people can only be achieved by enabling people's militant access to the existing forums of the state (Chapter Two). And the only civilised method of ensuring such access is to expand the space of electoral democracy in terms of widespread mass movements on basic issues of life and livelihood (Chapter Five). Since Maoists reject this option outright, there is nothing to talk about.

Maoists may agree to 'the proposal of talks to give some respite for the people at large who are living under constant state terror and immense suffering', as they say. However, they want 'to achieve whatever is possible for the betterment of people's lives' without compromising on their 'political programme of new democratic revolution and strategy of protracted people's war' (Azad, 2010a). Commenting on the proposal of talks with Maoists, Menon (2009) observes, 'the very idea of talks is actually ruled out, but Maoists may periodically agree to talks in order to gain time and space to regroup and prepare for the "next stage". On the other hand, what message does the Indian state send when it offers to talk to those brandishing guns, but not to those who do not?'

Such a 'message' was in fact sent by the Union Home Minister P. Chidambaram in the summer of 2010. He asked CPI(Maoists) to 'abjure violence' and to come to talks. Specifically, Chidambaram did not require that Maoists lay down arms; he just wanted cessation of hostilities for now for talks to take place. The knotty issue of arms may be taken up later. Once this minimal condition is satisfied, Chidambaram was prepared to talk on all issues concerning *adivasi* welfare and rights, industrial policy, models of development, and the like. As far as I can tell, the offer still stands on paper.

Assume that the offer explicitly includes a halt to the armed operations of the state as well in the concerned areas. Then Chidambaram's conditions essentially match those of the Citizens Initiative for Peace and other civil society groups who have volunteered to negotiate between the government and Maoists to bring both sides to the table – provided hostilities cease. Should we view this apparently friendly offer as Chidambaram's attempt to walk that extra disarming mile to bring peace with dignity to *adivasis*?

The problem is that, in an earlier statement,[2] Chidambaram also regretted that previous attempts by various state governments to talk to Maoists, after a temporary halt to violence from both sides, had been unfailingly 'futile'. Why then is the home minister offering to enter into another futile exercise? Further, given that the government has declared CPI(Maoist) as a banned organisation, what does it mean, from the state's point of view, to negotiate with an adversary with arms in its hands? Also, knowing that Maoists will settle for nothing less than seizure of state power after a protracted war, as they have repeatedly affirmed, what does the state want to talk about? Is this just a ploy to buy some time to organise whatever it is that Chidambaram and his colleagues in the intelligence wings have in mind? If Chidambaram's appeal is such a ploy, then his offer sounds plausible, for it is unlikely that Maoists will ever agree to spend some time at the table without their arms safely in place. So, why does the home minister need some time?

To probe the issue from one direction, among others, we recall that the earlier talks were held, essentially in Andhra Pradesh, when Maoists were upbeat especially after People's War Group joined hands with Maoist Communist Centre under the banner of CPI(Maoist). As the Maoist influence spread, the state of Andhra responded with enhanced gunpower. In a scenario of escalating violence, both sides needed some respite to consolidate their forces. Hence the 'talks'; they were abandoned as soon as Maoists realised the trap (Chenoy and Chenoy, 2010). With the reported expansion of Maoist territory in Dandakaranya between 2006 and 2008, especially after *Salwa Judum* operations, does a similar situation of Maoists' gaining ground obtain there as well? Or, in contrast, is there some difference in the conditions themselves in the present situation for Chidambaram to believe that it might lead to meaningful talks? In other words, is Chidambaram willing to talk to obtain some respite from the apparently problematic security situation, or is he convinced that he will be talking from a position of strength?

Being in charge of anti-Maoist operations, Chidambaram surely knows the real picture. From whatever is available in the public domain, it looks like Maoists have lost considerable ground *since* 2008. For example, the alert observer Sumanta Banerjee suggested in 2009 that 'the state's dragnet is closing in to besiege [the Maoists'] narrow base'. They are now basically restricted to some forests in the tiny new states of Chhattisgarh and Jharkhand and some adjacent areas in Odisha and Bihar. Many of their top and middle-level leaders have been eliminated or arrested in the past years. Despite temporary setbacks including considerable loss of manpower, the security forces seem to be closing in on those jungles. It is well-known that secret, militaristic organisations engage in dramatic displays of public violence essentially out of desperation and to convey a false impression of strength. From this perspective, the series of violent operations by Maoists in 2010, and their attempts to penetrate and hide among popular uprisings in the neighbourhood of their headquarters, could in fact signal that they are losing ground.

Add to this the increased repression of the state of unarmed *adivasi* populations in those areas, including the unleashing of *Salwa Judum*, the introduction of special forces, and so on. The enhancement of paramilitary operations, with increasing assistance of the Indian army, belies Chidambaram's 'friendliness' towards *adivasi*s and the rebels. While these insidious operations do on occasion compel some of the victims to join the ranks of militancy and take up arms, they also leave such populations in a state of exasperation.[3] In sum, notwithstanding tall claims by their leaders, Maoists could be fast losing their ability to hide.

If these conjectures are even partly true, they explain Chidambaram's current, apparently friendly, gestures from a purely tactical point of view. The state will not only talk to Maoists from a relative position of strength, in allowing the rebels to retain their arms, the state will be free to retain its own to continue with 'normal' police operations to further encircle Maoists. Needless to say, if Maoists do agree to enter into dialogue under pressure from their friends in, say, the Citizens Initiative, it will be a huge propaganda victory for Chidambaram. If the talks fail – as they inevitably will when the issue of surrender of arms comes up sooner or later – Chidambaram can officially declare an all-out war, perhaps involving the Indian army, pleading the TINA (there is no alternative) factor.[4] It would be the most 'friendly' way of smashing the rebels and *adivasi* uprising, and pave the way for a 'peaceful' introduction of mining and other cartels in the scene.

The duplicity of both the state and Maoists, with the non-participating *adivasi*s caught in the middle, was starkly revealed with the incident of Azad's murder. As noted, Azad was the Maoist spokesperson until his death; reportedly, he was number three in the Maoist hierarchy. Azad became a central figure in the projected negotiations for peace following the peace mission of 6–8 May 2010 undertaken by some prominent citizens such as Swami Agnivesh and Prof Yash Pal (see Introduction). Although the peace mission itself had to be abandoned after it was repeatedly attacked by local hoodlums with ill-concealed approval from the BJP-led government in Chhattisgarh, Chidambaram appeared to appreciate the effort. In his (confidential) letter to Swami Agnivesh, Chidambaram encouraged Agnivesh to 'reach out to CPI(Maoist) and persuade them to accept the Government's offer for talks, the sole condition being that CPI(Maoist) should abjure violence.' The 'offer' included (a) cessation of 'operations' against each other by both sides for seventy-two hours from a fixed agreed date and (b) maintenance of the position of 'no violence' until talks concluded.

Azad responded on behalf of CPI(Maoist) when Agnivesh passed on Chidambaram's letter to them. Azad also appreciated the efforts at peace, but rejected the seventy-two hour clause proposed by Chidambaram as it was 'like a joke'. Instead, Azad asked for truce for a longer period of several months provided the government (a) lifted the ban on the party; (b) released its leaders; (c) withdrew the paramilitary forces from the concerned areas; both Ganapathy and Kishenji had laid down these preconditions earlier. Swami Agnivesh responded to Azad's proposals and it was handed over to Azad. While Azad was carrying this response to consult other leaders of CPI(Maoist) he was apparently picked up in Nagpur and subsequently killed in the Adilabad forests of Andhra Pradesh. We return to this killing later.

What do we make of the proposals and counter-proposals? As an ordinary citizen without access to secret confabulations in the North Block in New Delhi (where the Union home ministry is located), and the Maoist headquarters in Abujmaad, I can only make some speculative but hopefully reasonable gestures. Consider first the surprisingly small window of seventy-two-hours which Azad called a 'joke'. From Chidambaram's letter to Swami Agnivesh, it appears that Agnivesh himself made this offer to Maoists, although Chidambaram had proposed this idea in his meeting with Agnivesh prior to the peace march.[5] It could be that Agnivesh conveyed this time-frame in good faith to Maoists to begin the groundwork for talks; seventy-two hours looks neither too short nor too long a duration for the warring sides to halt operations such that some signal of their peaceful intentions can be gauged by the peacemakers. It was perhaps hoped that the ceasefire would hold even after the first seventy-two hours.

Why then did Azad think of the suggestion as a joke? Perhaps Maoists were immediately alarmed by the fact that the suggestion had originated from Chidambaram. We recall that Chidambaram had proposed a mutual halt of operations from a fixed date. In his letter to Agnivesh of 11 May, he cited 1 June as an example; he said the date could be even *earlier*. In other words, he expected the truce to begin almost immediately and continue for at least seventy-two hours. Two facts need consideration. First, Maoist forces are scattered secretly and disjointedly over thousands of kilometres of forests; so, it cannot be easy for these dozens of units of uneven size to move into safe and secured positions mostly by foot within a short time. Second, one of the safe methods of communication developed by Maoists is to use foot-couriers who carry (carefully folded) handwritten messages called 'biscuits'. The method is safe but obviously time-consuming. In order to inform all the units to stop offensive operations and move into secured defensive positions, Maoists need to activate and coordinate the entire network carefully. To attempt to do this within a couple of weeks might very well expose the network at crucial joints. Perhaps that is precisely what Chidambaram wants: to pry the Maoist network open in the name of peace! Further, an activation of the network in haste might leave some units uncovered such that there will be a chance of someone somewhere violating the truce and, thereby, giving Chidambaram the opportunity to abandon the peace process from a moral high-ground, and arrest the interlocutors. If I can see this, Maoists obviously can.

Assuming that the preceding speculation explains why Azad thought of Chidambaram's proposal as a joke, Maoists' own proposals are no less ridiculous. In its interview with Azad (2010a), *The Hindu* raised the basic problem with Maoist proposals as follows:

> Usually in negotiations of this kind around the world between governments and insurgent groups, the lifting of a ban is one of the objects of talks rather than a precondition and the release of political prisoners an intermediate step. Is the Maoist party not putting the cart before the horse, making demands that the government may be unlikely to accept as a starting point, rather than positing the same as one of the end points of the proposed dialogue?

Swami Agnivesh made basically the same point succinctly when he wrote to Azad, 'the steps you suggest can all be discussed during the talks.' In the said interview, Azad responded by saying that (a) without lifting the ban, the party cannot engage in open mass work; and (b) unless some of the leaders are released from jail, there will be no one to represent the party because 'we cannot bring any of our leaders overground for the purpose of talks.'

One can debate whether banning an organisation, whatever its programme, is ever an option in democracy. But the fact is that the government is currently not interested in the debate as the relevant acts have been passed by the parliament; if the ban is lifted without Maoists rectifying anything that led to the ban in the first place, the government will be charged by the opposition and much of the civil society with violation of its own norms. As to the leaders in jail, they have been charged with grave violations of the law and most of these charges are non-bailable. So these prisoners can only be brought to the negotiating table after due sanction from the courts. How can the courts allow non-bailable prisoners to be bonafide negotiators with the government without Maoists giving something beforehand? Also, what is the guarantee that the decisions reached by a handful of imprisoned and ageing leaders like Kobad Ghandy and Narayan Sanyal will in fact be respected by the party itself, especially when there is intense division in the party on this issue? So, the only valid option for Maoists is to engage some of their active leaders in the talks with a mixture of risk and guarantee from the government, and hope for the best. As to the safety of underground leaders, of course an agreement has to be reached in advance, as in the Andhra negotiations of 2004, regarding the security of these people even if the talks fail. It is inconceivable that Maoists do not know of these obvious responses from the government.

In his reported conversation with Swami Agnivesh,[6] Chidambaram was also making an essentially empty proposal that, once the talks begin, the government is prepared to place all signed MOUs on the table and discuss all problems concerning *adivasis* regarding water, land and forests. All he wanted for the talks to begin was for the Maoists to just halt operations *without* laying down arms or giving up the Maoist programme. Chidambaram knows very well that, if Maoists refuse to disarm during such talks, the question of lifting the ban and releasing their leaders does not arise, not to speak of negotiating with them on social policy like land reform, wages, right to habitat, MOUs with mining corporations, and the like. It goes without saying that Maoists know that too. Chidambaram also knows that Maoists will not disarm at his calling.

It is not difficult to discern that neither the government nor Maoists are particularly interested in reaching a peaceful solution. Each wants to use the occasion of a few days of meaningless talks for propaganda mileage ('we tried our best') and to secure whatever tactical advantage they can marshal before the violence begins afresh on a much higher scale. Notwithstanding his apparently aggrieved and earnest tone, Azad was not totally honest when he said that the 'proposal of talks' is not 'a ploy to buy time or regroup ourselves'.

Undeterred by Azad's clearly unacceptable response and Chidambaram's reported lack of further interest,[7] Swami Agnivesh wrote once again to Azad on 26 June 2010, reiterating Chidambaram's earlier condition and, in fact, suggesting three alternative dates from which the seventy-two hour truce might begin: 10 July 2010, 15 July 2010 and 20 July 2010. In effect, he offered a slightly longer time-frame for Maoists to organise themselves. According to Agnivesh, Azad seemed to have received the letter on 27 June and he spent the next three days in consultations with his colleagues at hand. After that Azad proceeded towards Dandakaranya for the final round of consultations with senior leaders. Agnivesh believes that he would have been told of the chosen date by the first week of July. We recall that Agnivesh did not concede to any of Azad's preconditions and insisted on a seventy-two-hour window. Azad's reported actions suggest that he was prepared to proceed nonetheless. Did that bold decision lead to his killing? Whatever his motivation, it appears that Azad was sincerely engaged in giving the prospect of talks – and of relief for *adivasi*s – a chance.

That was not to be as Azad's body was found in the Adilabad forests some time during the night of 1–2 July 2010, and the emerging prospect of peace abruptly collapsed. According to the Special Branch of Andhra Pradesh police (APSIB), Azad and Hemchandra Pandey, a journalist from Delhi, were killed during an encounter in which some thirty Maoists fired upon a police party engaged in combing operations. Several fact-finding teams, including one consisting of reputed rights people such as Amit Bhaduri, Prashant Bhusan, Gautam Navlakha, Kavita Srivastava, and others, tore the police story to shreds. The postmortem report clearly shows that Azad was killed from a point-blank range with the weapon pointing downwards (Bhaduri, 2011).

The police story is so ridiculously full of holes that the reports of various 'fact-finding' missions merely confirm the obvious. According to the story, after several hours of firing, Maoists retreated leaving just the bodies of Azad and Pandey behind. Therefore, according to the Andhra police:

1. The hapless journalist from Delhi, Hemchandra Pandey, was in fact a guerrilla in Andhra Pradesh. So, he worked as a journalist during the day in Delhi though as a guerrilla in Andhra during the night! Alternatively, he worked as a guerrilla during holidays. Maoists did not drag the bodies away as they always do even though Azad was number three in the Maoist hierarchy!
2. The police bullets found exactly these two men, perhaps they

had bullets with the names of Azad and Pandey written on them!
3. No one else from either side was hurt, specifically, no other Maoist was hurt or killed in trying to protect Azad, or if they did, their bodies were dragged away while Azad's was left behind.

If we want to believe that, we might as well believe in the parting of the Nile and Ganesha idols drinking milk.

Let me turn to the Maoist story; it is important to remember that we have only the Maoists' word for it.[8] According to them, at the end of his trip from 'somewhere in the North', Azad was roaming unarmed along with the hapless Pandey at the Nagpur railway station in Maharashtra, waiting for one comrade Sahadev to show up. Around that point in time, Andhra Pradesh police picked him up probably from the crowded station itself, took him to the Adilabad jungles probably in a helicopter, and killed him. No one apparently saw anything in this elaborate operation.[9] Maoists also said that Azad was to go to Dandakaranya to give political lessons to the cadres; they also suggested that he was going to meet his comrades to discuss Agnivesh's plan.

When the government was fully aware of his role as a peacemaker, why should the police kill him after arresting him? He would have been a prized catch on par with Kobad Ghandy, Amitabha Bagchi, Sushil Roy, Narayan Sanyal, Pramod Mishra, and others, to boost the morale of the state and the security forces after two big setbacks in April and June of 2010. An arrest would have increased Chidambaram's bargaining power manyfolds; it would have ensured that Azad himself took part in the talks. Instead, the home minister is now faced with a range of exposures after the alleged encounter, with glaring holes in the story as outlined.[10]

It has been suggested by some commentators that the whole peace initiative from the government was a sham with Swami Agnivesh merely an ignorant pawn. The exercise was meant to bring Azad to the surface, track him, and kill him at the appropriate moment to stall any further prospect of peace (Bhaduri, 2011).[11] Is it in the interest of the government to expose its sinister intentions in such an obvious fashion? If 'getting' Azad was the basic intelligence interest, he, along with some other Maoists, could have been picked up much earlier as he was 'moving fast' in the north to meet 'regional' colleagues, according to a Maoist source.[12]

In fact, it was in the government's interest to keep the 'peace process' alive, with Swami Agnivesh in the centre, so that it can continue to track Azad to get a fuller picture of the network as he proceeded to meet central leaders in the Maoist stronghold. By killing Azad, the government jeopardised its intelligence initiative after just one hit. Now Maoists will 'talk' to Agnivesh only through 'open letters' in the media.[13] And, as suggested above, the government desperately needed a peace interlude at that point both for propaganda and for paramilitary reorganisation after massive attacks on its security forces in April and June that year, and Azad looked like the prominent Maoist leader who could be relied upon. Thus, for purely tactical reasons, it is difficult to believe that either the Central or the provincial government ordered Azad's killing.

It has also been suggested that Azad was killed by a rogue unit of the Andhra police (APSIB) either because of the lucrative sum of money on his head or to take revenge for the Maoist attack in Narayanpura in which twenty-seven people were killed. However, as Swami Agnivesh points out, it is extremely unlikely that local police would have dared to act on their own on such an important leader as Azad. Agnivesh also points out that a senior

Maoist like Azad would have taken every precaution to guard his movements especially after the experience of the 'peace process' in Andhra in 2004 in which he took prominent part. Thus, there is little credibility to the suggestion that Azad let his guard down as the peace process started and the government took advantage of his carelessness.

In this connection, Agnivesh also suggests that 'it is worth pondering if someone from the [Maoist] ranks did not want the peace process to continue. There are people who are against peace talks inside and outside Maoist circles. It is possible that one of them informed the police.'[14] So, a third possibility is that some section of Maoists themselves is responsible for Azad's killing. It could be either because, as hinted above, some Maoists do not want to take any of the security risks which inevitably arise in a peace process, or because they simply do not want to negotiate with the state and are determined to continue with the war. Or perhaps there was a power struggle: The Maoist source cited above suggests that Azad was very close to the general secretary Ganapathy and was tipped to be the next chief.[15] If these people merely 'informed' the police, the police would have arrested Azad and taken the credit as suggested above. It is obvious that Pandey was killed because he was the sole witness. The Andhra police of course know what happened, but they are not going to tell unless they are compelled to do so by the highest court in the country.

A similar perspective applies to the recent killing of one of the most prominent Maoist leaders, Koteshwar Rao, popularly known as Kishenji. Both Azad and Kishenji belonged to reasonably well-off upper caste families in Andhra who were able to go to college. Both joined the revolutionary movement in their teens to fight for the people. In college, although Azad and Kishenji excelled in studies (with Azad going on to secure an M. Tech degree in engineering), they devoted most of their energy to build the massive revolutionary student movement that rocked the state of Andhra during the 1970s and the early 1980s. Apart from impressive on-campus and urban resistance, the student movement motivated hundreds of more militant students to go to villages and fight directly for and with the peasants, especially on the issue of land distribution. In time, as fatigue set in and repression mounted, most left the resistance and looked for greener pastures.

In contrast, Azad, Kishenji and many others left the academia and turned into fulltime political workers in the agrarian struggle initiated by one of the factions of the naxalite movement. While Azad devoted more attention to political organization, Kishenji emerged as one of the principal peasant organisers with many thousands of landless peasants and adivasis confronting one of the most brutal repressions launched by a state in republican India. Eventually, both Azad and Kishenji joined the People's War Group (PWG) founded by Kondapalli Sitaramaya and went underground. For nearly three decades since, these fearless spirits roamed the hills and forests of Central India to spread the fire of revolution among the destitutes left behind by the Indian state. I am no admirer of their politics, but I am honoured to pay my tributes to these noble spirits especially when one examines with disgust the life-histories of most of the official politicians that rule the country.

Azad's cold blooded murder and Kishenji's 'encounter' death are not only infuriating, these are clear signals that even limited talks with a short-term respite from violence for *adivasi*s is no longer feasible. Thus, repeated appeals for talks from well-meaning individuals,[16] and organisations such as Citizen's Initiative for Peace, are likely to fall on deaf ears of the parties that matter. In any case, as we saw, even if some token talks were to take place for a while, they cannot lead to any lasting peace for *adivasi*s. To emphasise that, the character of the Maoists' demands are such that there are no intermediate points for the government to agree with. For example, can the government agree to the full implementation of NREGA, PESA, FRA, minimum wages and so on, in the Dandakaranya area *under* Maoist supervision *with* Maoists holding on to their arms and liberated zones? It is clear that this must be Maoists' minimum demand while it (already) far exceeds the maximum that any government can even contemplate. Generally, as one commentator pointed out, we cannot expect a state to negotiate its own disappearance. This is the reason why, unlike the insurgencies in the North-East and Kashmir, there has never been any meaningful dialogue with Maoists in the four decades of their operations. As things stand, *adivasi*s have no respite from the war.

This observation is not in conflict with recent initiatives by the West Bengal government to engage in talks with Maoists in the Jangalmahal area of the state. Maoists may well agree to hold some talks there since they have only marginal presence in that area, especially after they lost much ground in recent months. They have nothing like guerrilla zones, not to mention 'liberated zones'. Most armed Maoists have been forced to retreat to dense forests in neighbouring states after a determined attack by CPM cadres and paramilitary forces. Also, the recent elections were a setback to their efforts to penetrate and control the population (see Chapter Five). Hence, TMC leader, Mamata Bannerjee's initiatives will in fact enable them to re-enter the area.[17] The situation in Dandakaranya is entirely different.

In any case, the situation in Jangalmahal itself seems to have changed significantly in recent months. Immediately after Kishenji's killing, the Maoist poet-ideologue Varavar Rao has claimed that, like Azad, Kishenji was also engaged in negotiations for peace with the newly elected regime in West Bengal, as promised by the TMC leader Mamata Bannerjee during her election campaign. As we saw, the unholy alliance between TMC and Maoists was a significant factor in the resounding electoral victory for TMC in the Jangalmahal area. Reportedly, as the negotiations with his commanders led to a deadlock, Kishenji himself moved into Jangalmahal from the Jharkhand forests to attempt a breakthrough. The state forces surrounded him and killed him alongwith three other Maoist guerrillas. According to Varavar Rao, Kishenji was first apprehended, tortured, and then killed in cold-blood. As suggested above, it could be that Kishenji's move for peace was purely tactical to find a safe haven for Maoist forces retreating from Jharkhand; or, it could be that he had a more lasting peace-plan in mind. It is obvious though that, having secured power, Mamata Bannerjee is no longer interested.

In the war, notwithstanding temporary initial advantages for Maoists, the state has the ultimate advantage of arms and other means of warfare – including sections of law – in its possession. Given the opportunity, the state will not hesitate to use them against its own people even in a quasi-democratic condition such as ours. However, compared to dictatorial and directly fascist regimes, quasi-democratic regimes face the problem of somehow aligning the repression with propaganda-with-a-human-face to muster popular support. In the current case, the propaganda advantage of the state comes from the operations of the CPI(Maoist).

Consider again Maoist actions such as the creation of 'liberated zones' to block the functioning of the state in particular areas, the killing of police personnel, killing of 'informers' and other 'class enemies', torching of trains, police stations and other public property, possession and use of vast quantities of sophisticated weapons, etc.[18] Maoists and their urban supporters no doubt justify these operations in terms of unilateral declaration of 'revolutionary violence and justice'. But the fact remains that these operations supply exactly the propaganda advantage needed by the state. As a result, Maoists cannot ultimately win this war, as I remarked at the outset of this work. The basic reason is that they never had – and never will have – the support of the people of India.

Thus, in theory at least, Maoists can pull the rug from below Chidambaram's tactics by unilaterally disarming themselves and joining democratic struggles against the predatory state. They do enjoy considerable support among some *adivasi* populations and sections of urban intellectuals, as noted. It is important that their 'enemies' such as the Union Home Ministry, the Congress party, and the CPM continue not to attach the 'terrorist' tag to them although, as we saw, most naxalites do! Even this minimal support may not last long if their increasingly desperate armed operations, perhaps even involving non-*adivasi* civilians in urban areas, escalate as in the 1970s; *adivasi* civilians have already paid a heavy price due to Maoist violence. In contrast, given their militancy, self-sacrifice and some acceptance among the poorest and the marginalised, they will be a major force in Indian politics if they give up arms and join democratic struggles.

Both Swami Agnivesh and Medha Patkar made similar appeals to Maoists in their speeches during the historic rally at Lalgarh on 9 August 2010. More recently, the writer-activist Dilip Simeon (2011) made the same point eloquently:

> Comrades, consider the impact if you were to give up the armed struggle and challenge the ruling class to adhere to the Constitution, reform the monstrous flaws in the criminal justice system, root out corruption in the police and judiciary ... develop the forest and tribal areas for the benefit of the people rather than corporate interests. A step such as this ... will electrify the situation. It will also place you in a central political position, for

> you will be challenging the entire Indian establishment. And the precious lives of thousands of ordinary people, including women, children and the elderly, quite apart from those of your committed cadres, shall be saved. There has been too much bloodshed. Violence is predictable. Do something different and unpredictable. It will bring a smile to millions of faces.

It is not difficult to understand that if Maoists do respond positively, their action will essentially deprive the state of the advantage of propaganda, for, if history is a guide, the state would *want* the current form of operations of CPI(Maoist) to continue. As long as Maoist violence continues, the state will be able to progressively enlarge the scope of Operation Green Hunt to ultimately smash the prospect of the far more dangerous broad, unarmed democratic alliance of all people. In this context, it is interesting that Chidambaram wants Maoists to keep their arms!

Once Maoists begin to transmit credible signals that they are prepared to lay down arms, the entire civil society, especially the hundreds of resistance movements and democratic organisations, can join hands to secure the best possible condition of surrender. This will include withdrawal of all paramilitary forces from *adivasi* lands, total and meaningful rehabilitation of all *adivasi* guerrillas and militias, release of all *adivasi* prisoners and withdrawal of charges, absolutely minimum and token sentencing of Maoist leaders, cancellation of all habitat-encroaching MOUs, and most importantly, a transparent and vigorous effort to implement all welfare measures for *adivasi*s available on paper. Once these conditions are substantially met, Maoists can surrender before civil organisations and join the resistance movements to ensure justice and welfare for the rest of the impoverished masses in the country. This will certainly 'bring a smile to millions of faces'.

This is a dream laced with plenty of hope. If the democratic sections of the civil society can somehow persuade Maoists to lay down arms, it will in fact strengthen the democratic struggle in India even if it will mean a temporary setback to Maoists before they spring back to genuine mass action. I can still recall the general enthusiasm — and the concern in the establishment media — when Maoists came out into the open before the Andhra talks in 2004 and organised impressive rallies in different parts of the country. By now, Maoists are far better organised and their identity is more firmly established in people's consciousness, albeit for the wrong reasons such as regular reports of blasts and killings. Given the turbulent character that mass mobilisation has assumed with the Lokpal movement, the presence of Maoists will certainly 'electrify the situation', as Simeon hopes.

Under the circumstances, the prospects of realising the sketched dream are not exactly promising. We recall Azad's words that 'the proposal of talks is [not] a part of the general re-evaluation of the political strategy of the party that could lead to its coming overground ... [or] ... compromising on our political programme of new democratic revolution and strategy of protracted people's war' (Azad, 2010c). The party has not spent decades in forests, and lost thousands of leaders and cadres in the process, only to give up their basic goal because some well meaning peace loving friends so desire. There is a sharp reference to Nepal in Azad's remarks. Although Maoists in Nepal were in a far better condition to carry on with their protracted war and seize state power on their own, they decided to give up arms and join the multiparty parliamentary system. I consider this decision to be a singular act of bold statesmanship. The Indian Maoists viewed this turn around essentially as a betrayal of MLM.

The party has confronted the issue of arms and protracted war throughout its history. Each time the issue reached a boiling point, the party had split only for this strand of Maoists to shift to an even more war-mongering leadership. One of the more recent of these divisions occurred when the veteran leader and the then general secretary of PWG, K. Sitaramaya, was expelled from the party in the early 1990s (Raychaudhury, 2010). Sitaramaya was no 'Gandhian with a gun'; he was the prime mover for initiating widespread guerrilla action and the shift to Dandakaranya for that purpose.[19] But he was also a long-standing mass leader. After Sitaramaya's expulsion, Mupalla Laxman Rao, alias Ganapathy – a strong believer in Charu Mazumdar's 'squad politics' – assumed leadership. Ganapathy's ascent to power facilitated dialogue – and ultimately unification – with the most ultra of the ultra-extremists, Maoist Communist Centre (MCC), to form CPI(Maoist). Several naxalite writers trace the current blood-thirsty character of Maoists to this merger with the MCC.

This short history of the current ideological state of the party negates real possibilities for laying down arms in the foreseeable future. It will not be surprising at all if Azad's – and later, Kishenji's – murders are found to be linked to this issue. Even if some of the saner sections of the party might be willing to reconsider peaceful options, it will only lead to even more bloodshed within the party and outside it. Finally, as indicated repeatedly in this work, the Maoist party never had it so big before in its long career in terms of visibility, area coverage, acquisition of arms and personnel, and intellectual support.[20] For the more militant sections in the organisation, this would obviously be seen as a victory of the party-line. Most leaders thus are likely to opt for the continuation and expansion of the protracted war, even if it means increased repression of *adivasi*s. There is no prospect of peace in so far as the Maoist leadership is concerned.[21] I must add though that this is one of those rare cases where, as a political thinker, I would *like* to be proved wrong.[22]

Turning to Maoist cadres, especially its armed forces, the salient aspect of the Maoist army is that its lower to middle level armed cadre constitutes almost entirely of *adivasi*s most of whom joined the forces as children. The significance of this singular fact is not fully grasped even in the Left-liberal circles. Thus, in one extreme, we are told that there is no difference between a Maoist and an *adivasi*, the Maoist army is a 'people's army', etc. (Roy, 2010a). In Chapter Four, we saw in some detail how this army is formed by recruiting hapless and hungry *adivasi* children. We may add that, by the same token, the Chhattisgarh state also could claim to have launched a 'people's army' since its over 6,000-strong Koya commandos consisted basically of *adivasi* youth of roughly the same age group as the Maoist armed cadre; importantly, a large number of Koya commandos were in fact deserters from Maoist ranks.

The phenomena of Maoist guerrillas and militias, on the one hand, and the state's Koya commandos, on the other, bring out the darkest side of the catastrophe faced by *adivasi*s of Dandakaranya. A vast unarmed population is not only caught in the crossfire between two insidious forces at war with each other for control of land and people, the children of this population are actually incorporated in the war itself by both sides to face the first line of fire. In thousands. In a triumph of democracy, the Supreme Court of India, following a writ petition from the civil society, has ordered disarming and safe rehabilitation of Koya commandos (see Chapter One). Who will bell the Maoists?

In a recent piece, the anthropologist Ramachandra Guha (2011) – who was one of the said petitioners – suggests a twin course of action: (a) Make *adivasi*s equal partners in economic growth; and (b) contain extremism through a well-trained, well-paid, and highly focused police force. The problem with this prescription is that 'extremism' in this context constitutes almost entirely of *adivasi*s themselves. So, the actions of the 'well trained, well paid, and highly focused police force' will be directed mostly at *adivasi*s. How can you make *adivasi* 'equal partners' while you plan to kill them in droves? Most bullets that are fired in Dandakaranya today hit an *adivasi* (Bhatia, 2011a; Mitra, 2011). For instance, *adivasi* SPOs have borne the major brunt of Maoist violence. In the 'celebrated' attack on the police camp in Rani Bodili, twenty-seven SPOs were killed. As Balagopal (2006) reminded us, 'all militant movements have killed more people of their own social base than their purported enemy classes'. As for the police bullets, *adivasi*s, armed and unarmed, are the *only* targets. Thus, while Roy fails to see the historical distinction between *adivasi*s and Maoists, Guha makes too sharp a statist distinction between them. Apart from the bullets and IEDs, the fate of *adivasi*s is now caught in this verbal crossfire.

My basic point is that these guerrillas and militias joined the Maoists as children largely due to famine-like conditions in their homes. They were carefully picked one by one over decades; there was no revolutionary upsurge. In that sense, they are not voluntary 'revolutionaries' determined to pursue a well understood ideology. It is understandable that after spending years in forests with constant indoctrination on 'class enemies', some of them might have turned into doctrinaire Maoists themselves. However, the very phenomenon of Koya commandos also shows that thousands of them have no ideological attachment to the Maoist party. Even when they do, they have been subjected to historical duress both from the callous state and Maoists. Now these *adivasi* young people face grave danger to their lives because of the mindless adventurism of their leaders overzealous to seize state power. The singular civilisational goal right now is to save them even if they are armed. That's one side of the story.

The other side is that, no matter how vociferous a tiny section of the civil society is about the atrocious Operation Green Hunt, the state is unlikely to listen largely because, especially after the 2009 elections, the Left-liberal forces in the country are in complete disarray in terms of their ability to influence government policies. In any case, the official Left is party to the aggression of the state on this issue (see Chapter One). For the rest of the splintered Left, meetings at the Gandhi Peace Foundation and sit-ins at Jantar Mantar in the national capital Delhi and occasional online petitions, etc., will not have any effect beyond creating a few ripples in respected but peripheral journals and websites. I am not suggesting that these efforts should be discontinued; just that they won't help save *adivasi*s right now when the bullets are already being fired. So, OGH will continue in one form and another until Maoists lose or decide to surrender arms. The Maoist leadership itself won't surrender voluntarily. As a result, *adivasi* young people will continue to get killed, and a wide *adivasi* population will be held hostage to massive state and vengeful Maoist violence.

Insofar as the state is concerned, security 'experts' such as K.P.S. Gill advocate the belligerent view that talking to insurgents can be meaningful only in a context in which the state has the military upperhand; presumably, such was the context in Andhra Pradesh in 2004 when some talks with Maoists took place. As noted, those talks failed. Setting aside the cynical militarism underlying Gill's proposal, the real issue is that the non-participating *adivasi*s will be subjected to mass violence until Gill's preferred scenario obtains.

Looking at the problem militarily, there are two conflicting aspects to the projected length of the protracted war. On the one hand, compared to Maoists, far more restricted armed insurgencies in the North-East have continued for decades. On the other, a far better equipped insurgency in Sri Lanka – with LTTE's loads of foreign money, armored vehicles, missiles, boats, and airplanes – was ultimately comprehensively defeated by a rather primitive Sri

Lankan army after nearly two decades of horrifying civil war. To emphasise, this time the Maoist war preparations are such that it will take many years before they can be militarily subdued. In the year 2009 when the full scale paramilitary offensive started, Home Minister Chidambaram asked for three years. More recently in mid-2011, retiring Home Secretary G. Pillai stretched the upper-limit to between five and seven years.[23] Jairam Ramesh, who is the current Central minister for rural development, does not see the 'conflict vanishing in the next 20 years.'[24] Except for meaningless quips about 'development', the government is apparently unconcerned about what happens to the millions of *adivasi*s in the meantime. Unless some non-statist direction to peace is found, *adivasi*s will be subjected to a repeat of catastrophic history.

The only option for saving *adivasi* lives then is to create conditions for *adivasi*s themselves to surrender and return to safety. The safety of these children is primarily the responsibility of the allegedly democratic state. But beyond the routine mechanism of surrender to the police, the state is unlikely to initiate any broad humanitarian action. Given the record of the police, including the sinister method of turning ultras into 'surrendered militants' which is a euphemism for police informer, *adivasi* communities are not likely to encourage their children, and especially their women, to surrender to the police.[25]

However, if the policy of universal amnesty and genuine rehabilitation of the guerrillas and militias after their surrender is supervised transparently by eminent civil society persons – especially those who are known for their peace initiatives and have a long history of respectable grassroots work among *adivasi*s – the people might view the policy in a different light, and might encourage their children to return to safety. There is a slim opening in this, but any straw afloat needs to be given a chance in this otherwise abysmal, sinking situation.

I am fully aware that a programme of surrender of perceived resistance forces is viewed as 'reactionary' from the radical perspective, whatever the character of the resistance. Perhaps it is also 'politically incorrect' to propose a separation between the leaders and foot soldiers of a movement. I myself shared this opinion for several decades before I realised that it was based on insufficient facts about the Maoist upheaval together with a myopic radical imagination. Hence, a book was needed to disentangle the parts that formed the suggested radical perspective to show that each of them is untenable in context. And so, the standard radical perspective does not apply here, just as it also does not apply to a variety of non-state forces across the world.

Specifically, it is simply false that the Maoist upheaval signals genuine resistance in the Indian context. Notwithstanding its stated egalitarian goals and some initiatives in that direction in its early phase, the Maoist insurgency in India has progressively degenerated into despotic militarism; as such it has turned into another instrument for controlling and humiliating the poor and the marginalised. A 'movement' whose basic resource of militancy constitutes of starving, illiterate, and gun-toting *adivasi* children cannot be glorified as 'resistance'. What is the radical priority in this context, some preconceived radical imagination unsubstantiated by facts or the life and livelihood of millions of people?

In the preceding discussion, I attempted to show that every other option to save *adivasi*s from massive disaster — except the one just proposed — is unavailable. The only available option is to make a determined humanitarian effort to enable *adivasi*s to return to safety. To that end, I propose that the state announce total and universal amnesty to the young *adivasi* people in the militias and the PLGA — and a safe and concrete programme for their rehabilitation — once they surrender (only) to a citizen's body comprising eminent individuals. Beyond the half-hearted and token appeals to Maoists made by a variety of individuals and organisations so far, the proposed peace committee must announce a transparent and nationwide call in various languages asking Maoists to lay down arms. The programme should be such that, even if the Maoist leadership is initially opposed or reluctant to lay down arms, the foot soldiers of the Maoist army are able to locate a safe and dignified passage for doing so. It is hoped that, once the process begins with increasing approval from *adivasi* communities, the Maoist leadership itself will return to sanity and follow suit.

The proposed citizen's body may consist of individuals who are already involved in the peace process with Maoists such as the Independent Citizen's Initiative, the people who took part in the earlier peace process in Andhra, the eminent citizens who undertook the recent peace march in Chhattisgarh, and the like. In general, the most important criterion is that the selected individuals should be acceptable to the besieged *adivasi*s. For that, the peace process must locate individuals who have devoted their lives to grassroots work to save *adivasi* habitats. It should also include people who have long been associated with human rights issues and have taken active part in people's tribunals opposing the state's security-centric approach to the issue. It is not difficult to chart an impressive list of individuals who meet the suggested criteria.[26]

Further, once a broad-based organisation is contemplated, it will naturally include representatives from the higher judiciary, present and past administrators of *adivasi* areas known for their commitment to and popularity with *adivasi* communities, members of human rights, minorities, and women's commissions, and the like. It will also be important to incorporate honest and sincere local politicians such as the known CPI leaders in Bastar, and the local activists and missionaries in Chhattisgarh. It is not going to be easy. It has to take the form of an *andolan*, bargaining fiercely with the state to protect the returning youth.

In the face of the vested interests of the state and the Maoists in continuing the war, the only option for saving *adivasi*s is for civil society to intervene massively as outlined. As noted, the Left-liberal section of civil society does not have the resources of resistance to compel either Chidambaram or Maoists to drop arms. It can try to reach the people concerned, but without expecting miracles. This was the point of the peace initiative by Swami Agnivesh, Prof Yash Pal, and others. It collapsed because it had no content. The project of universal amnesty with security and dignity might just offer that content, assuming of course that *adivasi*s are rational people not given to mass suicide. They know the middle to lower level Maoists, they are their children; that is precisely why they are likely to be interested to bring them back to safety, provided other things are equal.

More importantly, the Union Home Ministry may be also interested both for propaganda purposed and for a possible way out of the escalating conflict involving massive losses to the security forces. There are other logistic issues such as (a) the demoralisation of paramilitary troops attacked by Maoists and shunned by the local population; and (b) the relocation of forces from other theatres of conflict. If civil society helps the guerrillas lay down arms, the government might heave a sigh of relief for now. In that sense, the government may be willing to 'empower' such an initiative with the full backing of the state if the civil society is able to build up the meaningful pressure to demand it.

It stands to reason that no programme for laying down arms will be acceptable to the *adivasi* population if the violence of the state continues. Therefore, as a first confidence building measure, the government must unilaterally announce a complete halt to

OGH for a specified period of, say, one month. A second measure is to release all *adivasi* prisoners charged with Maoist affiliations unconditionally. A third is to pursue all human rights violations by the security forces in that area vigorously and transparently through a comprehensive tribunal.

Many of these measure have been implemented in the past to bring peace in conflict zones. As noted, the Left Front government in West Bengal released almost all naxalite prisoners after assuming power in 1977. Later, similar steps were taken in Mizoram. However, the scale of the conflict in Dandakaranya – and, hence, the suffering of the people – is unprecedented in contemporary Indian history. Extraordinary circumstances require special efforts of statesmanship and involvement of citizens.

To emphasise, the government must

- Halt operation green hunt and announce a unilateral ceasefire for a specific period
- Unconditionally release all *adivasi* prisoners charged with Maoist affiliations
- Announce a transparent programme for laying down of arms by *adivasi* insurgents with guaranteed safety and rehabilitation with dignity
- Constitute a civil society organisation composed of eminent citizens whom *adivasi*s can recognise and trust
- Endow the civil society organisation with full facilities to monitor the laying down of arms and rehabilitation of *adivasi* insurgents
- Withdraw paramilitary forces from areas of conflict in phases as laying down of arms progresses

If the process succeeds while the Maoist leadership continues to resist it, the essentially non-tribal leadership of CPI(Maoist), in their politbureau and central committee, must be brought to justice by a 'well-trained, well-paid, and highly-focused police force', as Ramachandra Guha phrases the security option. After all, no Operation Green Hunt was needed to pursue and arrest leaders like Kobad Ghandy, Amitabha Bagchi, Sushil Roy, Narayan Sanyal, Pramod Mishra, and others.

It is hoped that such a 'security' measure will not be required. As I have tried to indicate during the discussion, there are signs that Maoist leaders like Azad and Kobad Ghandy, perhaps even Kishenji, might have entertained a more peaceful and democratic solution to the problem keeping *adivasi* welfare centrally in mind. There is no doubt that the Maoist upheaval has compelled many wings of the callous state and sections of its priviledged citizenry to finally take strong notice of the plight of *adivasi*s in Dandakaranya and elsewhere. A range of powerful voices, as recorded above, has brought the plunder of the neo-liberal order and its effects on the poorest of the poor to international attention.

The Indian state, including the judiciary, has initiated remedial measures (belatedly) for *adivasi*s such as action against illegal mining and severe punishment to powerful violators, cancellation of problematic MOUs, re-enforcement of *panchayat* in scheduled areas, introduction of forest rights and education acts, additional welfare-funding in conflict zones, and the like. These steps can be extended and significantly implemented only if resistance by the people continues to grow as well. At least subliminally, some of these positive developments have ensued from the challenge thrown by Maoists.

In that crucial sense, the Maoist movement has indeed achieved some of its stated democratic goals even if the Maoist party itself has failed to seize state power. Hopefully, the Maoist leadership will realise the significance of this triumphant moment in the history of the Indian nation and will seize the momentum by laying down arms and joining the growing unarmed resistance.

As Simeon stated, this will 'electrify' the situation. However, if they continue with the futile 'protracted war', the moment will be lost with horrifying consequences for the people they claim to defend.

As for dismantling other undemocratic policies and operations of the state enshrined in the neo-liberal order, there cannot be a single prescription. It will need a 'million mutinies' by democratic organisations of people. Some of these mutinies are already in progress in non-Maoist areas.

Appendix I

INTERVIEW WITH GANAPATHY, GENERAL SECRETARY OF CPI (MAOIST), 2009

[Reproduced with permission from *Open Magazine* and Rahul Pandita]

The supreme commander of CPI(Maoist) talks to *Open Magazine* in his first-ever interview. At first sight, Mupalla Laxman Rao, who is about to turn sixty, looks like a school teacher. In fact, he was one in the early 1970s in Andhra Pradesh's Karimnagar district. In 2009, however, the bespectacled, soft-spoken figure is India's Most Wanted Man. He runs one of the world's largest Left insurgencies – a man known in Home Ministry dossiers as Ganapathy; a man whose writ runs large through fifteen states. The supreme commander of CPI(Maoist) is a science graduate and also holds a B.Ed degree. He still conducts classes, but now they are on guerrilla warfare for other senior Maoists. He replaced the founder of the People's War Group, Kondapalli Sitaramaya, as the party's general-secretary in 1991. Ganapathy is known to change his location frequently, and intelligence reports say he has been spotted in cities such as Hyderabad, Kolkata and Kochi. After months of requests, Ganapathy finally agreed to give a first-ever interview. Somewhere in the impregnable jungles of Dandakaranya, he spoke to Rahul Pandita on issues ranging from the Government's proposed anti-Naxal offensive to Islamist Jihadist movements.

Q. *Lalgarh has been described as the New Naxalbari by CPI(Maoist). How has it become so significant for you?*

A. The Lalgarh mass uprising has, no doubt, raised new hopes among the oppressed people and the entire revolutionary camp in West Bengal. It has great positive impact not only on the people of West Bengal but also on the people all over the country. It has emerged as a new model of mass movement in the country. We had seen similar types of movements earlier in Manipur, directed against army atrocities and the Armed Forces Special Powers Act (AFSPA), in Kashmir, in Dandakaranya and to some extent in Odisha, after the Kalinganagar massacre perpetrated by the Naveen Patnaik government.

There have also been mass movements in Singur and Nandigram but there the role of a section of the ruling classes is also significant. These movements were utilised by the ruling class parties for their own electoral interests. But Lalgarh is a more widespread and more sustained mass political movement that has spurned the leadership of all the parliamentary political parties, thereby rendering them completely irrelevant. The people of Lalgarh had even boycotted the recent Lok Sabha polls, thereby unequivocally demonstrating their anger and frustration with all the reactionary ruling class parties. Lalgarh also has some distinctive features such as a high degree of participation of women, a genuinely democratic character and a wider mobilisation of *adivasi*s. No wonder, it has become a rallying point for the revolutionary-democratic forces in West Bengal.

Q. *If it is a people's movement, how did Maoists get involved in Lalgarh?*

A. As far as our party's role is concerned, we have been working in Paschim Midnapur, Bankura and Purulia, in what is popularly known as Jangalmahal since the 1980s. We fought against the local feudal forces, against the exploitation and oppression by the forest officials, contractors, unscrupulous usurers and the goondaism of both the CPM and Trinamool Congress. The ruling CPM, in particular, has become the chief exploiter and oppressor of *adivasi*s of the region, and it has unleashed its notorious vigilanté gangs called Harmad Vahini on whoever questions its authority. With the state authority in its hands, and with the aid of the police, it is playing a role worse than that of the cruel landlords in other regions of the country. Given this background, anyone who dares to fight against oppression and exploitation by the CPM can win the respect and confidence of the people. Since our party has been fighting uncompromisingly against the atrocities of the CPM goons, it naturally gained the confidence and respect of the people of the region. The police atrocities in the wake of the landmine blast on 2 November [in 2008, from which West Bengal Chief Minister Buddhadeb Bhattacharjee had a narrow escape] acted as the trigger that brought the pent-up anger of the masses into the open. This assumed the form of a long-drawn mass movement, and our party played the role of catalyst.

Q. But not so long ago, the CPM was your friend. You even took arms and ammunition from it to fight the Trinamool Congress. This has been confirmed by a Politburo member of CPI(Maoist) in certain interviews. And now you are fighting the CPM with the help of the Trinamool. How did a friend turn into a foe and vice-versa?

A. This is only partially true. We came to know earlier that some ammunition was taken by our local cadre from the CPM unit in the area. There was, however, no understanding with the leadership of the CPM in this regard. Our approach was to unite all sections of the oppressed masses at the lower levels against the goondaism and oppression of Trinamool goons in the area at that time. And since a section of the oppressed masses were in the fold of the CPM at that time, we fought together with them against Trinamool. Still, taking into consideration the overall situation in West Bengal, it was not a wise step to take arms and ammunition from the CPM even at the local level when the contradiction was basically between two sections of the reactionary ruling classes. Our central committee discussed this, criticised the comrade responsible for taking such a decision, and directed the concerned comrades to stop this immediately. As regards taking ammunition from the Trinamool Congress, I remember that we had actually purchased it not directly from the Trinamool but from someone who had links with the Trinamool. There will never be any conditions or agreements with those selling us arms. That has been our understanding all along. As regards the said interview by our Politburo member, we will verify what he had actually said.

Q. *What are your tactics now in Lalgarh after the massive offensive by the Central and state forces?*

A. First of all, I wish to make it crystal clear that our party will spearhead and stand firmly by the side of the people of Lalgarh and entire Jangalmahal, and draw up tactics in accordance with the people's interests and mandate. We shall spread the struggle against the state everywhere and strive to win over the broad masses to the side of the people's cause. We shall fight the state offensive by mobilising the masses more militantly against the police, Harmad Vahini and CPM goons. The course of the development of the movement, of course, will depend on the level of consciousness and preparedness of the people of the region. The party will take this into consideration while formulating its tactics. The initiative of the masses will be released fully.

Q. *The government has termed Lalgarh a 'laboratory' for anti-Naxal operations. Has your party also learnt any lessons from Lalgarh?*

A. Yes, our party too has a lot to learn from the masses of Lalgarh. Their upsurge was beyond our expectations. In fact, it was the common people, with the assistance of advanced elements influenced by revolutionary politics, who played a crucial role in the formulation of tactics. They formed their own organisation, put forth their charter of demands, worked out various novel forms of struggle, and stood steadfast in the struggle despite the brutal attacks by the police and the social-fascist Harmad gangs. The Lalgarh movement has the support of revolutionary and democratic forces not only in West Bengal but in the entire country. We are appealing to all revolutionary and democratic forces in the country to unite to fight back the fascist offensive by the Buddhadeb government in West Bengal and the UPA government at the Centre. By building the broadest fighting front, and by adopting appropriate tactics of combining the militant mass political movement with armed resistance of the people and our PLGA (People's Liberation Guerilla Army), we will defeat the massive offensive by the Central-state forces. I cannot say more than this at the present juncture.

Q. *The Centre has declared an all-out war against Maoists by branding CPI (Maoist) a terrorist organisation and imposing an all-India ban on the party. How has it affected your party?*

A. Our party has already been banned in several states of India. By imposing the ban throughout the country, the government now wants to curb all our open activities in West Bengal and a few other states where legal opportunities exist to some extent. The government wants to use this draconian UAPA (Unlawful Activities (Prevention) Act) to harass whoever dares to raise a voice against fake encounters, rapes and other police atrocities on the people residing in Maoist-dominated regions. Anyone questioning the state's brutalities will now be branded a terrorist. The real terrorists and biggest threats to the country's security are none other than Manmohan Singh, Chidambaram, Buddhadeb, other ruling class leaders and feudal forces who terrorise the people on a daily basis. The UPA government had declared, as soon as it assumed power for the second time, that it would crush the Maoist 'menace' and it began pouring in huge funds to the states for this purpose. The immediate reason behind this move is the pressure exerted by the comprador bureaucratic bourgeoisie and the imperialists, particularly US imperialists, who want to plunder the resources of our country without any hindrance. These sharks aspire to swallow the rich abundant mineral and forest wealth in the vast contiguous region stretching from Jangalmahal to north Andhra. This region is the wealthiest as well as the most underdeveloped part of our country. These sharks want to loot the wealth and drive *adivasi* people of the region to further impoverishment. Another major reason for the current offensive by the ruling classes is the fear of the rapid growth of the Maoist movement and its increasing influence over a significant proportion of the Indian population. The *Janatana Sarkars* in Dandakaranya and the revolutionary people's committees in Jharkhand, Odisha and parts of some other states have become new models of genuine people's democracy and development. The rulers want to crush these new models of development and genuine democracy, as these are emerging as the real alternative before the people of the country at large.

Q. *The Home Ministry has made preparations for launching a long-term battle against Maoists. A huge force will be soon trying to wrest away areas from your control. How do you plan to confront this offensive?*

A. Successive governments in various states and the Centre have been hatching schemes over the years. But they could not achieve any significant success through their cruel offensive in spite of murdering hundreds of our leaders and cadres. Our party and our movement continued to consolidate and expand to new regions. From two or three states, the movement has now spread to over fifteen states, giving the jitters to the ruling classes. Particularly after the merger of the erstwhile MCCI and People's War in September 2004 [the merger between these groups led to the formation of CPI(Maoist)], the UPA government has unleashed the most cruel all-round offensive against the Maoist movement. Yet our party continued to grow despite suffering some severe losses. In the past three years, in particular, our PLGA has achieved several significant victories. We have been confronting the continuous offensive of the enemy with the support and active involvement of the masses. We shall confront the new offensive of the enemy by stepping up such heroic resistance and preparing the entire party, PLGA, the various revolutionary parties and organisations and the entire people. Although the enemy may achieve a few successes in the initial phase, we shall certainly overcome and defeat the government offensive with the active mobilisation of the vast masses and the support of all the revolutionary and democratic forces in the country. No fascist regime or military dictator in history could succeed in suppressing forever the just and democratic struggles of the people through brute force, but were, on the contrary, swept away by the high tide of people's resistance. People, who are the makers of history, will rise up like a tornado under our party's leadership to wipe out the reactionary blood-sucking vampires ruling our country.

Q. *Why do you think CPI(Maoist) suffered a serious setback in Andhra Pradesh?*

A. It was due to several mistakes on our part that we suffered a serious setback in most of Andhra Pradesh by 2006. At the same time, we should also look at the setback from another angle. In any protracted people's war, there will be advances and retreats. If we look at the situation in Andhra Pradesh from this perspective, you will understand that what we did there is a kind of retreat. Confronted with a superior force, we chose to temporarily retreat our forces from some regions of Andhra Pradesh, extend and develop our bases in the surrounding regions and then hit back at the enemy. Now even though we received a setback, it should be borne in mind that this setback is a temporary one. The objective conditions in which our revolution began in Andhra Pradesh have not undergone any basic change. This very fact continues to serve as the basis for the growth and intensification of our movement. Moreover, we now have a more consolidated mass base, a relatively better-trained people's guerilla army and an all-India party with deep roots among the basic classes who comprise the backbone of our revolution. This is the reason why the reactionary rulers are unable to suppress our revolutionary war, which is now raging in several states in the country. We had taken appropriate lessons from the setback suffered by our party in Andhra Pradesh and, based on these lessons, drew up tactics in other states. Hence we are able to fight back the cruel all-round offensive of the enemy effectively, inflict significant losses on the enemy, preserve our subjective forces, consolidate our party, develop a people's liberation guerilla army, establish embryonic forms of new democratic people's governments in some pockets, and take the people's war to a higher stage. Hence we have an advantageous situation, overall, for reviving the movement in Andhra Pradesh. Our revolution advances wave-like and periods of ebb yield place to periods of high tide.

Q. *What are the reasons for the setback suffered by the LTTE in Sri Lanka?*

A. There is no doubt that the movement for a separate sovereign Tamil Eelam has suffered a severe setback with the defeat and considerable decimation of the LTTE. The Tamil people and the national liberation forces are now leaderless. However, the Tamil people at large continue to cherish nationalist aspirations for a separate Tamil homeland. The conditions that gave rise to the movement for Tamil Eelam, in the first place, prevail to this day. The Sinhala-chauvinist Sri Lankan ruling classes can never change their policy of discrimination against the Tamil nation, its culture, language, etcetera. The jingoistic rallies and celebrations organised by the government and Sinhala chauvinist parties all over Sri Lanka in the wake of Prabhakaran's death and the defeat of the LTTE show the national hatred for Tamils nurtured by Sinhala organisations and the extent to which the minds of ordinary Sinhalese are poisoned with such chauvinist frenzy. The conspiracy of the Sinhala ruling classes in occupying Tamil territories is similar to that of the Zionist rulers of Israel. The land-starved Sinhala people will now be settled in Tamil areas. The entire demography of the region is going to change. The ground remains fertile for the resurgence of the Tamil liberation struggle. Even if it takes time, the war for a separate Tamil Eelam is certain to revive, taking lessons from the defeat of the LTTE. By adopting a proletarian outlook and ideology, adopting new tactics and building the broadest united front of all nationalist and democratic forces, it is possible to achieve the liberation of the oppressed Tamil nation [in Sri Lanka]. Maoist forces have to grow strong enough to provide leadership and give a correct direction and anti-imperialist orientation to this struggle to achieve a sovereign People's Democratic Republic of Tamil Eelam. This alone can achieve the genuine liberation of the Tamil nation in Sri Lanka.

Q. *Is it true that you received military training from the LTTE initially?*

A. No. It is not a fact. We clarified this several times in the past.

Q. *But, one of your senior commanders has told me that some senior cadre of the erstwhile PWG did receive arms training and other support from the LTTE.*

A. Let me reiterate, there is no relation at all between our party and the LTTE. We tried several times to establish relations with the LTTE but its leadership was reluctant to have a relationship with Maoists in India. Hence, there is no question of the LTTE giving training to us. In spite of it, we continued our support to the struggle for Tamil Eelam. However, a few persons who had separated from the LTTE came into our contact and we took their help in receiving initial training in the last quarter of the 1980s.

Q. *Does your party have links with Lashkar-e-Tayyeba or other Islamic militant groups having links with Pakistan?*

A. No. Not at all. This is only mischievous, calculated propaganda by the police officials, bureaucrats and leaders of the reactionary political parties to defame us and thereby justify their cruel offensive against the Maoist movement. By propagating the lie that our party has links with groups linked to Pakistan's ISI, the reactionary rulers of our country want to prove that we too are terrorists and gain legitimacy for their brutal terror campaign against Maoists and the people in the areas of armed agrarian struggle. Trying to prove the involvement of a foreign hand in every just and democratic struggle, branding those fighting for the liberation of the oppressed as traitors to the country, is part of the psychological war of the reactionary rulers.

Q. *What is your party's stand regarding Islamist jihadist movements?*

A. Islamic jihadist movements of today are a product of imperialist – particularly US imperialist – aggression, intervention, bullying, exploitation and suppression of the oil-rich Islamic and Arab countries of West Asia, Afghanistan, Pakistan, Somalia, etcetera, and the persecution of the entire Muslim religious community. As part of their designs for global hegemony, the imperialists, particularly US imperialists, have encouraged and endorsed every war of brazen aggression and brutal attacks by their surrogate state of Israel. Our party unequivocally opposes every attack on Arab and Muslim countries and the Muslim community at large in the name of 'war on global terror'. In fact, Muslim religious fundamentalism is encouraged and fostered by imperialists as long as it serves their interests – as in Saudi Arabia, other Gulf countries and Kuwait, Afghanistan, Iraq and Pakistan.

Q. *But what about attacks perpetrated by the so-called 'Jihadis' on innocent people like it happened on 26/11?*

A. See, Islamic jihadist movements have two aspects: one is their anti-imperialist aspect, and the other their reactionary aspect in social and cultural matters. Our party supports the struggle of Muslim countries and people against imperialism, while criticising and struggling against the reactionary ideology and social outlook of Muslim fundamentalism.

It is only Maoist leadership that can provide correct anti-imperialist orientation and achieve class unity among Muslims as well as people of other religious persuasions. The influence of Muslim fundamentalist ideology and leadership will diminish as communist revolutionaries and other democratic-secular forces increase their ideological influence over the Muslim masses. As communist revolutionaries, we always strive to reduce the influence of the obscurantist reactionary ideology and outlook of the mullahs and maulvis on the Muslim masses, while uniting with all those fighting against the common enemy of the world people – that is, imperialism, particularly American imperialism.

Q. *How do you look at the changes in US policy after Barack Obama took over from George Bush?*

A. Firstly, one would be living in a fool's paradise if one imagines that there is going to be any qualitative change in American policy – whether internal or external – after Barack Obama took over from George Bush. In fact, the policies on national security and foreign affairs pursued by Obama over the past eight months have shown the essential continuity with those of his predecessor. The ideological and political justification for these regressive policies at home and aggressive policies abroad is the same trash put forth by the Bush administration – the so-called 'global war on terror', based on outright lies and slander. Worse still, the policies have become even more aggressive under Obama with his planned expansion of the US-led war of aggression in Afghanistan into the territory of Pakistan. The hands of this new killer-in-chief of the pack of imperialist wolves are already stained with the blood of hundreds of women and children who are cruelly murdered in relentless missile attacks from Predator drones in Afghanistan and Pakistan. And, within the US itself, bail-outs for the tiny corporate elite and attacks on democratic and human rights of US citizens continue without any change. The oppressed people and nations of the world are now confronting an even more formidable and dangerous enemy in the form of an African-American president of the most powerful military machine and world gendarme. The world people should unite to wage a more relentless, more militant and more consistent struggle against the American marauders led by

Barack Obama and pledge to defeat them to usher in a world of peace, stability and genuine democracy.

Q. *How do you look at the current developments in Nepal?*

A. As soon as the Communist Party of Nepal (Maoist) [CPN(M)] came to power in alliance with the comprador-feudal parties through the parliamentary route in Nepal, we had pointed out the grave danger of imperialist and Indian expansionist intervention in Nepal and how they would leave no stone unturned to overthrow the government led by CPN(M). As long as Prachanda did not defy the directives of the Indian government, it was allowed to continue, but when it began to go against Indian hegemony, it was immediately pulled down. CPN-UML withdrew support to the Prachanda-led government upon the advice of American imperialists and Indian expansionists. We disagreed with the line of peaceful transition pursued by the UCPN(M) in the name of tactics. We decided to send an open letter to the UCPN(M). It was released in July 2009. We made our party's stand clear in the letter. We pointed out that the UCPN(M) chose to reform the existing state through an elected constituent assembly and a bourgeois democratic republic instead of adhering to the Marxist-Leninist understanding on the imperative to smash the old state and establish a proletarian state. This would have been the first step towards the goal of achieving socialism through the radical transformation of society and all oppressive class relations. It is indeed a great tragedy that the UCPN(M) has chosen to abandon the path of protracted people's war and pursue a parliamentary path in spite of having de facto power in most of the countryside. It is heartening to hear that a section of the leadership of the UCPN(M) has begun to struggle against the revisionist positions taken by Comrade Prachanda and others. Given the great revolutionary traditions of the UCPN(M), we hope that the inner-party struggle will repudiate the right opportunist line pursued by its leadership, give up revisionist stands and practices, and apply minds creatively to the concrete conditions of Nepal.

Q. *Of late, the party has suffered serious losses of party leadership at the central and state level. Besides, it is widely believed that some of the senior-most Maoist leaders, including you, have become quite old and suffer from serious illnesses, which is also cited as one of the reasons for the surrenders. What is the effect of the losses and surrenders on the movement? How are you dealing with problems arising out of old age and illnesses?*

A. (Smiles...) This type of propaganda is being carried out continuously, particularly by the Special Intelligence Branch (SIB) of Andhra Pradesh. It is a part of the psychological war waged by intelligence officials and top police brass aimed at confusing and demoralising supporters of the Maoist movement. It is a fact that some of the party leaders at the central and state level could be described as senior citizens according to criteria used by the government, that is, those who have crossed the threshold of sixty years. You can start calling me too a senior citizen in a few months (smiles). But old age and ill-health have never been a serious problem in our party until now. You can see the 'senior citizens' in our party working for sixteen to eighteen hours a day and covering long distances on foot. As for surrenders, it is a big lie to say that old age and ill-health have been a reason for some of the surrenders. When Lanka Papi Reddy, a former member of our central committee, surrendered in the beginning of last year, the media propagated that more surrenders of our party leaders will follow due to ill health. The fact is that Papi Reddy surrendered due to his loss of political conviction and his petty-bourgeois false prestige and ego. Hence he was not prepared to face the party after he was demoted by the central committee for his anarchic behaviour with a woman comrade. Some senior leaders of our party, like comrades Sushil Roy and Narayan Sanyal, had become a nightmare for the ruling classes even when they were in their mid-sixties. Hence they were arrested, tortured and imprisoned despite their old age and ill-health. The government is doing everything possible to prevent them from getting bail. Even if someone in our party is old, he/she continues to serve the revolution by doing whatever work possible. For instance, Comrade Niranjan Bose, who died recently at the age of ninety-two, had been carrying out revolutionary propaganda until his martyrdom. The social fascist rulers were so scared of this nonagenarian Maoist revolutionary that they had even arrested him four years back. Such is the spirit of Maoist revolutionaries – and power of the ideology of Marxism-Leninism-Maoism which they hold high. When there are serious illnesses, or physical and mental limitations to perform normal work, such comrades are given suitable work.

Q. *But what about the arrests and elimination of some of your senior leadership? How do you intend to fill up such losses?*

A. Well, it is a fact that we lost some senior leaders at the state and central level in the past four or five years. Some leaders were secretly arrested and murdered in the most cowardly manner. Many other and state leaders were arrested and placed behind bars in the recent past in Jharkhand, Bihar, Chhattisgarh, Odisha, West Bengal, Maharashtra, Haryana and other states. The loss of leadership will have a grave impact on the party and Indian revolution as a whole. We are reviewing the reasons for the losses regularly and devising ways and means to prevent further losses. By adopting strictly secret methods of functioning and foolproof underground mechanisms, by enhancing our mass base, vigilance and local intelligence, smashing enemy intelligence networks and studying their plans and tactics, we hope to check further losses. At the same time, we are training and developing new revolutionary leadership at all levels to fill up the losses.

Q. *How do you sum up the present stage of war between your forces and those of the Indian State?*

A. Our war is in the stage of strategic defence. In some regions, we have an upper hand, while in others the enemy has the upper hand. Overall, our forces have been quite successful in carrying out a series of tactical counter-offensive operations against the enemy in our guerilla zones in the past few years. It is true that our party has suffered some serious leadership losses, but we are able to inflict serious losses on the enemy too. In fact, in the past three years, the enemy forces suffered more casualties than we did. The enemy has been trying all means at their disposal to weaken, disrupt and crush our party and movement. They have tried covert agents and informers, poured in huge amounts of money to buy off weak elements in the revolutionary camp, and announced a series of rehabilitation packages and other material incentives to lure people away from the revolutionary camp. Thousands of crores of rupees have been sanctioned for police modernisation, training and for raising additional commando forces; for increasing Central forces; for training Central and state forces in counter-insurgency warfare; and for building roads, communication networks and other infrastructure for the rapid movement of their troops in our guerilla zones. The Indian state has set up armed vigilante groups and provided total support to the indescribable atrocities committed by these armed gangs on the people. Psychological warfare against Maoists was taken to unheard of levels. Nevertheless, we continued to make greater advances, consolidated the party and the revolutionary people's committees at various levels, strengthened the PLGA qualitatively and quantitatively, smashed the enemy's intelligence network in several areas, effectively countered the dirty psychological war waged by the enemy, and foiled the enemy's all-out attempts to disrupt and smash our movement. The successes we had achieved in several tactical counter-offensive operations carried out across the country in recent days, the militant mass movements in several states, particularly against displacement and other burning issues of the people, initiatives taken by our revolutionary people's governments in various spheres – all these have had a great impact on the people, while also demoralising enemy forces. There are reports of desertions and disobedience of orders by the jawans posted in Maoist-dominated areas. Quite a few have refused to undertake training in jungle warfare or take postings in our areas, and had to face suspension. This trend will grow with the further advance of our people's war. Overall, our party's influence has grown stronger and it has now come to be recognised as the only genuine alternative before the people.

Q. *How long will this stage of strategic defence last, with the Centre ready to go for the jugular?*

A. The present stage of strategic defence will last for some more time. It is difficult to predict how long it will take to pass this stage and go to the stage of strategic equilibrium or strategic stalemate. It depends on the transformation of our guerrilla zones into base areas, creation of more guerrilla zones and red resistance areas across the country, the development of our PLGA. With the ever-intensifying crisis in all spheres due to the anti-people policies of pro-imperialist, pro-feudal governments, the growing frustration and anger of the masses resulting from the most rapacious policies of loot and plunder pursued by the reactionary ruling classes, we are confident that the vast masses of the country will join the ranks of revolutionaries and take the Indian revolution to the next stage.

Appendix II

SANHATI STATEMENT AGAINST THE GOVERNMENT OF INDIA'S PLANNED MILITARY OFFENSIVE IN ADIVASI-POPULATED REGIONS

To Dr Manmohan Singh, Prime Minister, Government of India, South Block, Raisina Hill, New Delhi, India-110 011.

We are deeply concerned by the Indian government's plans for launching an unprecedented military offensive by army and paramilitary forces in the adivasi (indigenous people)-populated regions of Andhra Pradesh, Chattisgarh, Jharkhand, Maharashtra, Odisha and West Bengal states. The stated objective of the offensive is to 'liberate' these areas from the influence of Maoist rebels. Such a military campaign will endanger the lives and livelihoods of millions of the poorest people living in those areas, resulting in massive displacement, destitution and human rights violation of ordinary citizens. To hunt down the poorest of Indian citizens in the name of trying to curb the shadow of an insurgency is both counter-productive and vicious. The ongoing campaigns by paramilitary forces, buttressed by anti-rebel militias, organised and funded by government agencies, have already created a civil war like situation in some parts of Chattisgarh and West Bengal, with hundreds killed and thousands displaced. The proposed armed offensive will not only aggravate the poverty, hunger, humiliation and insecurity of the adivasi people, but also spread it over a larger region. Grinding poverty and abysmal living conditions that has been the lot of India's adivasi population has been complemented by increasing state violence since the neoliberal turn in the policy framework of the Indian state in the early 1990s. Whatever little access the poor had to forests, land, rivers, common pastures, village tanks and other common property resources has come under increasing attack by the Indian state in the guise of Special Economic Zones (SEZs) and other 'development' projects related to mining, industrial development, Information Technology parks etc. The geographical terrain, where the government's military offensive is planned to be carried out, is very rich in natural resources like minerals, forest wealth and water, and has been the target of large scale appropriation by several corporations. The desperate resistance of the local indigenous people against their displacement and dispossession has in many cases prevented the government-backed corporations from making inroads into these areas. We fear that the government's offensive is also an attempt to crush such popular resistances in order to facilitate the entry and operation of these corporations and to pave the way for unbridled exploitation of the natural resources and the people of these regions. It is the widening levels of disparity and the continuing problems of social deprivation and structural violence, and the state repression on the non-violent resistance of the poor and marginalized against their dispossession, which gives rise to social anger and unrest and takes the form of political violence by the poor. Instead of addressing the source of the problem, the Indian state has decided to launch a military offensive to deal with this problem: Kill the poor and not the poverty, seems to be the implicit slogan of the Indian government. We feel that it would deliver a crippling blow to Indian democracy if the government tries to subjugate its own people militarily without addressing their grievances. Even as the short-term military success of such a venture is very doubtful, enormous misery for the common people is not in doubt, as has been witnessed in the case of numerous insurgent movements in the world. We urge the Indian government to immediately withdraw the armed forces and stop all plans for carrying out such military operations that has the potential for triggering a civil war which will inflict widespread misery on the poorest and most vulnerable section of the Indian population and clear the way for the plundering of their resources by corporations. We call upon all democratic-minded people to join us in this appeal.

Signatories include Arundhati Roy, Amit Bhaduri, Prashant Bhushan, Arvind Kejriwal, Anand Patwardhan, Dipankar Bhattacharya, Sumit Sarkar, Tanika Sarkar, Gautam Navlakha, Sumanta Banerjee, Vandana Shiva, D. N. Jha, Uma Chakravarty, Amiya Dev, Kavita Krishnan, Shereen Ratnagar, Mira Shiva, Noam Chomsky, David Harvey, John Bellamy Foster, Gayatri Chakravorty Spivak, James C. Scott, Michael Watts, Mahmood Mamdani, Mira Nair, Howard Zinn, Abha Sur, Gilbert Achcar, Gyanendra Pandey, Justin Podur, Shefali Chandra, Angana Chatterji, Joseph Levine and Ania Loomba.

NOTES

INTRODUCTION

1. For historical reasons, communist China under Mao aligned with Stalin's Russia. Also, the Chinese form of governance adopted Stalinist principles. Consequently, Maoist groups across the world embrace Stalinism as a political doctrine. Mao characterised post-Stalin Russia first as 'revisionist' and then as 'social imperialist'. These terms are used by Maoist groups as well.
   Mao Tse Tung was the transliteration of the Chinese characters by the Wade-Giles romanisation system. It has been superceded by the current official Pinyin style: Mao Zedong.
2. See '30 years of Naxalbari,' http://naxalresistance.wordpress.com/2007/09/17/30-years-of-naxalbari/ [Last Accessed 4 November 2011].
3. See a list of anti-revisionist Leftist parties in the world at www.broadleft.org/antirevi.htm [Last Accessed 4 November 2011]
4. The Philippine model consists of three things: (a) preference, if possible, for a formally elected government over outright dictatorships; (b) near-absolute control over the electoral process by forces favoured by US; and (c) subservience of the elected government to the US's geo-political, military and economic interests. In effect, these are

client states with a formal democratic face. Currently, the Philippines, Colombia and Nicaragua among others satisfy this model; Pakistan is an unstable case. With the Sandinistas coming back to power, Nicaragua may eventually follow an independent course.

5. Indian Maoists are sometimes compared to the Senderistas in Peru in terms of similar tactics such as Batir el campo (hammer the countryside); see Banaji (2010).
6. For a list of these factions, see www.massline.info/India/Indian_Groups.htm [Last accessed 4 November 2011]. The list is slightly dated but fairly accurate.
7. See Florig 2008. Although the report carries the usual disclaimers about the personal views of the author, the US Army wouldn't have cleared the paper for official posting on the Internet if its findings went against US interests.
8. Officially, the Government of India claims that 60 districts of the country are 'affected' by 'Left-Wing Extremism'. The government has announced an Integrated Action Plan for the development of these districts.
9. The Hindu, 19 October 2003. For the programme of CCOMPOSA, see http://kasamaproject.org/2011/03/27/ccomposa-conf-politicalresolution-of-south-asian-maoists/#more-29065 [last accessed 28 December 2011].
10. Ram (1971), Mohanty (1977), Banerjee (1980), Ghosh (2009), Chenoy and Chenoy (2010), Chakravarty and Kujur (2010). TNMT (2008) contains a wealth of original documents, including hitherto secret ones, of the crucial period up to 1972. Bose (2010) depicts largely the point of view of the parliamentary Left. Also, there are some recent personalised accounts of travels in Maoist territory that include dramatic descriptions of armed operations by Maoists and the police, and plenty of 'human' side-stories (Chakravarty, 2008; Satnam, 2010; Mishra and Pandita, 2010; Pandita, 2011); in between, there is some useful information as well, usually undocumented.
11. This third voice includes Balagopal (2007), Banerjee (2009b), Bhattacharya (2010), Chatterjee (2010), Ramachandran (2010), Rana (2010), Sanyal (2010) and others.

CHAPTER 1: DARK CLOUDS OVER DANDAKARANYA

1. 'Report on the Peasant Movement in the Terai,' cited in Sengupta (1970/1983).
2. Recently, these 18 districts have been redivided into 27.
3. http://censusindia.gov.in/2011-prov-results/data_files/ Chhattishgarh/2.%20 Chhattishgarh%20Figures%20at%20a%20 glance. pdf [Last accessed 4 November 2011].
4. I am simplifying a bit here since the actual history of splinter groups that continued with the policy of annihilation is more complex. For example, a faction in Bihar, later called CPI (ML-Liberation) and led by Jauhar, continued the policy alongwith some form of mass line up to about 1975. After Jauhar was killed, Vinod Mishra took over the Liberation-group and adopted more democratic policies that continue today. These details are largely irrelevant by now since CPI (Maoist) is the only major MLM group that continues with versions of the annihilation policy (see Chapter Three).
5. As noted, Maoist military headquarters are located in the Abujmaad area of the Narayanpur district of Chhattisgarh. A former governor of Chhattisgarh reports that the state government made an attempt some years ago to conduct a land-survey of the area which covers about 10,000 of forests. The governor states that 'the surveyors could not move even 2–3 km inside the region because it was mined extensively in concentric circles and remains to be that way even today.' 'Naxalism: threat to internal security,' Center for Security Analysis, 21 May 2010.
6. 'UAVs deployed for anti-naxal ops,' *The Hindustan Times*, 3 September 2011. Apparently, deployment of drones is not proving effective in thick foliage, See 'Heron drone proves a dud in tracking Maoists in Chhattisgarh,' *India Today*, 3 January 2012. http://indiatoday.intoday.in/story/heron-uav-fails-to-track-maoists-in-chattisgarh/1/166919. html [Last accessed 3 January 2012].
7. See Iqbal (2011).
8. These are typically former adivasi rebels who are used by the state both for their murderous skills acquired at a young age and for securing information about rebel hideouts, movements, etc.

9. For a vivid description see Mahaprashasta (2011).
10. See Simeon (2010) for a list of civilian killings, mainly of adivasis, by Maoists in a few months of 2006 alone.
11. Supreme Court of India, Writ Petition (Civil) No. 250 of 2007, order of 5 July 2011. For a comprehensive report, see Venkatesan (2011).
12. 'Chhattisgarh to absorb SPOs in police,' The Times of India, July 23 2011. Also, 'SPOs may be absorbed as auxiliary force in Red zone,' The Times of India, 27 July 2011. These decisions were reached within weeks of the Supreme Court judgment.
13. See Hardikar (2011)
14. See Swami (2011).
15. For a series of recommendations in that direction to tackle the Maoist issue, see Ajai Sahni (2006).
16. On these issues, distinguished authors have published primary work which is easily accessible. This includes economists such as Utsa Patnaik (2007a; 2007b; 2010), Jean Dreze (Dreze and Sen, 1991; Deaton and Dreze, 2009), Arjun Sengupta (2008; 2009), and investigative journalists like Palagummi Sainath (1996; 2009).
17. Planning Commission figures, released 21 May 2001, The Times of India.
18. 'Unions pick up reforms gauntlet,' Government Business, p.viii, The Times of India, 25 May 2001.
19. Ibid.
20. It is another matter that when the parliamentary left happened to gain access to substantial money- and muscle-power as in West Bengal, their electoral strategies began to resemble those of right-wing parties (see Chapter 5).
21. Hardikar, op. cit.
22. I must note that the erstwhile PWG in Andhra did engage in some mass work and brought some relief to adivasis and peasants in the early years, as the late K. Balagopal (2006) points out. Thus, some sections of the poor, especially the older generation, retained some affection for Maoists after they were driven out. Maoist methods seem to have changed drastically on this score since the merger of PWG and MCC in 2004.

23. Another impressive struggle, among many others of a similar character, is the valiant resistance put up by villagers in Odisha in association with urban resistance groups against the giant multinational POSCO. I did not mention it in the main text since the resistance is currently unfolding at the time of writing. For a recent report, see P. Sainath, (2011).
24. Maoists themselves were quite appreciative of the effort, as was Mr. Chidambaram (see Chapter 6).
25. This was written before the historic assembly elections of 2011 in West Bengal in which the left was routed. It will be interesting to observe the stand of the left on operation Green Hunt as they occupy the opposition benches in both the Indian parliament and the West Bengal assembly.
26. The draconian Unlawful Activities Prevention Act hastily adopted in 2004 by the first United Progressive Alliance, (UPA) supported by parliamentary left. The speaker of the Indian parliament at that point, Somnath Chatterjee, who presided over the quick and smooth adoption of this Act, was himself an important leader of parliamentary left.

CHAPTER 2: FRAGILE DEMOCRACY

1. Unsurprisingly, spokespersons for the elites have always repented the fact that Indian democracy has failed to replicate the two-party system enshrined in the 'Westminster' model of parliamentary democracy. For a recent exposition, see P.S. Appu, 2011.
2. See Appu 2011 above, for a quick survey.
3. The growing 'anti-state' role of the corporate media explains in part the otherwise puzzling phenomenon of impressive space given to some of the radical critics of the state and the enthusiasm with which young, elite sections of the population have embraced these critiques. Even when these write-ups promote the Maoist cause, their ire is typically directed at state functionaries such as the prime minister, home minister, finance minister, police, human rights commission and judiciary. They also focus primarily on cases of massive corruption or diversion of funds that involve public

servants. Beyond a general mention of 'corporate loot' and extreme cases such as the mining mafia, these write-ups seldom engage in a detailed and direct exposure of big business whose actions characterise the 'rapaciousness' of the neo-liberal order.

4. As we will see in Chapter 4, during the season a large section of the Gond tribe in Dandakaranya, especially the women, is engaged in harvesting tendu leaves. In the 'liberated zones', this economic activity is completely controlled by the the Maoist party in collusion with private contractors and other forms of mafia. However, instead of using this control to drive the Gonds to the ballot-box, Maoists drive their children to armed struggle with a much larger aim in mind. Prabhat Patnaik (2010) rightly comments that 'underneath the veneer of "Maoism" we are witnessing a particularly vicious form of "identity politics".'
5. See Palshikar, 2011.
6. See the report on the rapid expansion of various armed groups, typically as 'liberation armies' in Assam, *The Statesman*, 21 January 1998. For more recent coverage including the Maoist groups, see Mishra and Pandita (2010).
7. The recent attempts by the parliamentary left to form a 'united front' with these regional fiefdoms – instead of forming alliances with an impressive range of other left-Socialist forums and grassroots organisations – is a clear sign of its political bankruptcy.
8. Lecture at the panel on Religion and Material Life, 64th session of the Indian History Congress, Mysore, 29–30 December 2003.
9. See Dharkar 2002. Also, 'State Sponsored Genocide: Factsheet Gujarat 2002', CPM Publications, 2002.
10. Within months after the carnage in Gujarat, the same media turned around and vigorously supported the regime in its 'India shining' campaign. The attack on Muslims in Gujarat, though still held to be condemnable, was systematically projected as an aberration.
11. Domesticism: Although religions such as Christianity, Islam, and, growingly, Hinduism aim for universal coverage, all religions typically embed themselves in local cultures to attain a variety of ethnic identities. 'Black' Christianity has a markedly different cultural form than 'white' Christianity. I was most impressed with telling

cultural differences between 'French' and 'Tamil' Christianity during Christmas celebrations in Pondicherry in 2010. In that sense, religious institutions are common grounds for preservation of local cultures in the face of cultural onslaughts from outside. When the cultural onslaught is accompanied by imperialist agenda, these institutions can in fact play a limited anti-imperialist role, culturally speaking.
12. It also explains why the elite, intellectual sections of the people feel less attracted to religions: They have other secular resources in which these universal human dimensions are satisfied – access to a high-culture, for example.

CHAPTER 3: ROLE OF INTELLECTUALS

1. There is growing evidence by now that many of the terrorist attacks that were previously ascribed to 'jehadists' are actually the handiwork of Hindu terror groups. For a detailed and powerful account of this phenomenon, see Teesta Setalvad (2008); also, Smruti Koppikar et al. (2010) and Gatade (2011).
2. *Revolutionary Democracy*, Vol. 9, No. 2, p. 51 for the full text of the letter. See this journal for information on Delhi University Teachers in Defence of S.A.R. Gilani.
3. For the role of the media, see the press statement of September 18, 2003 from Delhi University Teachers in Defence of S.A.R. Gilani reported in *The Statesman, The Hindu, Navbharat Times, The Asian Age*, and other papers on 19 September. See *The Times of India* (X-files, 21 September 2003) for another example of the biased role of the media; see the responses from Delhi University teachers (*The Times of India*, Letters to the Editor, 7 and 10 October 2003). For a general survey and analysis, see Mukherji (2005).
4. See the JTSA report, '"Encounter" at Batla House: unanswered questions', http://document.teacherssolidarity.org/Encounter%20at%20Batla%20House-%20Unanswered%20Question-%20JTSA%20REPoRT.pdf [Last accessed 28 December 2011]. Also Mukherji (2008b).
5. Azamgarh is alleged to be the origin of the 'terrorists' involved in the serial blasts according to the police.

6. See Mukherji (2009c) for more details and links to all the petitions mentioned above.
7. See 'Alternative platform for India's dynamic politics", *The Sunday Guardian*, 22 December 2011.
8. http://sanhati.com/excerpted/1824/ [Last Accessed 4 November 2011]. Also, Appendix II. The statement also contained a 'background note' that basically elaborated on the points mentioned in the statement without adding any new dimensions.
9. For example, see the maps in Chakravarty (2008) and Chakravarty and Kujur (2010). See also the rather colourful map (apparently produced by Maoists themselves) reproduced in Ajai Sahni (2006). Also, the map produced by South Asia Terrorism portal reproduced in 'The red scourge returns: the strategic challenge of maoist insurgency in India and South Asia,' by Lieutenant Colonel William R. Florig, United States Army Reserve, US Army War College, Carlisle Barracks, 9 May 2008.
10. In an interview to the journal *Mainstream*, Maoist spokesperson Azad traced the demise of the LTTE to its 'non-proletarian' character (Azad, 2010c). I will evaluate the 'proletarian' character of the Maoist movement as I proceed.
11. It is important to record that, in the intellectual campaigns against the Indian state's 'war on terror', mentioned above, not even a hint of indirect support to the 'jehadi' terrorists was ever offered. It was always felt that if the 'civil society' is to be in genuine solidarity with the people, it must maintain opposition to all forms of terror directed against the people. This criterion applies to Maoist terror as well.
12. This is probably an unfair analogy – unfair to Pol Pot – because General Pol Pot, after all, was a tall leader of the Cambodian revolution who fought for decades in the jungles to liberate Cambodia from a brutal US invasion. According to Kanu Sanyal (2010), Charu Mazumdar did not even physically participate in the original peasant uprising in Naxalbari although he contrived to steal the credit for it.
13. The qualification 'almost' is needed because there were prominent objections to the thoughts of Mao in the Indian communist

movement throughout. In fact, there were objections to Mao's thoughts in the broad naxalite movement also. one of the prominent voices was comrade Moni Guha who was not included in the AICCCR orchestrated by Charu Mazumdar and his group which at that point included the likes of Kanu Sanyal, Sushital Roychoudhury, Souren Bose, Jangal Santhal and Ashim Chatterjee.

14. From Simeon (2010), emphasis added. Simeon cites from Mazumdar (1970). A jotedar is a landlord who owns substantial tracts of agricultural land.
15. See Sengupta (1970/1983) for a vivid 'on-line' account of vicious divisions in the movement from the earliest stages. Sengupta, a veteran revolutionary of those times, specifically targets Charu Mazumdar and the coterie around him which, at that time, included Kanu Sanyal and Satya Narain Sinha (SNS).
16. It is unclear if the decisions to 'expel' Mazumdar and 'elect' SNS in his place, as reported by Banaji, were formally adopted in a meeting of either the central committee or the party congress of the original CPI(ML) itself. SNS, no doubt, broke away to form his own organisation, as noted. Maoists and a number of other groups of course maintain that SNS and others simply betrayed the movement: 'erstwhile leaders of the CPI(ML) like SNS, Kanu Sanyal, Ashim Chatterjee etc. merely sought to throw blame on [Charu Mazumdar] and escape into the revisionist camp'. See '30 years of Naxalbari,' http://naxalresistance.wordpress.com/2007/09/17/30years-of-naxalbari/ [Last Accessed 4 November 2011].
17. Banerjee's piece was published months before Roy's (2010a).
18. *WikiLeaks* cable 10MUMBAI12, Anti-Maoist operations In Chhattisgarh Begin: Activists Worry About Potential Human Rights Violations, Item #11.
19. However, it is quite possible that the consuls are themselves biased or inadequately informed about the issues they report on.
20. Yeddyurappa has obtained bail recently on ground of poor health!
21. See the *WikiLeaks* disclosure cited above.
22. A careful study of reports from the ground suggests that for the first year of Salwa Judum operations, Maoists did nothing to protect

the victims; they just retreated to their hideouts in the unaffected areas. Only when the repression escalated further and the victims started blaming Maoists for their plight that Maoists decided to attack Salwa Judum camps in order to save their adivasi support.
23. For some recent evidence, see 'Naxals put price tag on road projects in Bihar', *Indian Express*, 2 August 2011. See also 'Tendu leaves, illegal mining dictate game plan in Naxal heartland', *The Hindu*, 9 August 2011.
24. Except, of course, the classic case of Bailadila mines in Rajnandgaon which supplies iron ore to the Bhilai steel plant. The legendary activist Shankar Guha Neogi organised the mine-workers splendidly under the banner of Chhattisgarh Mukti Morcha (CMM) until he was brutally murdered in 1991 by state agents in collusion with the mining mafia. Although Maoists were already well-established in the nearby Bastar area, they had no role in the wonderful resistance put up by the miners under the leadership of Guha Neogi. The CMM, founded by Guha Neogi, continues to organise worker's struggle in the area.

CHAPTER 4: ARMS OVER PEOPLE

1. Nigam (2010a) observes that the 'real challenge lies in finding ways of decoding the mass of materials that are produced by the partisans of the movement. For one of the myths being endlessly reiterated in this genre of writings is that of virtually complete identity between the poor adivasi or peasant and the insurgents – a subsumption of adivasi voice into the voice of the Maoist vanguard.'
2. *The Times of India*, 18 March 2010.
3. As noted, there are other recent travelogues by journalists depicting the Maoist movement (Chakravarty, 2008; Mishra and Pandita, 2010; Pandita, 2011); none of them were given comparable access to the Maoist infrastructure in their guerrilla bases.
4. For records, Roy (2009) did contain some well-tempered critical remarks; they are totally absent from Roy (2010a) after her travels in Maoist territory in early 2010.
5. To put the point differently, right now in this chapter I will not

use even the left-of-the-CPM, anti-state write-ups that are critical of Maoists. (Balagopal, 2006; Balagopal, 2007; Ramachandran, 2009; Banerjee, 2009a; Banerjee, 2009b; Nigam, 2009a; Nigam, 2010a; Menon 2009, etc.) I will discuss this range of 'naxalite' views in Chapter Five.

6. According to Rajat Kujur, an academic expert on insurgencies in India, six squads entered Dandakaranya in 1979 and five more next year (Kujur, 2006).
7. Speaking to *NDTV*, 13 April 2009.
8. In a recent paper, Banerjee and Saha (2010) contend – without citing source, base year, and actual wages – that the rates for tendu leaf collection in Maoist areas has 'doubled'. I have followed a direct Maoist document to report a quadruple increase; even then the daily rates are less than rupees thirty.
9. The Maoist poet-ideologue Varavar Rao is another prominent proponent of this patently false view of Maoist efforts at development; see his claims in Chakravarty (2008). Similar 'facts' of development are repeated in Mishra and Pandita (2010, 51 53) without citing any independent evidence and quoting Maoist 'ideologues' or 'leaders'.
10. See also 'Tendu leaves, illegal mining dictate game plan in Naxal heartland', *The Hindu*, 9 August 2011, for a very similar picture for the forested areas of Kaimur hills in Bihar.
11. According to government reports, Chhattisgarh is one of the fastest growing states in terms of agricultural output.
12. In fact, there is one clear instance where Maoists disrupted community-oriented developmental work initiated by people themselves in Lalgarh, West Bengal. Instead of joining the people to expand this work, Maoists initiated their 'squad politics' to control the area. As a result, these interesting developmental initiatives soon collapsed as rule of the gun took over. See Nigam (2009b); Sarkar and Sarkar (2009).
13. According to Pandita (2011), who claims to tell the 'untold story' of Maoist movement, the decision to construct a base area in Dandakaranya was reached over a family dinner (p.53). The question of seeking consent from adivasis never arose.

14. A recent report states: 'The centre of Dandakaranya region is Abujmad which is an area of 10,000 sq km. This is more than the geographical area covered by the State of Tripura....The area has no roads, no tracks and nothing else except about 20,000 people spread over small villages numbering about 237. This area is the nerve centre for all the planning meetings of [CPI(Maoist)] Central Committees, and Polit Bureaus'. See http://internalconflict. csachennai.org/2010/05/lt.html [last accessed 28 December 2011]15. Unsurprisingly, the squads of the non-military cultural wing Chetana Natya Manch do engage with people on a regular basis.
16. What is 'contributions of people'? Are there remittances from abroad from wealthy sympathisers as with LTTE and similar organisations? Also, it is hard to document the 'income' from direct extortion and ransom money from kidnappings often reported by people working near Maoist zones.
17. 'The slippery arithmetic and the sly system of measurement that converts bundles into manak boras into kilos is controlled by the contractors, and leaves plenty of room for manipulation of the worst kind in a business running into several hundred crores' (Roy, 2010a). Roy fails to remind the readers that the 'sly system' must have had Maoist approval.
18. After surveying the implementation of the rural employment guarantee scheme in Bastar, Banerjee and Saha (2010) contend that the scheme is well implemented in 'Maoist-influenced' areas. However, Bastar is a vast region with Maoists controlling only a fraction of it in the forest areas. A survey of the entire Bastar area, therefore, does not throw light on Maoist achievements unless specific data from the areas that are fully under Maoist control are separately furnished. This the authors fail to do unsurprisingly; it is unclear what would such data mean even if available. In fact a positive comment on the implementation of the scheme in Bastar in general favours the state government rather than Maoists.
19. For instance, see 'Teaching in the shadow of the gun,' *The Hindustan Times*, Chhattisgarh, 5 September 2011. Also, 'No teacher has come to this school in last five months....28 October, Chhattisgarh

net, www.cgnetswara.org/index. php?id=8194. [Last Accessed 4 November 2011].
20. To me, it is a moral concern that this argument is made at all.
21. But see Menon (2009) and Dixit (2011).
22. Letter from Ganapathy, secretary general, CPI (Maoist), to the Independent Citizen's Initiative, 10 October 2006, para. 5. Subsequently published as Ganapathy,(2007) see also www.cgnet.in/N1/maoistrep-lytoici/view?searchterm=reply
23. According to some reports, the 'help' to the families amounts to rupees two thousand per month, roughly matching what the SPos get from the Chhattisgarh state. If this is true, then, for the reported ten thousand guerrillas, the total 'help' alone amounts to rupees two crores per month. Where does this money come from? Unfortunately, we cannot use RTI to find out.
24. The food-intake by the guerrillas reported in Satnam (2010) was much poorer. But Satnam's report is based on travels in late-2001. Things seem to have improved for the guerrillas by the time Navlakha undertook his trip in 2010.
25. 'Six Naxals held for Dantewada massacre', *The Hindu*, 25 May 2010. For a picture of Barsa Lakhma, see www.outlookindia.com/article.aspx?265603
26. See Dutta (2011)
27. See *Human Rights Watch*, 'Being Neutral Is Our Biggest Crime', p. 128.
28. *Human Rights Watch*, 21 May 2010, www.hrw.org/en/news/2010/05/21/india-protect-children-maoist-conflict [Last accessed 4 November 2011].
29. *Human Rights Watch*, Sabotaged Schooling, 2009.
30. 'Maoists target tribal areas to further propaganda', *The Times of India*, 4 December 2011.
31. *Human Rights Watch*, op. cit.
32. On a personal note, I did talk to some people about the plight of children under the state and Maoists. one of them launched into a historical lesson into China, Vietnam, and other theatres of revolution. Another one suggested that there will be collateral damages until the violence ends. Hope this gives long term solace to the parents

of Barsa Lakhma. I wonder if those who applaud Maoists for their military successes will send their own children to become guerrillas.

CHAPTER 5: FORMS OF RESISTANCE

1. For a list of these factions, see www.massline.info/India/Indian_ Groups.htm [Last accessed 4 Novembe, 2011].
2. http://sanhati.com/articles/2431/ [Last accessed 4 November, 2011]
3. http://sanhati.com/articles/2610/ [Last accessed 4 November 2011] Navlakha has formed the interesting belief that 'be it NREGA, the forest bill or the decision to enforce Panchayat Extension to Schedule Areas, which was passed in 1996 but not implemented and so many other such issues figure on the agenda thanks to the fear that were this not done the poorest among the poor will continue to turn to Maoists'. So, the credit for NREGA, FRA, PESA, Right to Education, planned legislations on right to healthcare, right to food, etc. goes to Maoists (I wonder why RTI wasn't mentioned)! Hence, 'it would be a recipe for disaster to surrender the right to offer armed resistance until such time that the State outlaws war against the people,' Navlakha insists.
4. The chances of such a broad front with Maoists at the Centre is remote since, according to Prabhat Patnaik (2010), in the name of Marxist politics, Maoists are in fact engaged in an 'identity politics'. 'Class politics,' Patnaik holds, is 'inclusive,' it unites people leaving a small minority as the 'enemy'. 'Identity politics,' in contrast, is essentially exclusionary, 'it is not system-transcending'. 'This exclusionary nature of identity politics', Patnaik suggests, 'makes most such movements unthreatening from the point of view of imperialism (except of course those directly aimed against imperialism itself, and even in their case it is more a nuisance, even a serious nuisance, than a real threat)'. In any case, the chances of this 'united front' winning even 10 parliamentary seats out of about 545 are even more remote.
5. Closer to home, it is clear that one of the main reasons for the

downfall of the Left-Front government in West Bengal in recent elections is the increasingly authoritarian character of governance orchestrated with a complex network of cadres, party apparatchiks and the police. See Mukherji (2008; 2009a; 2011a).

6. Chomsky's remarks are based on the earlier stint of the Sandinistas. There have been significant changes in the politics of Latin America in the last two decades to enable the Sandinistas to come back to power recently.
7. I am not aware of any protests against this murder from prominent rights organisations. Unsurprisingly, Maoists are spreading the word that Kendruka Arjun was a 'police agent'. Not only that these allegations were found to be baseless on subsequent inquiry, later reports from CMAS state that many thousands of *adivasis* joined the funeral procession carrying comrade Arjun's body; more recently, several thousand gathered to mark his first death anniversary.
8. See www.tehelka.com/story_main50.asp?filename=Ne060811First. asp
9. See CPI (Maoist) 'Urban Perspective Plan,' reproduced in Chakravarty (2008).
10. See also the detailed and insightful review of Pandita (2011) by the journalist from Bastar, Rajiv Ranjan Prasad, at *pravakta.com* (in Hindi). The site looks like generally pro-statist, but the mentioned write-up seems objective and based on verifiable facts.
11. Maoists and their intellectual supporters such as Varavar Rao often explain the 'developmental' initiatives in Dandakaranya in terms of what was achieved during the revolutionary peasant movements in China and Vietnam.
12. In a subsequent interview to Al Jazeera TV, Chatterjee is severely critical of Maoists; he calls them 'social terrorists' – socialist in words, terrorist in deeds. www.aljazeera. com/programmes/aljazeeracorre spondent/2011/10/20111019124251679523. html. [Last accessed 4 November 2011] The *Al Jazeera* film, 'India's Silent War', gives a brief but reasonably accurate depiction of the Maoist issue, especially the condition of adivasis caught in the crossfire.
13. See Vinod Mishra, 'Political-organisational Report adopted at the Third Party Congress', December 1982.

14. Thus much of the doctrinal criticisms are directed at the 'cliques' engineered by Khrushchev in Russia and Lin Piao in China with Leon Trotsky as the universal target. Personally, I am yet to meet a naxalite intellectual-activist who has actually read Trotsky.
15. See '30 Years of Naxalbari,' http://naxalresistance.wordpress.com/2007/09/17/30–years-of-naxalbari/ [Last accessed 4 November, 2011].
16. Maoists are very clear on this point about inconsistency, but from the opposite direction. According to their policy document, 'it is an error to hold that, alongwith other war-strategies, [participation in elections] is another war-strategy if it fits in with the strategy of seizure of power through protracted war'. It is an error because participation in elections 'has nothing to do with the ebb and tide of revolution'. 'Tactics and strategies of Indian Revolution' (in Bengali), *Aneek*, July 2010.
17. In the article, although Ghandy mentions the 'assertiveness' of 'Lula's Brazil' and the fact that a 'pro-Lula candidate defeated a US puppet in the recently held elections', he fails to note that even though the Lula government did submit to some of the IMF conditions to secure loan, the government was able to divert much of the resources to poverty-alleviation and other welfare measures (Chomsky, personal communication).
18. The post-Mao China – apparently orchestrated by the 'Deng clique' – is strongly denounced by Maoists for adopting a neo-liberal path. Yet, Ghandy (2011c) praises the emergence of China as a superpower in the 'last ten years'.
19. The latest shining example is the massive nation-wide anti-corruption movement for the constitution of a Lokpal, a strong ombudsman. The structure and the content of this fascinating movement are yet to be fully understood. For much enlightened discussion, see Kafila.org. See also Mukherji (2011d).
20. Chomsky sometimes views corporations as 'commisariats' and corporate proclamations as 'Maoist'.
21. Even in the recent elections of 2011 in the state of West Bengal with massive turnouts as noted below, it is now reported that over thirty-five percent of the newly-elected members of the

state assembly have criminal cases pending against them. About twenty-six percent of MLAs have very serious charges against them. Also, over sixteen percent of MLAs are *crorepatis*. These are substantial increases from the assembly elections of 2006. Source: Report by Association for Democratic Reforms, compiled from official data submitted to the election commission by the candidates. Full report at *myneta.info*. Thanks to Abhijit Guha for sending me this report.
22. For a perceptive account, see Nigam (2009b), also Sarkar and Sarkar (2009).
23. 'CPM Pays for Netai', *Indian Express*, 14 May 2011.
24. Op. cit. Also, see www.wsws.org/articles/2011/feb2011/beng-f12.shtml [Last accessed 4 November,2011],the official site of the Fourth International. The site states that 'in a CD released to the media Sunday, 7 February (2011) and a written statement last month, CPI (Maoist) leader Bikram declared Maoists' support for the coming to power of the TMC [Trinamool Congress], which he labeled the 'bourgeoisie alternative', in West Bengal. 'Due to our joint efforts', declared Bikram, who is a member of Maoists' Bengal-Jharkhandorissa regional committee, 'the demon called CPM is on the back foot in West Bengal ... people want this ... we also want to maintain and strengthen our relationship with [TMC leader] Banerjee'. The Maoist leader ... declared that 'for the sake of peace and development,' Maoists will 'not boycott the elections and will participate in the peace process'. See also Sharmistha Chowdhury (2011). The CD and the statement were also reported by *The Hindu*, Monday, 7 February 2011.

CHAPTER 6: QUEST FOR PEACE

1. See 'Differences "narrowed",' *The Times of India*, 19 July 2011.
2. *The Times of India*, 30 October 2009.
3. See Supriya Sharma's report, 'Death threats to disarmed tribals,' *The Times of India*, 9 July, 2011.
4. See the ominous advice from the ex-Army chief, Shankar Roychowdhury, 'Ballerina in boots', *Deccan Chronicle*, 13 July 2011: 'The [Chhattisgarh] state has always demanded the deployment and

involvement of the Army against the Naxalites, which is one reason the training areas near Abujmarh [Abujmaad] were so readily allotted, and it is expected that the clamour for military involvement in the Naxalite problem will now increase. The Army finds itself in the position of a ballerina dancing in combat boots, treading warily between the minefields of IEDs and civil rights. But the Army has also made its rules of engagement clear – it is not a sitting duck; if fired upon, it will fire back'. See also 'Need 65,000 troops to fight naxals: army assessment,' *Indian Express*, 19 July, 2011. This report says that the army plans to use at least six divisions, including new battalions of Rashtriya Rifles.
5. See Teesri Dunia, August 2010, p. 21.
6. Op. cit., p. 22.
7. Op. cit., August 2010, p. 23.
8. 'The war is on,' Open Magazine, 9 July 2010, www.openthemagazine. com/ article/nation/the-war-is-on
9. How did Maoists get to know these details? Who reported to them? What does comrade Sahadeb know?
10. To raise doubts about the Maoist story concerning the specific case of Azad's murder is not to deny that Andhra police had sometimes picked up Maoist leaders from towns such as Bangalore to kill them somewhere in the forests of Andhra. See Chakravarty (2008) for several examples.
11. Also Arundhati Roy in conversation with Karan Thapar on *CNN IBN*.
12. Op. cit.
13. 'Open Letter to Swami Agnivesh from Srikant, Central Committee member of CPI (Maoist),' http://sanhati.com/articles/2626/ [Last accessed 4 November, 2011].
14. Op. cit., August 2010, p.25.
15. See 'The war is on,' *Open Magazine*, 9 July 2010, www. openthemagazine. com/article/nation/the-war-is-on
16. See, for example, Nandini Sundar et al, 'As much a lesson for Maoists as for the government,' *Outlook Online*, 10 July, 2011
17. See Chowdhury (2011) for an insightful review of the options before Maoists in West Bengal after Trinamool Congress assumed

power. The situation seems to have changed once again after the gunning down of Kishenji (see above).
18. According to the Home Ministry's report to the Indian Parliament, Maoists had between 2006 and 2011 destroyed over 1,100 economic targets, including telephone towers, electricity transmission lines, power plants and mining and railway infrastructure. The Times of India, 4 December 2011.
19. See Pandita (2011) for a somewhat personalised biographical sketch of KS.
20. There is no conflict between this general observation and the suggestion made above that Maoists may be on the run. As noted, the Maoist influence in Dandakaranya increased sharply after the Salwa Judum campaign and the subsequent attack by the state. Thus by 2009, they probably reached the peak in their history. The situation since then could have changed in favour of the state due to the massive induction of paramilitary forces in several states around the conflict area.
21. Raychaudhury (2010) holds the contrary view that only a dialogue with the leaders can prevent the otherwise inevitable anarchy as the movement splinters into roving armed bands of various sizes. While the movement degenerating into 'roving armed bands' is a real possibility, it is unclear if Maoist leaders are inclined to meaningful dialogue at all, as argued above. The only solution thus seems to be to promote a rehabilitation programme for the armed bands to return to the mainstream.
22. I hope, unknown to me, some back-channel negotiations are going on and some dramatic developments are in store.
23. *The Telegraph*, 30 June 2011.
24. See 'The long road ahead,' *Tehelka*, 31 December 2011.
25. Hence, the recent circular on amnesty from the centre – re-issued by the West Bengal government – is a non-starter. It is just the old programme, thinly sugar-coated.
26. Earlier, I presented a list of names of relevant individuals in an article (Mukherji, 2010a) which is basically a detailed critique of Maoists in Dandakaranya. The material is essentially covered in Chapter 4 of this book. The names were obviously suggestive to illustrate the

kind of civil society campaign I had in mind. I don't seem to have the authority (or the desire) to actually install a peace committee to the satisfaction of Mr Chidambaram! Instead of responding to the substantive issues raised in the article about Maoist efforts at 'welfare,' some intellectuals – whose names did not happen to appear in my list – concentrated entirely on the list itself. While one of them objected to the inclusion of individuals 'hand picked' by one 'university professor', the other preferred straight insult. I have decided not to display this list of names here because the scene has changed considerably in the meantime.

ABBREVIATIONS

AFSPA	Armed Forces Special Powers Act
AICCCR	All India Coordination Committee of Communist Revolutionaries
ANC	African National Congress
APDR	Association of People for Democratic Rights
APSIB	Andhra Pradesh Special Intelligence Branch
CCOMPOSA	Coordination Committee of Maoist Parties and Organisations in South Asia
CMAS	Chasi Muliya Adivasi Sangh
CMM	Chhattisgarh Mukti Morcha
COBRA	Commando Battalion for Resolute Action
COC	Central Organising Committee
CPC	Communist Party of China
CPI (Maoist)	Communist Party of India (Maoist)
CPI (ML)	Communist Party of India (Marxist-Leninist)
CPI	Communist Party of India
CPM	Communist Party of India (Marxist)
CPN (M)	Communist Party of Nepal (Maoist)
CPSU	Communist Party of Soviet Union
CRPF	Central Reserve Police Force
CSPSA	Chhattisgarh Special Public Security Act

DAKMS	Dandakaranya Adivasi Kisan Majdoor Sangh
FARC	Fuerzas Armadas Revolucionarias de Colombia
FIR	First Information Report
FRA	Forest Rights Act
IED	Improvised Explosive Device
JASM	Jharkhand Andolan Samanway Manch
JKLF	Jammu and Kashmir Liberation Front
JTSA	Jamia Teachers' Solidarity Association
KAMS	*Krantikari Adivasi Mahila Samity* (Tribal Women's Revolutionary Front)
LTTE	Liberation Tigers of Tamil Eelam
MCC	Maoist Communist Centre of India MLM Marxist-Leninist-Maoist
MISA	Maintenance of Internal Security Act
MLM	Marx, Lenin, and Mao ZeDong
MOU	Memorandum of Understanding
MRD	Ministry of Rural Development
NAPM	National Alliance of People's Movements
NBA	*Narmada Bachao Andolan* (Save Narmada Movement)
NDA	National Democratic Alliance
NMDC	National Minerals Development Corporation
NREGA	National Rural Employment Guarantee Act
OBC	Other Backward Castes
OGH	Operation Green Hunt
PCC	Provisional Central Committee
PCPA	People's Committee Against Police Atrocities

PESA	Panchayat Extension to Scheduled Areas Act
PLGA	People's Liberation Guerrilla Army
POTA	Prevention of Terrorism Act
PUCL	People's Union of Civil Liberties
PUDR	People's Union of Democratic Rights
PWG	People's War Group
RPC	Revolutionary People's Committee
RSS	*Rashtriya Swayam Sevak Sangh* (National Self-help Organisation)
RTI	Right to Information Act
SEZ	Special Economic Zone
SIB	Special Intelligence Branch
SPO	Special Police Officer
TADA	Terrorist and Disruptive Activities Act
TMC	Trinamool Congress
UAPA	Unlawful Activities Prevention Act
UAV	Unarmed Aerial Vehicles
UCPN(M)	Unified Communist Party of Nepal (Maoist)
UPA	United Progressive Alliance
VHP	*Vishva Hindu Parishad* (World Hindu Forum)

REFERENCES

Unsigned or short newspaper and magazine reports are not listed here. They are referenced in the notes. For bibliographical items in which an URL is given, the date of last access is 4 November 2011.

Apoorvanand. 2010. On regret and control. *Kafila*, 20 May.
Azad (Chemkuri Rajkumar). 2010a. Interview. *The Hindu*, 14 April. Text at www.thehindu.com/news/resources/article396694.ece
———. 2010b. A last note to a neo-colonialist. *Outlook*, 19 June. www.outlookindia.com/article.aspx?266164
———. 2010c. Let us not make truth a casualty in this war. *Mainstream*, Vol. 48, No. 29, 10 July.
Balagopal, K. 2006. Maoist movement in Andhra Pradesh. *Economic and Political Weekly*, 22 July.
———. 2007. The limits of violence. *Himal*, December Vol. 20, No. 12.
Banaji, Jairus. 2010. The Maoist insurgency in India: end of the road for Indian Stalinism? *Platypus Review* 26, August.
Banerjee, Kaustav and Partha Saha. 2010. The NREGA, Maoists and the developmental woes of the Indian State. *Economic and Political Weekly*, 10 July, Vol. 45.
Banerjee, Sumanta. 1980. *In the Wake of Naxalbari: A History of the Naxalite Movement in India*. Calcutta: Subarnarekha.

———. 2006a. Beyond Naxalbari. *Economic and Political Weekly*, 22 July, Vol. 14, No. 29.

———. 2006b. Hour of the assassins. *Economic and Political Weekly*, 14 October, Vol. 41, No. 41.

———. 2009a. Revisiting the 'underground'. *Economic and Political Weekly*, 14 February, Vol. 44, No. 7.

———. 2009b. Critiquing the programme of action of Maoists. *Economic and Political Weekly*, 14 November, Vol. 44, No. 46.

———. 2010. A station called Maobad (in Bengali). *Aneek*, July.

———. 2011. West Bengal's next quinquennium, and the future of the Indian Left. *Economic & Political Weekly*, 4 June, Vol. 46, No. 23.

Bhaduri, Amit. 2011. The magic-realistic slaughter of Azad. *Outlook Magazine*, 31 January.

Bhatia, Bela. 2011a. Judging the judgment. *Economic and Political Weekly*, 23 July, Vol. 46, No. 30.

———. 2011b. Awaiting nachiso: Naga elders remember 1957. *Himal Southasian*, August.

Bhattacharya, Dipankar. 2010. Communist movement in India and armed struggle (in Bengali). *Aneek*, July.

Bose, Prasenjit (ed.). 2010. *Maoism: A Critique from the Left*. New Delhi: Leftword.

Chakravarty, Bidyut and Rajat Kujur. 2010. *Maoism in India: Reincarnation of Ultra-Left Wing Extremism in the Twenty-First Century*. London, Routledge.

Chakravarty, Sudeep. 2008. *Red Sun: Travels in Naxalite Country*. New Delhi, Penguin Books.

Chatterjee, Ashim. 2010. Maoist path of armed struggle (in Bengali). *Aneek*, July.

Chatterjee, Partha. 1983. Introduction. In Sengupta (1970/1983).

Chaudhury, Shoma. 2009. Weapons of mass desperation: operation green hunt, the offensive against naxals might blow up in our faces. *Tehelka Magazine*, Vol. 6, No. 39, 3 October.

———. 2011. The inconvenient truth of Soni Sori. *Tehelka Magazine*, Vol. 8, No. 41, 15 Oct.

Chenoy, Anuradha, M. and Kamal Mitra Chenoy. 2010. *Maoists and Other*

Armed Conflicts. New Delhi, Penguin Books.

Chomsky, Noam. 1986. *Knowledge of Language*. New York, Praeger.

———. 1996. *Class Warfare*. London, Pluto Press.

———. 1998. *Talking about a Revolution*. Boston, South End Press.

———. 1999a. *Powers and Prospects*. Boston, South End Press.

———. 1999b. *The Common Good*. Berkeley, Odonian Press.

———. 2003. *Hegemony or Survival: America's Quest for Global Dominance*. New York, Henry Holt and Company.

———. 2010. An Interview with Noam Chomsky. Jean Bricmont and Julie Franck (ed.) *Chomsky Notebooks*. New York, Columbia University Press.

———. 2011. US's savage imperialism, Part 2: The Israel/Palestine issue. *ZMagazine*, Vol. 24, No. 1, January.

Chowdhury, Sharmistha. 2011. Maoists and the CPM: the crisis of the Left in West Bengal. *Red Star*, August.

DCEAA. 2008. *Development Challenges in Extremist Affected Areas: Report of an Expert Group to Planning Commission*. New Delhi, Government of India.

Deaton, Angus and Jean Dreze. 2009. Food and Nutrition in India: Facts and Interpretations. *Economic and Political Weekly*, 14 February, Vol. 44, No. 7

Dixit, Neha. 2011. Maoists creating child warriors in Jharkhand's Sardana. *Headlines Today Bureau*, Ranchi, 21 April.

Dec13. 2006. *December 13: A Reader*. New Delhi, Penguin.

D'Mello, Bernard. 2009. What is Maoism? *Monthly Review*, November.

Dreze, Jean and Amartya Sen. 1991. *Hunger and Public Action*. Oxford, Clarendon Press.

Ganapathy. 2009. Interview with Rahul Pandita. *Open Magazine*, 17 October. Text at www.openthemagazine.com/article/nation/we-shall-certainly-defeat-the-government. Included in this book as an appendix.

———. 2010a. Interview with Jan Myrdal and Gautam Navlakha. 12 February. Text at http://sanhati.com/articles/2138/

———. 2010b. Nobody can stop the revolution. *Kafila*, November 10. http://kafila.org/2010/11/10/nobody-can-stop-the-revolution/

Gatade, Subhash. 2011. *Godse's Children: Hindutva Terror in India*. New Delhi, Pharos Media and Publishing Private Limited.

Ghandy, Kobad. 2008. Interview with Suvojit Bagchi. BBC South Asia (Bengali).

———. 2011a. Comrade Anuradha Gandhi and the idea of India. In Pandita (2011).

———. 2011b. World economy splutters: dark clouds on the horizon. *Mainstream*, Vol. 49, No. 17, 16 April.

———. 2011c. Geo-politics of the present-day international economic crisis. *Mainstream*, Vol. 49, No. 34, 13 August.

Ghosh, Suniti Kumar. 2009. *Naxalbari Before and After: Reminiscences and Appraisal*. Kolkata, New Age Publishers.

Gopalakrishnan, Shankar. 2010. Forest areas, political economy and the 'Left-Progressive line' on operation green hunt. *Kafila*, 25 June.

Guha, Ramachandra. 2007. *Adivasi*s, naxalites and Indian democracy. *Economic and Political Weekly*, 11 August.

———. 2011. People versus the people. *Hindustan Times*, 10 July.

Gupta, Smita. 2010. Searching for a third way in Dantewada. *Economic and Political Weekly*, 17 April, Vol. 45, No. 16.

Habib, Irfan (ed.). 2007. *Religion in Indian History*. New Delhi, Tulika.

Hensman, Rohini. 2010. Heading for a bloodbath. *Outlook Online*, 22 April.

Koppikar, Smruti, Debarshi Dasgupta and Snigdha Hasan. 2010. The Mirror Explodes. *Outlook Magazine*, 19 July.

Kujur, Rajat. 2006. Left extremism in India: naxal movement in Chhattisgarh & Orissa. New Delhi, *Institute of Peace and Conflict Studies Special Report* No. 25, June.

Mahaprashasta, Ajoy. 2011. Terror force. *Frontline*, Vol. 28, Issue 17, 13-26 August.

Mamdani, Mahmood. 2003. *Good Muslim, Bad Muslim: America, the Cold War and the Roots of Terror*. Pantheon Books.

Mander, Harsh. 2011. Barefoot: Injustice, resistance and violence. *The Hindu*, 30 July.

Mazumdar, Charu. 1970. A few words about guerrilla actions. *Liberation*, February 1970.

Menon, Nivedita. 2009. Radical resistance and political violence today. *Economic and Political Weekly*, 12 December, Vol. 44, No. 50.

Ministry of Rural Development (MRD). 2009. *Report of the Committee on Agrarian Relations and Unfinished Tasks of Land Reforms*. New Delhi.

Mishra, Nilesh and Rahul Pandita. 2010. *The Absent State: Insurgency as an Excuse for Misgovernance*. New Delhi, Hachette India.

Mitra, Ashok. 2011. Streams of *adivasis* are joining the Maoist camp. *The Telegraph*, Friday, 2 December.

Mohanty, Manoranjan. 1977. *Revolutionary Violence: A Study of the Maoist Movement in India*. New Delhi, Sterling Publishers.

Mukherji, Nirmalangshu. 1999. Some reasons for the State. *Indian Social Science Review*, Vol. 1, No. 2.

———. 2001. A Parliament adjourned. *Economic and Political Weekly*, 29 December, Vol. 36, No. 52.

———. 2002. Gujarat and the world order. *Znet*, 12 June. www.zcommunications.org/zspace/nirmalangshumukherji

———. 2003. Teachers and war on terrorism. *Economic and Political Weekly*, 25 October, Vol. 38, No. 43.

———. 2004. 2004 elections and after. *Revolutionary Democracy*, Vol. 10, No. 2. www.revolutionarydemocracy.org/

———. 2005. *December 13: Terror over Democracy*. New Delhi, Bibliophile South Asia.

———. 2006. Last chance to know what really happened. *Economic and Political Weekly*, 7–13 October, Vol. 41, No. 40. Reprinted in Dec13 (2006). Also *Outlook Online*, www.outlookindia.com/article.aspx?232879

———. 2007a. Textuality and mass culture. In Habib (2007). Download from http://people.du.ac.in/~nmukherji/work.htm

———. 2007b. Revisiting the Kashmir Issue. *ZNet*, 13 April. www.zcommunications.org/zspace/nirmalangshumukherji

———. 2008a. Left and the nuclear deal. *Revolutionary Democracy*, Vol. 14, No. 2, September. www.revolutionarydemocracy.org/

———. 2008b. Trail of the terror cops. *Znet*, 17 October, also *Revolutionary Democracy*, November. www.zcommunications.org/zspace/nirmalangshumukherji

———. 2009a. Requiem for the Left. *Revolutionary Democracy*, Vol. 15, No. 1-2, April-September. www.revolutionarydemocracy.org/

———. 2009b. Open letter to Noam Chomsky. *Kafila*, October 21.

For a full discussion on this article, see http://kafila.org/2009/10/21/open-letter-to-noam-chomsky- nirmalangshu-mukherjee/. Reprinted in *Outlook Online*, 22 October.

———. 2009c. Politics of petitions. *Outlook Online*, 27 October.

———. 2009d. Lay down arms. *Indian Express*, 3 November. www.indianexpress. com/news/lay-down-those-homemade-arms/536483/

———. 2010a. Arms over the People: What have Maoists achieved in Dandakaranya? *Economic and Political Weekly*, June 19, Vol. 45, No. 25. A longer version appeared in *Outlook Online*, May 19, 2010, and in *ZNet*, 22 May, 2010.

———. 2010b. Have you looked at Barsa Lakhma's face?. *Mainstream*, June 5, Vol. 48, No. 24. Also in *Outlook Online*, 27 May, 2010.

———. 2010c. New 'Bush' doctrine. *Kafila*, 28 May. http://kafila.org/2010/05/28/ the-new-bush-doctrine-nirmalangshu-mukherjee/

———. 2010d. Charu Mazumdar's vision. *Outlook Online*, 1 June. www.outlookindia. com/article.aspx?265655

———. 2010e. Children of war. *Red Star*, Volume 11, June, Issue 6. Follow-up discussion 'Response to the Letter on Article 'Children of War", in *Red Star*, September, Vol. 11, Issue 9.

———. 2011a. The writing on the wall. *Outlook Online*, 16 May. www.outlookindia. com/article.aspx?271846

———. 2011b. The state of the war. *Outlook Online*, 14 July. www.outlookindia. com/article.aspx?277662

———. 2011c. Talking to Maoists. *Outlook Online*, 5 August. Also, *Mainstream*, Vol. 49, No. 42, 8 October.

———. 2011c. Response to Gail Omvedt. *Kafila*, 26 August. Reprinted as 'Three Components of Jan Lokpal Campaign', *Mainstream*, Vol. 49, No. 37, 3 September.

———. Mukhopadhyay, Ashoke Kumar (ed.). 2006. *The Naxalites: Through the Eyes of the Police: Select notifications from the Calcutta Police Gazette, 1967–1975*. Kolkata, Dey's Publishing.

Nandy, Vaskar. 2001. War against terrorism: perspective on protests. *Economic and Political Weekly*, 27 October.

Navlakha, Gautam. 2010. Days and nights in the heartland of rebellion. *Sanhati*. http://sanhati.com/articles/2250/

Nigam, Aditya. 2009a. Democracy, State and Capital: The 'Unthought'

of 20th Century Marxism. *Economic and Political Weekly*, 19 December, Vol. 44, No. 51.
———. 2009b. A million mutinies within. *Tehelka*, 4 July, Vol. 6, No. 26.
———. 2010a. The Rumour of Maoism. *Seminar*, No. 607, March.
———. 2010b. *After Utopia: Modernity, Socialism, and the Postcolony*. New Delhi, Viva Books.
Pandita, Rahul. 2011. *Hello Bastar: The Untold Story of India's Maoist Movement*. New Delhi, Tranquebar.
Patnaik, Prabhat. 2002. Market, morals and the media. *Frontline*, 20 July-2 August, Volume 19, Issue 15.
———. 2007. In the aftermath of Nandigram. *Economic and Political Weekly*, 26 March.
———. 2010. The choice before Maoists. *The Telegraph*, 15 July.
———. 2011. The Left in decline. *Economic and Political Weekly*, 16 July, Vol. 46, No. 29.
Patnaik, Utsa. 2007a. *The Republic of Hunger and Other Essays*. New Delhi, Three Essays Collective.
———. 2007b. Neo-liberalism and rural poverty in India. *Economic and Political Weekly*, 28 July, Vol. 42, No. 30.
———. 2010. A critical look at some propositions on consumption and poverty. *Economic and Political Weekly*, 6 February, Vol. 45, No. 6.
Peer, Basharat. 2003. Victims of 13 December. *The Guardian Weekend*, 5 July.
———. Prasad, Vijay. 2010. The antinomies of Maoism. In Prasenjit Bose (ed.) *Maoism: A Critique from the Left*. New Delhi: Leftword.
Ram, Mohan. 1971. *Maoism in India*. Delhi: Vikas Publications.
Ramachandran, K. N. 2010. The role of armed struggle in Indian Revolution. Translated into Bengali. *Aneek*, July.
Rana, Santosh. 2010. Interview. *Seminar*, March, 607.
Roy, Arundhati. 2009. Mr Chidambaram's war. *Outlook Magazine*, 9 November.
———. 2010a. Walking with comrades. *Outlook Magazine*, 29 March.
———. 2010b. Trickledown revolution. *Outlook Magazine*, 20 September.
Roy, Biswajit. 2010. The Azad murder and the CPM. *Kafila*, 6 September.

———. 2011. New phase in struggle for release of political prisoners in West Bengal. *Kafila*, 19 July.

Raychoudhury, Diptendra. 2010. The danger of fighting Maoists without knowing who they are. *Mainstream*, 10 July, Vol. 48, No. 29.

Sahni, Ajai. 2006. Left wing extremism in India: evolving strategies for containment. *CRPF Samachar*, New Delhi, October.

Sainath, Palagummi. 1996. *Everybody Loves a Good Drought: Stories from India's Poorest Districts*. New Delhi, Penguin India.

———. 2009. The largest wave of suicides in history. *Counterpunch*, 12 February.

———. Sanyal, Kanu. 2010. The history of the CPI (ML) from 1969–1972: An evaluation. *Class Struggle*, April. www.janasakthionline.com/downloads/history_en.pdf

Sarkar, Sumit and Tanika Sarkar. 2009. India: Notes on a Dying People [in Lalgarh]. *Economic and Political Weekly*, Vol. 44, No. 26 and 27 27 June–10 July.

———. Satnam. 2010. *Jangalnama: Travels in a Maoist Guerrilla Zone*. Translated from Punjabi by Vishav Bharti. New Delhi, Penguin India.

Sengupta, Arjun, K. P. Kannan and G. Raveendran. 2008. India's common people: who are they, how many are they and how do they live?. *Economic and Political Weekly*, 15 March.

———. 2009. Report for national commission for enterprises in the unorganised sector. http://nceus.gov.in/The_Challenge_of_Employment_in_India.pdf

Sengupta, Promode. 1970/1983. *Biplab Kon Pathe*. 1970. Translated from Bangla by Tanika Sarkar, *Whither Revolution?*, contained in the book *Naxalbari and Indian Revolution*, Calcutta, Research India Publications, 1983. The book also contains an interview with Promode Sengupta.

Setalvad, Teesta. 2008. Blast after blast: who is responsible?. *Communalism Combat*, July–August.

Simeon, Dilip. 2010. Permanent Spring. *Seminar*, March, 607.

———. 2011. Open letter to revolutionaries after Salwa judum judgment. http://groups.yahoo.com/group/chhattisgarh-net/message/19346

Singh, Mahi Pal. 2010. Fighting naxalism the democratic way. *Mainstream*, 17 April Vol. 48, No 17.

Subrahmaniam, Vidya. 2004. Two gods, one message. *The Hindu*, 11 November.

———. Sundar, Nandini. 2006. Bastar, Maoism and Salwa judum. *Economic and Political Weekly*, 22 July.

TNMT. 2008. *Historical and Polemical Documents of the Communist Movement in India*. Vijaywada, Tarimela Nagireddy Memorial Trust. In two volumes.

———. Venkatesan, V. 2011. A proven case. *Frontline*, Vol. 28, Issue. 16, 20 July–12 August.

———. Verma, Preeti (ed.) 2004. *The Terror of POTA and other security legislation: A report on the People's Tribunal on the Prevention of Terrorism Act and other security legislation*. New Delhi, Human Rights Law Network.

GLOSSARY

adivasis	indigenous people, tribals
akhara	place for ritualistic congregation for body-building, sermons etc.
andolan	literally, churning; wide-spread mass movement
Azad Hind	Free India campaign organised by Subhas Chandra Bose by recruiting Indian soldiers from the British armed forces engaged in WWII
Bajrang Dal	most militant forum of *Sangh Parivar*, devoted to lord Hanuman, the mythological monkey-devotee of lord Rama
bal sangam	children's association
bidi	local cigarettes made out of *tendu* leaf
crore	ten million
crorepati	multimillionaire
daal	lentil soup
dalam	literally, a group; in Maoist parlance, a squad of armed guerrillas
Dalit	scheduled caste at the bottom of caste-system
Dandakaranya	forests in East-Central India mentioned in mythologies
Ganesha	hindu deity with elephant's trunk
gram sabha	village council, typically the lowest tier of *panchayat*

Hindu	believer in Hinduism broadly speaking
hindutva	literally, doctrines of hinduism; often identified with communalism
jan adalat	people's court
janatanam sarkar	people's government
khap panchayat	forum of upper caste landed gentry in some areas of rural North India who dictate terms for maintenance of 'social order' based on 'ancient customs'
khichri	literally, gruel made out of rice and lentils; odd mixture
kumbhmela	six-yearly major Hindu festival on the banks of the Ganges
lakh	a hundred thousand
lingayat	a community in Karnataka devoted to lord *Shiva*
lokayukta	ombudsman appointed by a provincial government
lokpal	proposed national ombudsman, yet to be passed by parliament
mahua	a variety of forest flower used to make local liquor
panchayat	three-tier system of elected rural self-governance
panchayat pradhan	head of a *panchayat*, typically at district-level
patwari	village-level land revenue official
poha	cooked cereal made with flaked rice
Rama	mythological hero in *Ramayana*, a Hindu epic with many versions
Ranvir Sena	vigilante group organised by big landlords in Bihar to counter Maoists
rupee	local currency; one US dollar equals roughly 50 rupees
safai karmachari	cleaners and janitors
Salwa Judum	tribal vigilante force organised by Chhattisgarh state
Sangh Parivar	collection of bodies subscribing to *hindutva* agenda consisting of BJP, RSS, VHP, *Bajrang Dal*, among others
Santhal	specific indigenous people typically located in Eastern India
sarpanch	village-head, typically the chief of village-*panchayat*

Shiva	major Hindu deity
subzi	vegetables
Telugu	Dravidian language spoken mostly in Andhra Pradesh
tendu	plants bearing tobacco leaves

ACKNOWLEDGEMENTS

Some of the material included here appeared in various anthologies (Habib, 2007; Dec.13, 2006); in journals and newspapers *Economic and Political Weekly*, *Indian Social Science Review*, *Indian Express*, *Mainstream*, *Revolutionary Democracy*, and *Red Star*, and in online forums *ZNet*, *Outlook*, and *Kafila*. The original items are listed in the references. I have learned much from editorial advice from the concerned editors.

For fairness, I have supported my criticism of Maoists in India with extensive citations from recent Maoist literature – in particular, Ganapathy (2009; 2010a; 2010b) and Azad (2010a; 2010b). These are listed in the references with their site-addresses so that readers can look them up if they so desire. One of these documents (Ganapathy, 2009) is included here, with permission, as an appendix.

I am indebted to many people for helpful discussion and correspondence on the issues covered in this work: Mahtab Alam, Swami Agnivesh, Amiya Bagchi, Sourin Bhattacharya, Akeel Bilgrami, Ramratan Chatterjee, Anuradha Chenoy, Kamal Mitra Chenoy, Noam Chomsky, Biswabasu Das, Probal Dasgupta, Amiya Deb, Gopalkrishna Gandhi, Anuradha Ghosh, Hiren Gohain,

Abhijit Guha, Pervez Hoodbhoy, Javed Iqbal, Ali Javed, Sanjay Kak, Poonam Kaushik, Kavita Krishnan, Rimina Mohapatra, Nivedita Menon, Radhika Menon, Subodh Mitra, Gautam Mody, Bijoy Mukherjee, Aditya Nigam, Pratyush Nilotpal, Prabhat Patnaik, Utsa Patnaik, Justin Podur, Vijay Prashad, Badri Raina, K. N. Ramachandran, Dunu Roy, Rajat Roy, Tapas Ranjan Saha, Shuddhabrata Sengupta, P. K. Shahi, Dilip Simeon, and Vijay Singh, among others. A special word of thanks to Rimina Mohapatra for organising the maps in Chapter 1.

I have also learned much from several incisive reports on the manuscript commissioned by the publisher. David Castle and the editorial team at Pluto Press, who first published the book, made many helpful suggestions that, as well as sharpening the argument, made the book more accessible to a wider international audience. Needless to say, not everyone agrees with my evidence, analysis and proposals.

INDEX

9/11 attack, 66, 68, 75
26/11 attack, 223–224

Abujmaad hills, 20, 115, 120,
    125, 126, 190, 234n5
    as Central Guerrilla Base,
    109,126
*Adivasi*s
    atrocious actions of the police
        against, 23–24
    chronic illnesses, 121
    construction of harvesting
        structures, 119–120
    democratic rights of, 1
    displacement of, 107
    encroachment of habitats, 86
    exploitation, 118
    guerrillas, 202
    health aspects, 120–121
    history of resistance, 125

humanitarian disaster faced by,
    7
livelihood, 32, 117, 123
as Maoist, 113
Narmada Bachao Andolan, 81
panchayats controlled by,
    122–123
proposal for safety of, 11
quality of life, 120
villages in Bastar, 127
welfare measures for, 48,
    114–115, 132
women's health, 121
African National Congress
    (ANC), 96, 148
Afzal, Mohammad, 80, 82
Agnivesh, Swami, 37, 157,
    189–197, 201, 211
All India Coordination
    Committee of Communist

Revolutionaries (AICCCR), 16, 17, 100–101, 240n13
American imperialism, 224
Andhra Pradesh Special Intelligence Branch (APSIB), 101, 194, 196, 226 *See also* Operation Green Hunt (OGH)
Aneek (Bengali journal), 145
Annihilation campaign, 99, 101–102, 153, 161, 168, 170, 234n4
Ansari, Niyamat, 157–158, 164, 165
Arjun, Kendruka, 156–157, 159, 246n7
Armed Forces Special Powers Act (AFSPA), 26, 35, 74, 184, 216
Arms and drugs, smuggling of, 63
Association of People for Democratic Rights (APDR), 56, 78–79, 141, 179
Azad (Chemkuri Rajkumar), 102, 115–116, 122, 131–132, 145, 147, 190–192, 194–200, 204–205, 214, 250n10
Azad Hind movement, 169

Bagchi, Amitabha, 195, 213
Bajrang Dal, 72
Balagopal, K., 94, 159–161, 206, 233n11, 235n22
Banerjee, Sumanta, 37, 102, 160–162, 187, 231
Bangladesh Samajwadi Party (ML), 8
Bannerjee, Mamata, 179, 199–200
Basu, Jyoti, 14
Bharatiya Janata Party (BJP), 31–32, 37, 40, 52, 53, 60, 67–70, 76, 107, 120, 179, 189
Bhatia, Bela, 144
Bhattacharya, Amit, 144
Bhattacharya, Dipankar, 162, 175, 231
Bodoland movement, 183
Bolshevik Party, 169
Bose, Subhas Chandra, 169
Bourgeois state, 51, 54, 57
'Bretton Woods' world-order, 4
Budra, Kawasi, 137
Bush doctrine, 95, 171

Central Guerrilla Base, 126
Central Reserve Police Force (CRPF), 38, 110, 136, 140
Chasi Muliya Adivasi Sangh (CMAS), 156, 157
Chatterjee, Asim, 88, 153, 165
Chatterjee, Partha, 169
Chaudhury, Shoma, 9, 94, 111
Chhattisgarh Mukti Morcha (CMM), 132, 241n24
Chhattisgarh Special Public

Security Act (CSPSA), 26, 37
Chidambaram, P., 37–38, 140, 146, 186–193, 195, 202, 208, 211, 219
Children in Maoist armed guerrilla squads (*dalams*), 132–139, 206
reason for joining, 206
Children of war, 137
Chomsky, Noam, 5, 11, 39, 42, 45–51, 55–56, 63, 64, 75–77, 80, 83–85, 149–153, 177, 231, 246n6
Citizen's Initiative for Peace, 198
Civil rights movement, 56, 79
Civil society, 11, 37, 134, 186, 192, 202, 203, 205–206, 208, 211–212, 239n11, 251n26
Civil war, 4, 7, 86, 89–91, 169, 208, 230–231
Coal power project, tribal agitation against, 105
Communal-fascism, 40, 65–69, 71–73
Communist Party of Ceylon (Maoist), 8
Communist Party of Colombia (Marxist-Leninist), 4
Communist Party of India (Maoist), 1, 6, 10, 13, 14–16, 20–21, 83, 88, 92–93, 96, 102, 110, 145, 148, 153, 186–187, 189–190, 200, 202, 204, 215–217
all-India ban, 219–220
insurgency launched by, 13
links with Lashkar-e-Tayyeba, 223
non-tribal leadership of, 212
setback in Andhra Pradesh, 221
stand regarding Islamist jihadist movements, 223
Communist Party of India-Marxist (CPM), 13–16, 20, 35–36, 60, 84–85, 96, 103, 156–157, 162, 170, 181, 183, 200, 202, 218–219, 249n24
Communist Party of India [Marxist-Leninist, CPI (ML)], 14–15, 97, 100, 142, 153, 155, 156, 162–165, 168–170
Red Star, 164
Communist Party of Nepal (Maoist), 4, 8, 91–92, 225
Coordination Committee of Maoist Parties and Organisations in South Asia (CCOMPOSA), 8
Counter-insurgency warfare, 227–228
CPI (Maoist), *See* Communist Party of India (Maoist)

Dalits, 8, 20, 40, 52, 70, 75, 148, 153, 156, 158, 174, 182
Dandakaranya Adivasi Kisan Majdoor Sangh (DAKMS), 116
Dandakaranya forest, 87, 114, 115–117, 119, 121, 124, 130, 143, 148, 162, 205, 212, 213, 216
  advantages of, 124–125
  attack on *adivasi*s in, 85, 95
  exploitation by contractors, 164
  Janatana Sarkars, 114, 219
  Maoists insurgency in, 13–38, 48, 108
  picture of, 117
Democratic movement right, 21, 22, 45, 47, 55–57, 71, 92, 124
Devi, Mahasweta, 179
'Dig-and-decamp' mining, 109
Dreze, Jean, 157–158, 164

Election Commission, 41, 43, 180
Electoral politics, 3, 42, 44, 73, 152, 163, 171–172, 176–182
  in terms of mass movements, 185–186
Electoral system, 8, 40, 42, 45, 54, 174, 181

Farmer suicide, issue of, 27, 31

Forest Rights Act (FRA), 9, 123, 177, 199
Fuerzas Armadas Revolucionarias de Colombia (FARC), *See* Revolutionary Armed Forces of Colombia

Gadchiroli, 120–121
Ganapathy (General Secretary of CPI-Maoist), 18, 20, 38, 88–90, 96, 103, 114–115, 124, 133–136, 143, 144, 146, 189, 197
  change in American policy, views on, 224–225
  current developments in Nepal, views on, 225
  interview with, 215–228
Gandhi, Indira, 52, 69
Gandhi, Mahatma, 96
Gandhi Peace Foundation, 207
Gandhi, Sonia, 157, 173
Ganga, Oya, 137
Ganguly, Kaushik, 79
Geneva conventions, on prisoners of war, 101, 129
Ghandy, Kobad, 66, 117–118, 136, 145, 172–173, 192, 195, 213
Gill, K.P.S., 147, 207
Girijans, 1
Giri, Saroj, 144
Global capitalism, growth of, 49–51, 55

Global war on terror, *See* war on terror
Gorkhaland movement, 183
Grey Hounds, *See* Andhra Pradesh Special Intelligence Branch (APSIB)
Guerilla warfare, 125
Guerrilla forces of PWG, 125
Guerrilla zones, 22, 108, 124–128, 131, 132, 161, 199
Guha, Ramachandra, 205, 213

Haldia-Nandigram area, West Bengal, 60
Harmad Vahini, 217–218
Health centers, 120–122, 131, 132, 159
Hidma, Oyam, 137
Hidma, Podiyami, 137
Hindu community, religious practices of, 71
Human rights, violation of, 27, 36, 40, 50, 78, 94, 149, 178, 210, 212, 229, 236n3
Human Rights Watch report, 137–139

Independent Citizen's Initiative, 133–134, 210, 244n22
Indian democracy, 39–40, 64–65, 70, 73, 74, 92, 177, 230
anti-electoral doctrines, 42
election system, 40–41
Indian state

binary doctrine, 36–37
democratic opposition to, 48
law-enforcing institutions, 43–44
notion of, 43
peace mission, 37
predatory role of, 31, 34
Individual annihilation of 'class enemies,' doctrine of, 21
Infant socialism, 72
Iqbal, Javed, 23
Islamic jihadist movements, 223
Islamic terror, 68
Islamophobia, 68, 70

Jamat-e-Islam, 84
Jamia Teachers' Solidarity Association (JTSA), 80–82
Jammu and Kashmir Liberation Front (JKLF), 35
Janatanam Sarkars (JS), 38, 114, 116, 120, 122, 129, 219
Jangalmahal, 145, 153, 155, 158, 166, 179–182, 199, 200, 216, 218–219
Jehadi terror, 74, 239n11
Jharkhand Andolan Samanway Manch (JASM), 153
Jharkhand Unity Forum (JUF), 153
Joga, Dura, 137
Jungle warfare, 26, 228
training school, 22

Kashmir, insurgency in, 26,
    34–35, 75, 80, 82, 145,
    183–184, 199, 216
Khap panchayats, 33
Khasnabis, Ratan, 162
Kishenji (Koteshwar Rao), 114,
    131, 189, 197–200, 204,
    213, 250n17
Knutson, Jesse Ross, 144, 147
Koya commandos, 23–25, 127,
    205–206
Krantikari Adivasi Mahila Samity
    (KAMS), 116, 123
Krishak Sabha (Peasant
    Association), 14
*Krishak Samiti*s (Peasant Unions),
    14

Lakhma, Barsa, 137, 140, 244n25
Lalgarh, 82, 102, 145, 155, 158,
    180–181, 201
    developmental schemes in, 159
    Maoists involvement in,
        216–217
    mass uprising, 216
    tactics against offensive by
        government forces, 218
    use as 'laboratory' for anti-
        Naxal operations, 218–219
Latin America, 3, 66, 151, 168,
    173, 246n6
Left Front, 60, 79, 82–83, 153,
    165, 177, 178–180, 212,
    246n5

Left-liberal forces, 207
Liberated zones, 47, 93, 129–
    130, 199, 200, 237n4
Liberation Tigers of Tamil Eelam
    (LTTE), 6, 26, 33, 90–91,
    93, 165, 207
    arms training and other
        support to PWG, 90, 222
    operations, 155, 207
    reasons for the setback
        suffered by, 221–222
Lin, Piao, 170–171, 247n14
Lokayukta, 60, 106
Lokpal movement, 203
Lord's Resistance Army, Uganda, 6

Madhav, comrade, 134
Mahato, Chatradhar, 180, 182
Maintenance of Internal
    Security Act (MISA), 74
Mandela, Nelson, 96, 148, 175
Mangtu, 132
*Maobadi*s (Maoists), 37
Maoist discourse, 144–145, 147,
    153, 173
Maoist guerrillas, 13, 200, 205
Maoist insurgency
    *adivasi*s in, 113–114
    appeals and statements,
        155–156, 186
    armed insurgencies, 4, 5, 9,
        24, 29, 44, 160, 207
    authoritarian tendencies,
        160–161

Banerjee's analysis, 161–163
brief chronology of, 17–18
collapse of, 160–161
criticism of, 154–155
demand for separation from a State, 183–186
doctrines and practice, 41
effect of the losses and surrenders on, 226
electoral democracy, 167
forceful acquisition of land, 163–164
intellectuals support for, 103
major source of funding, 109–111
mass penetration of, 167–168
mass support, 163
military preparations, 25
in Nepal, 6–8, 10, 29, 34, 91–92, 172, 175
non-*adivasi* support, 113, 114
in Philippines, 5
priorities of, 114
psychological warfare against, 228
recruiting children for warfare, 132–139
resistance to aggressive neo-liberal policies, 106
revolutionary politics of, 147, 169–170
source of money, 128–129
'standard' operations of, 28
support base, 115, 161

and terrorism, 161
warnings issued, 157
Maoist organisations, 2–4
Maoists Communist Center of India (MCC), 8, 17, 18, 22, 143, 187, 204
Mao, Tse Tung, 97
Mao, Zedong, 16
contributions to revolutionary theory, 97
Marxist conception of state, 43
Marx, Karl, 71
Marx, Lenin, and Mao Zedong (MLM), doctrines of, 1–2, 226
Massachusetts Institute of Technology, 153
Mazumdar, Charu, 16–17, 21, 95–103, 125, 142–143, 153, 161, 163, 165–169, 171, 204
McNamara, Robert, 67
Mishra, Pramod, 136, 195, 213
Mishra, Vinod, 17, 163, 168, 234n4
Mizoram insurgency, 184
MLM organisation CPI (ML-Liberation), 6, 8, 167, 168
Mobile school programme, 122, 134–135
Moon, Ban Ki, 137
Mukherjee, Mahadeb, 168, 170
Murder manual, 98
Muslim fundamentalism, 84, 223–224

Muslim-sponsored terrorism, *See*
    Islamic terror
Myrdal, Jan, 144

Naga insurgency, 184
Nandigram uprising, 29, 60,
    82–85, 163, 176, 179–180,
    216
Narmada Bachao Andolan (NBA),
    81
National Alliance of People's
    Movements (NAPM), 81
National Democratic Alliance
    (NDA), 53
National Human Rights
    Commission, 81
National Patriotic Front and
    Movement for Democracy,
    Liberia, 6
National Rural Employment
    Guarantee Act (NREGA), 9,
    123, 158, 199, 245n3
National Socialist, 2
Navlakha, Gautam, 37, 75, 95,
    103, 104, 116–120, 121,
    125, 127–128, 135, 141,
    144, 147, 158, 162, 194, 231
Naxalbari village, peasant
    uprising in, 14–16, 29, 88,
    97, 173
'Naxalite' actions, 89
Naxalite criticism of Maoists,
    169–170
Naxalite movement, 10, 13–16,
    90, 96, 98, 103, 143, 146,
    154, 160–161, 168, 199
Naxalite politics, 171–172
Nazi movement, 2
Neogi, Shankar Guha, 132,
    241n24
Netai massacre, 180
Nigam, Aditya, 27, 159, 177,
    241n1
Non-Maoist naxalites, 36,
    171–172
Non-state terror, 36

Obama, Barack, 57, 224–225
October Revolution, 169
Operation Green Hunt (OGH),
    13, 22, 24, 29, 38, 85, 87,
    93, 104, 108, 143, 207, 212

Pal, Yash (Prof.), 37, 189, 211
Panchayat Extension to
    Scheduled Areas Act
    (PESA), 199, 245n3
Panda, Sabyasachi, 136
Pandey, Hemchandra, 194
Pandita, Rahul, 101, 216
Patkar, Medha, 81, 84, 201
Patnaik, Prabhat, 62, 65–67, 69,
    237n4, 245n4
Patnaik, Utsa, 30–31, 65, 119,
    235n16
Peace process, 186–194, 196–
    197, 210
Peer, Basharat, 68

People's Committee Against
   Police Atrocities (PCPA),
   156, 180–182
People's Democracy, 84
People's Liberation Guerrilla
   Army (PLGA), 18, 28, 91,
   108, 126–127, 129, 130,
   133–136, 147, 209, 219,
   220, 228
People's resistance, 146, 220
People's Union of Civil Liberties
   (PUCL), 56, 75, 78, 141
People's Union of Democratic
   rights (PUDR), 56, 75, 78
People's War Group (PWG), 8,
   18, 22, 92, 124, 143, 159,
   171, 187, 198, 215
   arms training and other
      support from LTTE, 222
   guerrilla forces of, 125
Pillai, G., 208
Politics of identity, 62, 73
Pol Pot, 96, 239n12
Poverty, 7, 27, 30, 33, 40, 117,
   173, 230
Prabhakaran, Velupillai, 90, 93,
   155, 222
Prachanda, 92, 225
Predatory insurgencies, 6
Prevention of Terrorism Act
   (POTA, 2002), 74–76, 80
Provident fund scheme, 30
Provisional Central Committee,
   Communist Party of
India, Marxist-Leninist
   (PCC (Provisional Central
   Committee), CPI (ML)),
   153
Public Distribution System, 30,
   40, 65
Purba Bangla Sarbahara Party, 8

Rajkumar, Chemkuri, 145
Ramakrishna, 136
Ramesh, Jairam, 208
Rana, Santosh, 17, 87–88, 153,
   158, 167, 182
Ranjan, Vishwa, 137
Ranvir Sena, 163
Rao, Koteshwar, *See* Kishenji
Rao, Mupalla Laxman, *See*
   Ganapathy (General
   Secretary of CPI-Maoist)
Rao, Varavar, 144, 199–200,
   242n9, 246n11
Rashtriya Swayamsevak Sangh
   (RSS), 32–33
Red terror, 21–22
Reformist movement, 150
Revolutionary Armed Forces of
   Colombia, 4, 6
Revolutionary Communist
   Centre of India (Maoist), 8
Revolutionary People's
   Committees (RPCs), 114,
   116, 128–129, 135, 219, 228
Revolutionary United Front,
   Sierra Leone, 6

Right to Education Act (RTE), 9
Right to Information Act (RTI), 9, 104, 123, 177
Royal Nepalese Army, 34, 91
Royalties, 109, 111, 119, 128–130
Roy, Aruna, 157, 164
Roy, Arundhati, 35, 95, 102, 104, 144, 162, 231
Roy, Biswajit, 36
Roy, Sushil, 195, 213, 226

Salwa Judum, 18, 24, 37–38, 104, 106–108, 114, 134, 143, 145, 187–188, 240n22, 250n20
Sandinista movement, 151
Sangh Parivar, 68, 70, 72–73, 80
Sanhati (online forum), 85, 87, 93–95, 103
   statement against military offensive in *adivasi* habitats, 229–231
Santhal, Jangal, 153, 240n13
Sanyal, Kanu, 14, 20–22, 87, 94, 97, 153, 156, 170, 239n12, 240n15
Sanyal, Narayan, 136, 192, 195, 213, 226
Sardar Sarovar Dam project, campaign against, 81
Satnam's report of Maoist territory, 108, 115, 127

Seizure of power, 35, 124, 130–131, 247n16
Sen, Binayak, 26–27, 37, 79
Sengupta, Promode, 100, 169, 171
Sharmila, Irom, 35, 184
Sheppard, Bede, 137–138
Shiva, Vandana, 117, 231
Simeon, Dilip, 99, 103, 201, 203, 214
Singur, 29, 82, 85, 163, 179–180, 216
Sitaramaya, Kondapalli, 198, 204

Social justice, 41, 168
Social organisation
   Marxist and Gandhian conceptions of, 46
   of *Santhals*, 158
Soma, Commander, 131
Special Economic Zones (SEZs), 86, 230
Special Police Officers (SPOs), 24, 132
Strategic defence, 227–228
Sunderban forests, 29, 166
Surrendered militants, 208

Taliban, 112
Tamil Eelam, 90–91, 221–222
Tamil nationalism, 89
Tata Steel, 107, 123
Tehrik-e-Taliban, 6, 32
Terrorist and Disruptive Activities Act (TADA), 74

TINA (there is no alternative) factor, 188–189
Tribal non-combatants, 144
Trinamool Congress, 32, 84, 181, 217–218, 248n24
  alliance, 179–180

Unarmed Aerial Vehicles (UAVs), 22–23, 234n6
United Front (UF), 6, 52
United Progressive Alliance (UPA), 53, 236n26
Universal amnesty, 165, 208–209, 211
Unlawful Activities Prevention Act (UAPA), 38, 80, 154, 177, 219, 236n26

Vedanta, 34
Verghese, B. G., 145

Vietnam War, 67
Village militias, 126
Village panchayats, 34, 122
Vinod, Comrade, 120
Vishwa Hindu Parishad (VHP), 33, 72

Wages, agricultural labour, 118–120
War on terror, 76, 79–80, 82, 178, 224, 239n11
Welfare institutions, 42, 48
WikiLeaks, 105, 110–111, 240n18
Working class movement, 53, 108

Young Communist Mobile School, 135